Humanism as Realism

Other Books of Interest from St. Augustine's Press

Thomas F. Powers, *American Multiculturalism
and the Anti-Discrimination Regime*

Richard Ferrier, *The Declaration of America:
Our Principles in Thought and Action*

Jeremy Black, *The Age of Nightmare*

Jeremy Black, *Defoe's Britain*

Joseph Bottum, *The Decline of the Novel*

Francisco Insa, *The Formation of Affectivity: A Christian Approach*

Rémi Brague, *The Anchors in the Heavens*

Rémi Brague, *Moderately Modern*

Marvin R. O'Connell, *Telling Stories that Matter: Memoirs and Essays*

Josef Pieper, *Traditional Truth, Poetry, Sacrament:
For My Mother, on Her 70th Birthday*

Marcel H. van Herpen, *History and Human Responsibility:
The Unbearable Weight of Freedom in a Dystopian World*

John von Heyking, *Comprehensive Judgment and Absolute Selflessness:
Winston Churchill on Politics as Friendship*

David Lowenthal, *Slave State: Rereading Orwell's 1984*

Gene Fendt, *Camus' Plague: Myth for Our World*

Jean-Luc Marion, *Descartes's Grey Ontology:
Cartesian Science and Aristotelian Thought in the Regulae*

Will Morrisey, *Herman Melville's Ship of State*

Roger Scruton, *The Meaning of Conservatism: Revised 3rd Edition*

Roger Scruton, *On Hunting*

Gabriel Marcel, *The Invisible Threshold: Two Plays by Gabriel Marcel*

Winston Churchill, *Savrola*

Winston Churchill, *The River War*

Humanism as Realism
Three Essays Surrounding the Thought of Paul Elmer More and Irving Babbitt
Paweł Armada

St. Augustine's Press
South Bend, Indiana

Copyright © 2024 by Paweł Armada

All rights reserved. No part of this book may be reproduced, stored in a retrieval system, or transmitted, in any form or by any means, electronic, mechanical, photocopying, recording, or otherwise, without the prior permission of St. Augustine's Press.

Manufactured in the United States of America.

1 2 3 4 5 6 29 28 27 26 25 24

Library of Congress Control Number: 2023947235

Hardback ISBN: 978-1-58731434-6
Ebook ISBN: 978-1-58731-435-3

∞ The paper used in this publication meets the minimum requirements of the American National Standard for Information Sciences – Permanence of Paper for Printed Materials, ANSI Z39.48-1984.

St. Augustine's Press
www.staugustine.net

Abba Anthony said, 'A time is coming when men will go mad, and when they see someone who is not mad, they will attack him saying, "You are mad, you are not like us.'"

The Sayings of the Desert Fathers: The Alphabetical Collection 25, trans. Benedicta Ward, SLG

TABLE OF CONTENTS

Preface ix

Introductory Remarks xi

On the Mixing Up and Explanation of Concepts 1

Un-Economic Ideals 87

The Ancient Mirror of Theology 189

Selected Literature 277

Index 280

PREFACE

This is a protreptic book. Its main goal is to encourage people to undertake independent studies or, more generally, simply to think independently. If we want to think for ourselves and not like preprogrammed humanoids, we can't do so in a vacuum. We have to lean on something. In the Author's view, the more than century-old writings of Paul Elmer More and Irving Babbitt are ideally suited to the role of such a support for us, living in the here and now. They make it possible for us to dig ourselves out from underneath the heaps of opinions, "principles," or "theories" that allegedly can't be rejected, that we're obliged to follow, but that have a paralyzing and dumbing-down effect on us, making our lives from the outset seems like the dream of a childish old man.

It will be up to the reader to decide whether heading toward humanistic realism was indeed the right thing to do. There is certainly no need to read the entire volume at once. Sometimes, it's necessary to entertain an outdated thought that is harder to digest for a long time before it makes one seriously consider the meaning of things holistically. But before that happens, our attention is focused on highlighted topics or even minor issues that seem closer, clearer, more tangible to us for some reason, for now. And the more vivid and troubling doubts remain with the reader, the better. Provided, of course, that these doubts do not eat him alive, that, on the contrary, they become food for his soul. This can happen as long as we seriously believe that we can become better than we are. Ultimately, what matters is that when you activate your thinking, you do so not merely "for the sake of art" but for your own benefit. What *truly* serves me (you) must be *beneficial* for everyone.

"Everyone" includes friends, in the first place. Without friendship, no endeavor is worth undertaking. Dariusz Bartula and Jakub Chmielniak will know what the author of this book thanks them for from the bottom of his heart. In addition, special thanks are due to Paweł Cieślarek, who has been an invaluable companion throughout the author's intellectual journey.

Paweł Armada
Bielsko-Biała – Kraków,
X 2017–VII 2018

INTRODUCTORY REMARKS

This book consists of three essays. Each relates to the findings of Paul Elmer More (1864–1937) and Irving Babbitt (1865–1933). Both gentlemen hailed from America. Friendship united them, creating opportunities for great discussions. They were both competent and well-educated. They lived in an age of upheavals – of the emergence of humankind as we know it today. Their approach to these changes was very critical. They tried to explain to a world rushing forward that there was something wrong, even deadly, where others only wanted to see good. They initiated a movement called the "New Humanism," which failed and was subsequently forgotten.

Ever since the Internet began to accompany us constantly, there has been no need to bore readers with detailed biographies of these or other figures. Finding information about More or Babbitt is not a problem – it is easy to access most of the texts they've left behind, as well as elaborations of their thoughts. After all, the fact that the "New Humanism" was forgotten does not mean that nothing has been written about it since the 1930s. It *does* mean that not much was written and that what was, were not necessarily works reaching the heights of humanistic reflection. Above all, no one has managed to arouse greater interest in what distinguishes the humanists' ideas from other important voices at the beginning of the last century. No meaningful debate to discover and reflect upon the astonishing content of More's and Babbitt's writings has occurred or is occurring. We aren't benefitting at all from their work. We argue that we should be reaping benefits, here and now: in our corner of the world and in the time given to us.

This book contains judgments and interpretations that are not self-explanatory, ones that may appear too far-reaching or not firmly grounded. To help the reader assess the credibility of these ideas, let us point out a few publications discussing More's and Babbitt's humanism from a slightly different perspective. The following monographs are certainly worth mentioning: J. David Hoeveler, Jr.'s *The New Humanism: A Critique of Modern America 1900–1940* (Charlottesville 1977); Robert Shafer's *Paul Elmer More and American Criticism* (New Haven–London 1935) – written during More's lifetime; Arthur Hazard Dakin's *Paul Elmer More* (Princeton 1960) – a model record of More's intellectual biography containing, among others, long passages from his private correspondence (we use this in our essays); Robert M. Davies' *The Humanism of Paul Elmer More* (New York 1958); Francis X. Duggan's *Paul Elmer More* (New York 1966); Stephen L. Tanner's *Paul Elmer More: Literary Criticism as the History of Ideas* (Provo, Utah 1987); *Irving Babbitt: Man and Teacher* (New York 1941) edited by Frederick Manchester and Odell Shepard – they are actually memories (relatively fresh, at the time of writing) of Babbitt's students and friends; Thomas R. Nevin's *Irving Babbitt: An Intellectual Study* (Chapel Hill – London 1984); Stephen C. Brennan and Stephen R. Yarbrough's *Irving Babbitt* (Boston 1987). We can add to this the penultimate chapter of Russell Kirk's much better-known work *The Conservative Mind: From Burke to Santayana* (Chicago 1953). As a curiosity, let us also indicate the lost work of Bogdan Suchodolski *Studja nad humanizmem współczesnym. Irving Babbitt* (Warszawa 1936) [Eng. *Studies on Contemporary Humanism. Irving Babbitt* (Warsaw 1936)], with the caveat that this Polish contribution did not result in anything permanent and there is no point in linking Babbitt with the "late" Suchodolski. This list could be extended, of course. However, that would mean including works by authors inspired by the "New Humanism" rather than presenting the original thoughts of More and Babbitt. On the other hand, some minor texts, interesting articles, and comments can be found online without prior instruction, using only one's research abilities.

Our essays do not form a scientific monograph in the strict sense. Each of them may be read separately, although at the same time, they are intentionally arranged to form an integral whole.

Introductory Remarks

The title of this book reveals the main idea: true humanism is realism. More's and Babbitt's legacy, consistently referred to by us as "humanism," includes a view of reality that provides an excellent basis for understanding and judging the modern state and modern society. In other words, what we have here is an unusually wise lesson in political philosophy. However, it is not a lesson in formulating and adopting short-term, superficial opinions on democracy or an efficient economy. On the contrary, it is conditioned by an outside perspective resulting from deep reflection on the nature of man and the possibilities of his spiritual development. This lesson seems especially worth studying for those who would prefer to perform as esteemed actors rather than cheap pushovers, decorations, or props on the stage of Western history.

The author of these essays would be inclined to consider his interpretation of More's and Babbitt's works as thoughtful and helpful, which is not to say that it is definitive or complete. This is especially true of the last essay, which is mainly devoted to matters of religion. It is not for us to settle the ultimate questions. We merely want to show that the way the humanists approach these questions may differ from what we have become accustomed to from both modernists and traditional defenders of the faith.

In the second essay, we try to apply the humanist diagnosis of modernity directly to today's ways of "sensing" the spheres of politics and economics, which brings with it a non-ideological story about transformations in the human imagination. Finally, the first essay attempts to explain what humanism (and its renewal) is all about, the purpose of the unfulfilled "Humanist Movement," and why this seemingly ancient idea doesn't seem to age.

ON THE MIXING UP AND EXPLANATION OF CONCEPTS

I.

People have always messed with each other's heads. They took away old words, introduced new ones. However, at times they valued precise keys over the hammer – intellectual tools that could be used to manipulate existing meanings and associations. A few skillful moves and what was black yesterday could be viewed as colorful and polka-dotted tomorrow. Demagogues, your everyday charlatans, and scammers operate in this way. There is nothing new under the sun. However, it is not absurd to think that this age-old mixing up of concepts has substantially increased with the development of mass communication, modern ideologies, propaganda, and sales techniques. It has also likely become more organized and more purposeful, and so all the more dangerous. The danger lies in the fact that playing around with the alteration of discourses may lead to us losing our basis for understanding ourselves and each other; that, therefore, the subject of humanistic reflection – man – may cease to exist; not because some higher-order entities, "terminators," or other "oddities" will replace us, but that what awaits us, people of flesh and blood, is a faster and faster transformation into elements of freely-moving fat- and bone-mass. Meanwhile, as Irving Babbit wrote in 1930, *though the humanist does not seek to define God and is in general chary of ultimates, he is wont in more mundane matters to put the utmost emphasis on definition. This Socratic emphasis would seem especially needed at a time like the present which has probably surpassed all previous epochs in its loose and irresponsible use of general terms. Unless this tendency is corrected, the day may come when, outside of words that stand for the measurements of science or the objects of sense, communi-cation between men will be well-nigh impossible.*[1] What can be said apart from the fact that the next era – our own – did not turn out to be any better? That the amount and ease of prattle concealing base motives and incompetence frighten anyone who tries, even from time to time, to "turn on" their thinking for so much as a moment? That it is difficult to escape the thought that we are plunging into something horrible, into some post-totalitarian al-gorithm – without labor camps and gas chambers (presumably), but how effective in not calling things by name, in simultaneously directing our opinions and exploiting our emotions?

However, the point isn't to jump out of the frying pan and into the fire; in our times, it is easier to change owners than to live in freedom. It seems that Babbitt's intention, like Paul Elmer More's and that of most other members of the movement called "New Humanism," was not to propose a new form of "negative" engagement – say, an individual's passionate reaction pitted against the passionate drift of entire societies, a solo by the last of the righteous, or a farewell insurrection of the defeated. None of the humanists was hysterical or sank into despair. If they preached a return to the classics of Western thought, with Socrates at the forefront, it was not because they indiscriminately wanted to twist the arrow of time. If they peered into the treasury of Far Eastern thought, it was not to extract and plant two pennies' worth of seeds of mystical spirituality in the rotten West. The goal was much more ambitious: to gain control of the course of what Babbitt called the "modern experiment," and thus remedy the great mixing up of concepts, which was giving rise to ever more dangerous political and moral consequences, with world war at the forefront (it's worth noting that for them, there was "only" one *such* war). This meant, in other words, a great service check of the vehicle of general concepts.

---

1   I. Babbitt, *Humanism: An Essay at Definition* [in:] *Humanism and Amer-ica: Essays on the Outlook of Modern Civilization*, ed. N. Foerster, New York 1930, p. 25.

On the Mixing up and Explanation of Concepts

Importantly, however, this was not a "check" done by "career" philosophers, professional analyzers, or reviewers of their own works. To understand the idea of humanism, one needs to adopt a perspective outside of academic (and peri-academic) philosophy as we know it. In one of his letters from 1925, More mentions a joint session of British scientific societies – the Aristotelian Society and the Mind Society, writing bluntly that this meeting turned out to be for him *an expense of spirit and a waste of words. It confirmed me in the opinion that modern philosophy is an intellectual nuisance. I never in my life felt so much out of place and so hopelessly stupid as when attending these sessions.*[2] Someone may consider this anecdotal experience a distant example of the typical trials faced by a sensitive outsider surrounded by learned experts, except that it is precisely the prevalence of such experiences, their normality, that should worry us. Occupying one place or another in the broad field of the humanities (or in the social sciences or sciences in the strict sense), we have simply become accustomed to treating universal philosophical issues as something almost hidden underneath the tarp of discourse, the most obvious function of which seems to be improving the self-esteem of participating intellectuals. Moreover, the degree to which successive generations of "knowledge coryphaei" make a real impact – especially when we take into account their "quotability" in the media or mass culture – appears to be inversely proportional to the quality of their findings or the depth of their reflection. After all, the para-scientific gibberish of a handful of dreamy aesthetes reflects, but also in a way conditions, prattle on a broad scale relatively well. What, if not the thoughtful gestures and wrinkled foreheads of academic "authorities" (and some of their students) could define the limits of intellectual freedom for us, average Joes, would-be- or not-yet-adepts? Who else stands guard over concepts – the entire heritage of human thought? Who else is so capable of obscuring or transforming this heritage?

2   Quoted in: A. H. Dakin, *Paul Elmer More*, Princeton, New Jersey 1960, p. 231.

HUMANISM AS REALISM

Between us and the works of the ancients, from which we oft unreflectively draw our most essential concepts, such as "happiness" or "justice," there lies a wide trench of once-assumed combinations and over-interpretations, as well as quite contemporary research grants, intellectual trends, and political correctness. One works through the other: new mistakes confirm old mistakes, and the worthlessness of concepts encourages worthless initiatives and worthless personalities. Vain intellectualism couples perfectly with moral rubbish, the hallmark of which is invariably the willingness to serve the highest bidder. How often one thinks *for* something other than a good reason! But we are not all so futile. Many of us take the search for truth very seriously, process what we read with the utmost care, strain our minds beyond measure, and nevertheless go astray, which we quietly admit and regret. According to More, *one of the hardest things for a student to learn, which yet, if he could but know it at the beginning, would save him from endless perplexities and perhaps from final despair, is just the simple fact that* brain-power is no guarantee for the rightness of thinking, *that on the contrary a restlessly outreaching mind, unchecked by the humility of common sense, is more than likely to lead its owner into bogs of duplicity if not into the bottomless pit of fatuity (…) there has been no more powerful intellect for the past hundred years than Kant's; I doubt if any writer ever filled the world with more confusion of thought or clouded the truth with a thicker dust of obscurity.*[3] Leaving what one thinks of Kant aside, what is this "common-sense humility"?

Properly understood, this humility may prove to be the key to the humanistic attitude, so we will return to it. For now, let us emphasize More's own words: "brain-power is no guarantee for rightness of thinking" – precisely! How many people "with a high IQ" do we meet, people gifted one way or another, very skilled in math, or endowed with a phenomenal memory, but at the same time extremely prone to having their heads "messed with"? How many are not mentally indifferent but are affected by a lack of will

---

3   P. E. More, *The Humility of Common Sense* [in:] *Humanism and America…*, pp. 64–65. Emphasis in the original text.

On the Mixing up and Explanation of Concepts

or some spiritual inertia, some fundamental character deficit, some falsehood that makes it impossible to pose questions or to think for themselves? Here, we need but mention Stalin's glorifiers and other disgraced intellectual titans.[4] In the age of the Internet, a whole lot of this type of human vermin – ostensibly smart, but stupid through and through – if they are not basking in the limelight before the cameras, one can be sure they are sitting at their keyboards. They are among usLeaving aside specific examples – since our goal is not to write a pamphlet but to demonstrate the basic premises of "humanism" as a way of thinking – we are slowly beginning to understand that what we previously called a "service check of the vehicle of general concepts" is not, and cannot be an ordinary "technical" enterprise. The goal is not to justify one's preferences or beliefs that, say – since I have a problem with Kant, for example, I'll join the "anti-Kantian" party, which will grow in strength and set things in order. Ha! You can consistently reject not just some chapter of the "meta-narrative" legacy of the Moderns, but the entire modern form of civilization in its literal, material version, with the megatons of garbage it produces, announce your release from the "matrix" or intent to overthrow the "system," and proceed to become part of another niche of unchained debunkers. So, what? Our "final" choices – between one matrix of engagement and another, action and reaction; in political life as well, the changes in which we will discuss separately – usually turn out to be much less final and severe than we previously thought. And perhaps it is this issue that is so perfectly grasped by Babbitt, who tried to declare himself the most modern of the Moderns, preaching ancient wisdom. Perhaps it would only seem far-fetched to juxtapose this peculiar claim with the method of interpreting Nietzsche's work that can be found in the correspondence between Karl Löwith and Leo

---

4   Cf. P. Johnson, *Intelektualiści*, trans. A. Piber, Poznań 1998; M. Lilla, *Lekkomyślny umysł. Intelektualiści w polityce*, trans. J. Margański, Warszawa 2006; L. Kołakowski, *Intelektualiści* [in:] idem, *Czy diabeł może być zbawiony i 27 innych kazań*, Londyn 1983, pp. 121–30.

Strauss. It discusses an attempt to "recreate antiquity at the heights of modernity,"[5] which may mean that the very momentum of modern thought gives hope for overcoming its harmful effects. Of course, one should not assume that the humanist critique will be consistent with Nietzsche's critique. After all, doctors can generally agree on a diagnosis (or at least a level of diagnosis) and yet propose utterly different treatment methods.[6] At this stage, we must be able to grasp what distinguishes humanists from fair-minded and smart critics of twentieth-century civilization, and what, in a sense, finds its counterbalance in humanist rhetoric: their ambitions; the actual, full (not apparent or occasional) radicalism of their thought; thought that would allow for a new interpretation of primary concepts, which were established centuries ago and have decayed over time.

However, let us give the floor to Babbitt. In his characteristic cautious tone, he states: *the whole modern experiment is threatened with breakdown simply because it has not been sufficiently modern. One should therefore not rest content until one has, with the aid of the secular experience of both the East and the West, worked out a point of view so modern that, compared with it, that of our young radicals will seem antediluvian.*[7] It is not difficult to guess who could be considered a radical in the 1920s. The brutal effects of radicalism at the time – a diverse and explosive cocktail of modern ideologies and personal grievances – were unfortunately revealed to the world quickly and directly. Before asking about the "secular experience of both the East and the West," we should consider whom Babbitt is addressing in that statement. To whom was the "offer" of humanism directed in that "market of ideas"? To whom are we marketing our service of "service checking concepts" and the

5 Cf. K. Löwith, L. Strauss, *Listy*, trans. P. Armada, A Górnisiewicz, "Kronos," 2/2010, especially p. 187 ff.
6 Cf. P. E. More, *Economic Ideals* [in:] id., *Shelburne Essays Eleventh Series: A New England Group and Others*, Boston–New York 1921, pp. 248–49; I. Babbitt, *Rousseau and Romanticism*, Boston–New York 1919, especially pp. 198, 250.
7 I. Babbitt, *Rousseau and Romanticism...*, p. xxiii.

On the Mixing up and Explanation of Concepts

development of an ultra-modern perspective on its basis? Above all, we are not targeting convinced traditionalists or obscurants, people living in the past who are offended by reality. In other words – having renounced allegiance to the current authorities – we aren't looking to return to former authorities (or to their present spokespeople). A true return is not possible. The whole issue is quite delicate and difficult to grasp at the level of assumptions. On the one hand, as we will unequivocally confirm, humanistic reflection on modern thought provides a fundamental critique of modernity encompassing not only the "young radicals" living on the surface of the "experiment," but also the majority who live as if in the middle and tend to consider their attitudes and choices to be "common sense." On the other hand, this criticism should be regarded as ultra-modern and not, in any case, as deriving from a sentimental attachment to – mostly – fading traditions. At the same time, in speaking of "traditions," we mean beliefs or ideals serious enough that, in principle, they can be reduced to a religion. To reiterate, humanism contains a radicalism of thought that does not retreat from any of the findings of modern thought and even exceeds them by definition. Consequently, Babbitt says that his *argument, if it makes any appeal at all, will be to those for whom the symbols through which the past has received its wisdom have become incredible.* He adds that *under existing conditions, the significant struggle seems to me to be not that between the unsound individualist and the traditionalist, nor again, as is currently assumed, that between the unsound individualist and the altruist, but that between the sound and the unsound individualist.*[8]

We may therefore presume that the task of the humanist would be to promote "sound individualism" or, more practically, it would amount to attempts to raise young people to be "sound individualists." If that is the case, "soundness" should be associated with a critical attitude or with "total positivism," in Babbitt's terminology. The systematic examination of one's individual experiences, the effort of intentional introspection – all in all, the

8   Ibid., p. xxii; id., *Democracy and Leadership*, Indianapolis 1979, p. 8.

habit of independent internal work – is opposed to obedience to those who wish to explain our experiences to us authoritatively from the outside. In the first place, it is necessary to teach *yourself* the ability to focus. Adequately raised, we get to know ourselves and take responsibility for ourselves. Is that all? On a certain level, yes. However, it is not difficult to see that in such an approach, everything hinges on our definition of "wisdom," the accompanying "symbols" of which may have been changed or weakened in the past. Wisdom, if understood seriously, lies in concepts. To reach concepts, we must tear down the symbolic layer that surrounds and protects them. To reach concepts is to establish their direct meaning, that is, their place in the order of immediate, universal human experience; to explain them is to shine the light of discourse on them with such an intensity that the result would not be worse than that known through symbols. The latter may not be final or perfect, but they also have their fundamental meaning or rooting in the order of human affairs. Thus, the tearing down of the symbolic layer – a prerequisite for our suprahistorical "review of concepts" – is by no means a job for the sluggish, reckless, or supine. Instead, to use More's phrase, it requires "a guarantee for rightness of thinking": you need to know what to ask and you cannot fear the answer; one has to be a "sound individualist" in the philosophical dimension.

In turn, we would call someone philosophically "unsound" if they got excited by the power of questioning (the "tearing away") itself, losing sight – if they ever saw it – of the object and purpose of intellectual work. An irresponsible killjoy riding a wave of self-satisfaction is a terrible thing. At the same time, it is worth considering the attitude opposed to Babbitt's "positivism," i.e., unconditional trust of traditional authorities (or authorities who refer to tradition). This attitude can quickly turn out to be merely a superficial or self-interested attachment to certain specific symbols (for example, those that define the status of a person born into a particular family) – a state of being accustomed to decorative staffage or a case of general inertia. Many seemingly noble forms conceal a void. On the other hand, the fall or discrediting of particular symbolic forms causes irreparable damage to *our* attitude towards concepts. After all, we have one life, in the here and now. Our search for wisdom is impacted by our status as painfully "one-time-only" creatures. It is more and more difficult for us to develop "rightness of thinking"; it is more and more challenging to move in the direction of something that today is indicated only by demolished or blurred signposts. Despite our respect for the people who put them up, many of these signposts should perhaps be rejected entirely, removed from our field of vision, since – manipulated, twisted – they can lead us astray, or at least discourage us. To continue, in Babbitt's words: *The positive and critical humanist would seem to have a certain tactical superiority over the religious traditionalist in dealing with the defects of the humanitarian programme* (we will get into what this flawed "humanitarian program" is shortly). *In the battle of ideas, as in other forms of warfare, the advantage is on the side of those who take the offensive. The modernists have broken with tradition partly because it is not sufficiently immediate, partly because it is not sufficiently experimental. Why not meet them on their own ground and, having got rid of every ounce of unnecessary metaphysical and theological baggage, oppose to them something that is both immediate and experimental – namely the presence in man of a higher will or power of control* (over himself)?[9] This quote raises further questions. At this point, we need only conclude that our review of concepts will not be conducted in peaceful conditions. Whether we like it or not, we are going to war together with the humanists.

II.

What does all this mean? After all, we were not supposed to fall out of the pan into the fire and get involved in creating another party, whose seats in the parliament of postmodernity would be numbered in advance or – in the event of deeper impertinence – swapped for cozy solitary confinement cells. A conviction that

9   Id., *Humanism: An Essay...*, p. 44.

our participation in the "battle of ideas" would not be siding with any of the factions we have come to recognize in the intellectual debate must underlie the choice not to change our minds. Henceforth, our fundamental question concerns the "transcendence" of humanism in relation to modern thought. Is this not too much? What could such immodestly conceived humanism be? And to top it all off, the "common-sense humility" in all of this! What can we be certain of? Besides the fact that, as we calmly assume in advance, being a "humanist" is not the condition or privilege of someone who does not like mathematics? We will follow this path – of a negative definition – by patiently asking: what is humanism (as understood by Babbitt, More, and most of their students) *not*?

First of all, humanism is not a doctrine. We may use the word "doctrine" in a colloquial and pejorative way, such as when we talk about "doctrinaires" and "doctrinairism," meaning a fossilization of viewpoints, their "staleness," especially someone's turning away from everyday life and disregarding teachings based on experience. Of course, such an attitude has nothing to do with "sound individualism," criticism, or "positivism" and "experientiality." We can also talk about a "doctrine" without reference to such contrasts, as any system of statements or set of views. At the highest possible level of generality, this would simply mean delineating a snippet of thought that is more "put together" or grounded. However, it is easy to descend into absurdity here since everything essential turns out to be someone's doctrine. From our point of view, it is much more useful to link doctrine with ideology, so that a doctrine would be a specific – still rather general – application of a "great narrative" such as "liberalism" or "socialism." At the same time, a "program" (political, economic, cultural) would be a practical way of implementing it. Here is not the time or place to consider the genesis or integrity of the known models of ideological attitudes. Suffice it to say that under the banner of "humanism" (sometimes known as "secular" or "new" humanism), we will quickly encounter more or less clever disciples of Voltaire's "Enlightenment," i.e., some versions of "liberals" or "socialists," and maybe even some

On the Mixing up and Explanation of Concepts

"secular conservatives." Moreover, this concept can serve as a euphemism similar to "social sensitivity": it is better to call yourself a "humanist" than a libertine or anti-clerical; "sensitive to inequality," rather than an advocate of social engineering. More's and Babbitt's legacy is not at all suitable for this type of image manipulation. Because he did write with his readers in mind, and with an eye toward rhetorical benefits, Babbitt develops a dichotomy between "false" and "true" liberals.[10] At the same time, More entangles himself in defining the conservatism of the Tories.[11] Trying to place either of them within a given party or labeling them an ideologue would mean one has understood nothing of what they wrote beyond these matters.

Does this mean we should acknowledge that the humanists' creativity emerges out of a void, that there were no connections, intellectual debts, or anticipation? Of course not. They were representatives of the educated strata of their time, undoubtedly immersed in the heritage of the previous century. As erudite but openly moralizing "critics of literature and life," they tried to draw on the best examples of nineteenth-century essay writing – today, we would call it "very cultured, but by no means 'correct'" – such as Charles-Augustin Sainte-Beuve or Matthew Arnold. Their bourgeois audience could rightly expect linguistic craftsmanship and wit from their writings. Among Americans, Ralph Waldo Emerson played an essential role in helping to sow the seeds of humanistic reflection, though More later criticized him. That being said, from the very beginning – let's assume that this refers to More's and Babbitt's meeting at Harvard in the early 1890s – the fundamental frame of reference here is fruitfully reinterpreted ancient literature, including texts from the Far East. So, is it not the case then that we can pick up, say, Aristotle's *Nicomachean Ethics* – a scientific, not religious or poetic text – and state

10 Cf. id., *Democracy and Leadership...*, especially pp. 246–49.
11 Cf. P. E. More, *Disraeli and Conservatism* [in:] tegoż, *Shelburne Essays Ninth Series: Aristocracy and Justice*, Boston–New York 1915, pp. 165 ff.

HUMANISM AS REALISM

simply: here is humanism, this is its doctrine? No, because the "service check of general concepts" requires taking into account the entirety of "Eastern and Western secular experience," which includes – as its culmination – the extensive range of findings made in modern thought. These findings may turn out to be not-much-better presentations of universal, eternal experiences, as successful or unsuccessful deductions from some creed imposed on the world. Yes, it is not certain that we humans understand ourselves better as a race than in antiquity. Nor do those who paid attention in history class find it hard to doubt moral progress. Generally speaking, there is no reason to believe that our age has any higher justification for its views. We have become unaccustomed to these kinds of questions, in any case. Either way, modernity may turn out to be illegitimate – just like that. So, we may want to go back to a time when the wisdom of philosophers seemed to be much more significant than it is today. Reaching for great intellectual works from the past may be useful or necessary for us, but it cannot be an end in itself. That would be a vain endeavor. It would surely be of no help to us to pretend that we are a lost tribe of the ancients, rather than part of the modern tribe, hungry for "something more" that this tribe does not have access to.

Thinking for ourselves, here and now, we should be talking about distilling the method rather than reconstructing the doctrine (as systematic teaching). Let us illustrate this point. In Babbitt's books, he repeatedly recapitulates judgments, the serious treatment of which opens up a new philosophical perspective. In doing so, he uses formulas explicitly given us by the classics – and is not satisfied with them. We can then learn (this is one of Babbitt's last statements) that the constitutive trait for "positive and critical humanism" of *the opposition between the two selves is well put by Cicero, one of the most influential of occidental humanists.* However, the question immediately arises: *why not simply reaffirm (...) the humanistic dualism in much the form in which Cicero stated it? Why complicate the situation by bringing in a discussion of grace, a purely religious problem? I have expressed the opinion on more than one*

On the Mixing up and Explanation of Concepts

occasion – Babbitt further states – *that there has been a serious omission in our modern attempts to construct sound philosophies of life – something that may turn out indeed to be the keystone of the arch. It may be that more is required, if we are to make good this omission, than simply to reassert 'reason' in the Ciceronian sense. A comparison may be of help at this point between occidental humanism and the great tradition of the Far East that is associated with Confucius.* In the latter, we find an idea *which is almost entirely absent, not only from Cicero but from Aristotle, who may be considered, doctrinally at least, as the most important of occidental humanists – the idea, namely, of humility.*[12] As we can see, humanistic humility returns in a vital context, but we still have to be patient. So far, we know that neither Cicero nor even Aristotle can have the last word. They are not the fathers of the humanist doctrine (understood as an existing and closed area of discourse). They are, on the other hand – if we can put it this way – great teachers of how to "do" humanism. Our task, then, is to take up and use their findings to explain concepts in our present situation. Similarly, though on a slightly different level, we can reach for Sir Thomas Elyot's Renaissance work *The Boke Named the Governour*, about which More stated that it is *the first treatise on education in the English tongue and still, after all these years, one of the wisest (...) naturally the method of training prescribed in the sixteenth century for the attainment of this goal is antiquated in some of its details, but it is not exaggeration, nevertheless, to speak of* The Boke Named the Governour *as the very Magna Carta of our education.*[13] Apart from the intrinsic value of Elyot's writings, it's easy to notice that such works as these separately constitute the heritage of numerous contemporary nations. In this sense, we, as Poles, also have our own humanists (native representatives of classical teaching, authors of works containing a non-modern

---

12 I. Babbitt, *On Being Creative and Other Essays*, New York 1968, pp. xv–xvi.

13 P. E. More, *Academic Leadership* [in:] id., *Aristocracy and Justice...*, pp. 53, 56. Cf. N. Foerster, *The American State University: Its Relation to Democracy*, Chapel Hill 1937, pp. 5, 44.

explication of concepts), from Master Wincenty Kadłubek to Jan Kochanowski, Łukasz Górnicki, and others; of course, this is not to say that we have our own doctrine of "polo-humanism," or anything of the sort – we do not.

Just as humanism cannot be forced into the Procrustean bed of doctrine, so also – this is the second step in our negative definition – we should not equate the term with the "substance" of any given historical epoch. In other words, it is not worth rushing to assess our heroes as posthumous children or epigones of the "age of humanism." Instead, we need to think more deeply – which we can only signal at this point – about how they captured historical tendencies or the fate of ideas. According to Babbitt, *the two most notable manifestations of the humanistic spirit that the world has seen, [were] that in ancient Greece and that in Confucian China.*[14] We are referring to particular works or, at best, intellectual formations constituting the ideals of ancient civilizations – important to us to the extent that they allow us to learn something about ourselves. The historical use of discussing "humanists" is associated with the figures of the Renaissance. We use this "historical meaning" to establish "psychological meaning," and this, according to Babbitt, applies to those who, *in any age, aim at proportionateness through a cultivation of the law of measure.*[15] However, when we take a closer look at the legacy of the Renaissance, it turns out that the protagonists of the intellectual scene of the time, who we are so eager to call "humanists," did not necessarily achieve the desired proportions and measures. Instead, we are dealing with the well-known swinging pendulum effect; or perhaps more precisely – the impact of the drunken horseback rider who, tilting to one side in the rush, goes faster and faster and so leans all the further (and more dangerously) to the opposite side.[16] *We have seen how the Renaissance protested against the supernaturalist excesses of*

14 I. Babbitt, *Humanism: An Essay...*, p. 37.
15 Ibid., p. 30.
16 Cf. P. E. More, *The Demon of The Absolute* (*New Shelburne Essays I*), Princeton 1928, p. 7.

the Middle Ages, against a onesidedness that widened unduly the gap between nature and human nature. Since that time the world has been tending to the opposite extreme; not content with establishing a better harmony between nature and human nature, it would close up the gap entirely.[17] What can we conclude from this? That, in short, we are the ones who are to regain the lost proportions and measures (meaning, as we shall see, the correct relationships between properly understood concepts). We should not follow the people of the Renaissance so much as correct their mistakes.

But again, there is something we have to factor out here. Earlier, we discussed the real and full radicalism of humanistic thinking (which should still be reconciled – however difficult it is – with "common-sense humility" and "proportioning"). But alongside this radicalism – or perhaps as a condition for it – we have a clear rejection of "hard" historiosophy. The presentation of historical phenomena and processes based on a deterministic schema cannot be reconciled with the sense of "free will" that ensures the significance of our individual decisions, the fundamental human perception of one's own experience as a whole directed toward a goal.[18] Addiction to history destroys the foundations of critical, "sound" individualism. To put it another way: if everything that happens has to happen, would it make sense to ask about past mistakes or to undertake any attempt at gaining control over the "modern experiment"? It would no longer be an "experiment," but the apparent result of centuries of homework in the subject of "humanity," as irrefutable as the answer to a math problem. Since things are progressing in the only possible direction, why voice your objections? A slight hesitation becomes an insult to reason, a cause for persecution or ostracism (a known curse for those who began to doubt the eschatological "givens" of the previous century, such as the "classless society" or the "end

17 I. Babbitt, *Literature and the American College: Essays in Defense of the Humanities*, Boston – New York 1908, pp. 28–29.
18 Cf. P. E. More, *The Sceptical Approach to Religion*, Princeton 1934, pp. 27 ff.

of history"). Meanwhile, the writing of humanists covers the years – decades, in fact, from the crisis point of faith in progress and decadence in the *belle époque* to the political and economic upheavals of the interwar period – when discussing the inevitable collapse and the necessary transformation of civilization was not unusual. But it was precisely the catastrophic and rationalizing vision of Oswald Spengler, characteristic of the period, that could draw nothing but severe and ironic criticism from Babbitt. *The whole conception – we read – not only implies a philosophy of history, but a philosophy of history that has, in my judgment, gone mad. This conception is based in any case on an utter denial of the quality of will in man on which I myself put supreme emphasis. In spite therefore of certain superficial resemblances in our respective views, Spengler and I are at the opposite poles of human thought. My own attitude is one of extreme unfriendliness to every possible philosophy of history (in the more technical sense of the term), whether it be the older type found in a Saint Augustine or a Bossuet, which tends to make of man the puppet of God, or the newer type which tends in all its varieties to make of man the puppet of nature. The Downfall of the Occident seems to me a fairly complete repertory of the naturalistic fallacies of the nineteenth century; it is steeped throughout in the special brand of fatalism in which these fallacies culminate, and as a result of which the Occident is actually threatened with "downfall."*[19] One can add with the same sarcasm that a humanist story is not meant to be a story about dying but about life. Suicidal desperation is the most obvious antithesis of humanism. It flows from the "metaphysical" consent to self-objectification and brings with it attempts to come to terms with an unacceptable situation by further mixing up and spoiling concepts to expose the allegedly rational premises of what we do with ourselves. Thus, the study of thoughts (concepts, discourses) should be understood as the study of what we (within the limits of human experience) *want* to be thought, not what the "epoch," "humanity" at a particular stage of development, or "nature" thinks for us. *Thought is the same yesterday and today* – More states

19 I. Babbitt, *Democracy and Leadership...*, pp. 42–43.

On the Mixing up and Explanation of Concepts

simply.[20] The modern is no more mature (or overripe) than the ancient. The course of history does not invalidate what humans can think.

The third point in our negative definition of "humanism" relates to the error of, and the temptation to treat More's and Babbitt's "offer" as the (unsuccessful) prediction of a substitute religion, of some kind of spiritual substitute for the intellectually agitated and lost. Religion is understood as more than a "doctrine" here. It would be appropriate to associate it with a life choice: not only what I preach, what I subscribe to, but a "way of life"; in this case – a life based on faith, recognizing the authority of the ministers of Revelation – since we are talking about a traditional religion in a form that Westerners would recognize. We are thus entering a vast area of findings concerning the current crisis – if not end – of the Christian faith treated seriously, permeating all aspects of everyday life. In the United States, at the beginning of the twentieth century, this meant an evident dissolution of the Puritan ethos, which, at the dawn of this mighty empire defined both the political system and commonly accepted moral principles. Babbitt discusses this quite picturesquely: *a few years ago I was walking one Sunday evening along a country road in a remote part of New England, and on passing a farmhouse saw through the window the members of the family around the lighted lamp, each one bending over a section of a "yellow" journal. I reflected that not many years before the Sunday reading of a family of this kind would have been the Bible. To progress from the Bible to the comic supplement would seem a progress from religious restraint to a mixture of anarchy and idiocy.*[21]

A man from whom the corset of tradition is removed becomes ideal prey for both sellers of cheap entertainment – in its "innocent," but wretched everyday form – as well as for all sorts of

---

20 P. E. More, *The Christ of the New Testament*, Princeton 1924, p. 4.
21 I. Babbitt, *Literature and the American...*, p. 64. Cf. A. Bloom, *The Closing of the American Mind: How Higher Education Has Failed Democracy and Impoverished the Souls of Today's Students*, New York 1987, pp. 170–71.

frauds, not to mention the prospect of having new, epoch-specific chains imposed: those of ideology or "correctness." An exceptionally accurate and suggestive description of this "in-between" state, referring to the spiritual condition of America in the 1920s, can be found in Walter Lippmann's writings (he was by no means a traditionalist; he was among Babbitt's students, although his own intellectual path fundamentally diverged from his master's teachings). According to Lippmann, there exist in this world *the gifts of a vital religion which can bring the whole of a man into adjustment with the whole of his relevant experience. Our forefathers had such a religion (...) the acids of modernity have dissolved that order for many of us, and there are some in consequence who think that the needs which religion fulfilled have also been dissolved;* the needs remained, however, and thus *the modern man who has ceased to believe, without ceasing to be credulous, hangs, as it were, between heaven and earth, and is at rest nowhere. There is no theory of the meaning and value of events which he is compelled to accept, but he is none the less compelled to accept the events. There is no moral authority to which he must turn now, but there is coercion in opinions, fashions and fads. There is for him no inevitable purpose in the universe, but there are elaborate necessities, physical, political, economic.* Events that concern man in the modern world contain *all the force of natural events, but not their majesty, all the tyrannical power of ancient institutions, but none of their moral certainty.*[22] The experience of the crisis (end) of religious life outlined this way should be considered constitutive for the reception of humanistic writing. An audience always wants answers to questions that it can and does pose. We are talking not about some niche phenomenon of *Weltschmerz* but about the growing and, for many, undoubtedly painful perception of change on a societal scale. But the humanists' response turns out to be quite heterogeneous. Its initial premise is the previously indicated identification of the addressees as young seekers. But what are the young to get? A new, more credible version of Revelation? Is this the

22 W. Lippmann, *A Preface to Morals*, New Brunswick–London 2009, pp. 8–9.

On the Mixing up and Explanation of Concepts

purpose of preaching the concepts? Or is it instead to overthrow traditional religion more wisely and effectively than the historic Renaissance or Enlightenment by proposing in its place a rational moral discourse – one different from the existing "theories" or justifications of what is necessary?

This seemingly most pressing issue for the self-determination of "humanism" as a movement in the academic and literary world of the interwar period – was "God dead" in their opinion? – was the subject of open controversy between the leading figures within this "movement." More's and Babbitt's subsequent texts reveal mutual tensions. When (in 1930) the most critical joint document of the humanist community was released, namely the collection of essays entitled *Humanism and America*, More (who had previously been reluctant to submit one of his numerous texts there) condemned in it *a divergence of views, although, perhaps for strategical reasons, perhaps in part because of a little uncertainty remaining in the minds of the contributors themselves, the matter has been kept rather in the background. However that may be, by reading between the lines or in some cases by taking into account knowledge otherwise obtained, one becomes aware that the allies are divided into three camps over the issue of religion. A few would appear to be actually hostile to any belief in the supernatural as essentially anti-humanistic (...) others, the majority I suspect, are friendly enough to religion in itself, but either have so vague a conception of its nature and function that practically it fades out of view, or, having clear views of what religion means to life, feel nevertheless that for the regeneration of art the program of humanism is adequate in and of itself. The remainder (...) hold that without a close Alliance between humanism and religion the former is shut off from its chief source of vitality. That is the issue; it cannot be bludgeoned into silence.*[23] Certainly, it may only surprise us that the crystallization of this controversy took place so late – be it "for strategic reasons" (it certainly had to do with rhetorical strategies, the art of gaining minds, or, to put it a bit more modestly, with reaching readers

---

23 P. E. More, *A Revival of Humanism* [in:] idem, *On Being Human* (*New Shelburne Essays III*), Princeton–London 1936, pp. 13–14.

with as consistent and unmistakable a message as possible) or for any other reason. This means that the shaping of humanism as a movement – especially in the 1920s – was burdened with tolerating a fundamental dispute and ambiguity internally. This burden also affects us, who are attempting to define "humanism" as a concept. This burden is especially palpable when reading the essays of the most famous of Babbitt's students, poet and later Nobel Prize winner, Thomas Stearns Eliot. He does not spare his fellow humanists venomous criticism, claiming that they are not humanistic enough. Eliot explains that *humanism depends very heavily upon the tergiversations of the word "human"; and in general, upon implying clear and distinct philosophic ideas which are never there. My objection is that the humanist makes use, in his separation of the "human" from the "natural," of that "supernatural" which he denies (...) man is man because he can recognize supernatural realities, not because he can invent them. Either everything in man can be traced as a development from below, or something must come from above. There is no avoiding that dilemma: you must be either a naturalist or a supernaturalist. If you remove from the word "human" all that the belief in the supernatural has given to man, you can view him finally as no more than an extremely clever, adaptable, and mischievous little animal.*[24] As we can see, Eliot's position concerns the very essence of humanism. His accusation is so painful because it negates the humanists' ability to take concepts seriously.

The immediate target of the attack is another prominent student of Babbitt's, Norman Foerster, about whom we read that he *is what I call a Heretic: that is, a person who seizes upon a truth and pushes it to the point at which it becomes a falsehood. In his hands, Humanism becomes something else, something more dangerous, because much more seductive to the best minds, than let us say Behaviorism.*[25] At this point, we should note that the argument cited consists of a mix of impertinence and valuable reflections (to which we will

24 T. S. Eliot, *Second Thoughts about Humanism* [in:] idem, *Selected Essays*, London 1999, p. 485.
25 Ibid., p. 488.

On the Mixing up and Explanation of Concepts

return when discussing religion). It is, however, a misguided attack – at least in the sense that it disregards the intent and level of expression of the abused adversary. The latter says of himself: *if, as a critical humanist – a "pure" or "mere" humanist – I cannot avail myself of all that* religion *offers, I can at least perceive that humanism and religion are in principle and in effect allied in opposition to what I have termed "naturism,"* (More and Babbitt would use the term "naturalism" instead), which in turn constitutes *the unsatisfactory program of the Occident since the seventeenth century (...) humanism is not a religion. It is possible, indeed, to conceive of a humanism without religion – an* alternative *to religion. Certainly humanism is capable of attracting the worldly as opposed to the otherworldly, because it offers, as naturism does not, order and happiness, if not the best order and happiness. It appeals to those who can find in themselves no vocation for spiritual humility, but who do find in themselves a steadying devotion to humane proportion. As an alternative to the ideal of the religious man, humanism in this incomplete sense offers the ideal of the civilized man. This is something; it is at least far better than the barbarism that prevails in most ages, including the present.*[26] Most importantly, the "incomplete" humanist does not preclude the "complete" humanist; we should think of the former as a specific stage, achievable here and now, of pulling people out of the modern form of barbarism. In any case, we cannot think of the "completeness" of humanism without reference to the supernatural, which allows for the spiritualization of some, and the "mere" civilization of others – and this should roughly correspond to Eliot's formula. We may presume that the essence of this controversy concerns the method: should the humanist refer to existing sources of religious authority, and if so, how? This method is implemented within a given historical context – the interwar period, which is far removed from our own. How and whom you should contact, what you may rely on when writing books or teaching courses at university, what you can achieve – all of these things depend on the circum-

---

26 N. Foerster, *Humanism and Religion*, "Forum," vol. 82, no. 3, September 1929, p. 147. Emphasis in original.

stances. In other words, this matter does not directly concern the "review" of the concepts discussed in this essay. So, for the time being, departing from the abyss of reflection on humanity, we can state quite unequivocally that the identification of humanism with religion – or an alternative (but "complete") version of life based on faith – is not what the humanists had in mind.

Let us dwell for a moment on the understanding of "Humanism" as a movement in its historical form. The basic approach is simple: it refers to a group of people directly inspired by Babbitt and More, their lectures and publications, and its duration spans less than four decades, counting from the beginning of the last century. We can consider the creation of such an environment as the result of the conscious actions of both thinkers. In his first book (from 1908), Babbitt provides an explicit formula for what constitutes the job of a serious academic teacher – *forming the minds and characters of the future citizens of a republic (...) those, who can receive the higher initiation into the Hellenic spirit will doubtless remain few in number, but these few will wield a potent influence for good, each in his own circle, if only from the ability they will thereby have acquired* (as the "initiated") *to escape from contemporary illusions.*[27] This is what the public disclosure of the humanist "program" looks like. On the other hand, one of Babbitt's later statements (from 1930) thoroughly explains his postulated *supreme emphasis on education. If the humanistic goal is to be attained, if the adult is to like and dislike the things he should – according to Plato, the ultimate aim of ethical endeavor – he must be trained in the appropriate habits almost from infancy. Occasional humanists may appear under present conditions, but if there is to be anything resembling a humanistic movement, the first stage would, as I have said, be that of Socratic definition; the second stage would be the coming together of a group of persons on the basis of this definition – the working out, in short, in the literal sense of that unjustly discredited word, of a convention; the third stage would almost inevitably be the attempt to make this*

27 I. Babbitt, *Literature and the American...*, pp. 178, 180.

On the Mixing up and Explanation of Concepts

convention effective through education.[28] We should immediately note that it would be wrong to take this description as retrospective. Despite his enormous didactic effort, the author did not achieve anything that could be considered a proper closing of the first stage. This is evidenced by, for example, the tensions surrounding the attitude towards religion signaled previously. The "service check of the vehicle of general concepts" has indeed begun – let the thesis be that this beginning is still worth our attention – but has not been completed. No true "unification" occurred, no effective *nomos* ("convention") emerged, the "future citizens of the republic" remained, en masse, completely unmoved. To put it sardonically, humanists have not influenced the history of the world all that much in the last hundred years. Historically, therefore, we have "Humanism" as a movement, but it is an unfulfilled movement, and its result does not fully reflect "humanism" as a concept.

The pinnacle of the "Humanist Movement" can be associated with the aforementioned publication of *Humanism and America*. The title itself should give one pause for thought, as it somewhat captures the relationship between the universal (humanism certainly concerns man in general, not only representatives of a given culture or nation) and the particular (America, well, isn't eternal). The editor of the entire volume is Norman Foerster (and one of the co-authors – his "persecutor," Eliot), from whom we learn that *being, in the main, historically educated men, however, humanists* (those belonging to the movement) *are well aware that a return to the past is impossible (...) if a present age appears to be bad, it can be changed only by the introduction of forces not vitally existing in that age, and since the future is always a blank, these forces can be found only through a reinterpretation of the past.* When we look back into the past, our eyes are drawn to great figures – as diverse as Homer, Buddha, and Dante – whose works are characterized by

28 Id., *What I Believe: Rousseau and Religion* [in:] id., *Spanish Character and Other Essays*, ed by. F. Manchester, F. Giese, W. F. Giese, Boston – New York 1940, pp. 243–44.

wisdom. We find in them excellent sources for reflection on "human perfection" and order. We are certainly not the first who wish to understand and use these resources to build (or rebuild) a civilization. *Yet, if humanism is never new, it must constantly confront new problems in time and place. In the Renaissance, its great foe was mediaeval otherworldliness; to-day its great foe is thisworldliness, obsession with physical things and the instincts that bind us to the animal order – in a word, the many forms of naturism that have all but destroyed humane insight, discipline, and elevation. In a given age, humanism may have the task of urging the claims of beauty; in another age the claims of science, or of conduct. It may have one problem in France, and another across the Channel. So long as America tends to set the pattern for the twentieth century, so long will the greatest problem of humanism lie here in the United States.*[29] Whatever one thinks about this approach to disagreement with modernity, one thing must be emphasized: we are dealing with a clear awareness of just how important it is – from the general human perspective, and not that of the good understood particularly (what is good for *us*) – to properly manage the most expansive political and civilizational creation that the United States was at that time (in 1930). Subsequent generations, staring in awe at the "stars" from across the ocean and pining over the great highways, have found themselves in the grip of this enormous success of *the American way of life*, which humanists would have preferred to prevent.

What we have said here about historical ("New") Humanism as a consciously "programmed" movement at the pinnacle of American society in the first half of the twentieth century will now allow us to close the first part of our attempt to negatively define "humanism" as a concept. Does it not simply signify an individual attitude? A kind of attitude that can and should be cultivated; self-development formulas based, above all, on reading the classics and drawing on their wisdom – for one's own benefit? If it is not a doctrine, not an epoch, not a religion, then maybe it is a special kind of personal choice, the aesthetic self-creation of

29   N. Foerster, *Preface* [in:] *Humanism and America...*, pp. xii, x.

On the Mixing up and Explanation of Concepts

a thinking individual against mass mediocrity? Thinking about ourselves, about the task of working on ourselves, we can find support, among others, in the Holy Bible, where we are asked a simple question (quoted with pleasure by More[30]): *what good is it for someone to gain the whole world, yet forfeit their soul?* (Mark 8: 36). Socratic philosophy, classical literature, the "Hellenic spirit" – all this is a school of practicing virtue, sculpting character, and caring for the soul. Far Eastern thought, which in turn is supposed to complement and support the humanist reinterpretation of the West's heritage, though full of idiosyncrasies, also focuses on the issue of what we can call "being decent." In general, we seem to be getting to the heart of the problem: premodern wisdom[31] does not focus on reforming societies or transforming humanity as a whole. If it proclaims progress, it is progress in improving a concrete, flesh-and-blood person, able to think for himself and, above all, control himself. This is our "sound individualist"! He might be "critical," as Babbitt wants, but his "critique" would not be suspended in the void of the passing moment; he would be, at best, the blood of the blood and bone of the bones of his noblest, most perfect spiritual ancestors, from whose experiences he would draw consciously, deliberately, never losing his sense of the specificity of his place and time. He would be the beneficiary of the concepts he had recovered for himself.

It would be "unsound," on the other hand, to succumb to momentary emotions – even those considered "positive" because they are rooted in sympathy. A life subject to a constant fluctuation of passions – such is the life of a bestialized man who would be less and less able to see himself from the side or from above; without sound judgment, without questioning, and without thinking – this the worst thing we can do to our souls. By losing

30 Cf. P. E. More, *The Religion of Plato*, Princeton–London 1921, especially p. 300.
31 Cf. id., *Delphi and Greek Literature* [in:] id., *Shelburne Essays Second Series*, New York–London 1907, p. 214.

sight of possible, though uncertain perfection – as the only true goal that brings forth real demands – we ensure ourselves certain, inevitable disintegration in our lifetime. Whoever understands this all-too-human dilemma may be called a "humanist." In Babbitt's opinion, *the humanist (...) as opposed to the humanitarian, is interested in the perfecting of the individual rather than in schemes for the elevation of mankind as a whole; and although he allows largely for sympathy, he insists that it be disciplined and tempered by judgment.*[32]

The humanist is, therefore, a realist. He knows the price of mediocrity and does not intend to pay it himself. Here, we must add a seemingly trivial caveat. If this "interest in the perfecting of the individual" were reduced to reasonably practiced egoism and the "auto-rationing" of sympathy, Babbitt's humanist would not write much of anything or would write only for himself, treating it as a purely individual test of character or an exercise of his intellect. His dedication to the cause and sacrifices in his role as a teacher would be a sham, and the movement he initiated would be nothing more than the byproduct of a rich personality. Perhaps this would constitute the "occasional" humanism he mentions. However, it was precisely this "occasionality" that Babbitt, openly confronted with the whole of the "modern experiment," decided to overcome. Why so? Is it enough to say that a sober person will not think himself to be an absolute monad, but rather – like the master Aristotle – will take the political dimension of his nature seriously? An affirmative answer seems appropriate, but it is also worth commenting further. Although critically focused on his soul, the humanist cannot accept the naive translation of perfect peace of mind – which would be *the peace of God, which transcends all understanding* (Philippians 4:7) – into peace in a political sense. We have a glaring example of the mixing up of concepts here. Babbitt states: *it is a matter of common sense and everyday experience that there can be no peace with the unrighteous and the unrighteous always have been and are extremely numerous (...) the virtue that sums up all other virtues in the secular order is, as every thinker worthy of*

32 I. Babbitt, *Literature and the American...*, p. 8.

On the Mixing up and Explanation of Concepts

the name has always seen, not peace but justice.[33] In short, the *real* work of a humanist – who does not give up life "in the secular order" while perfecting himself, but stands on the side of right-eousness – can mean going to war. In the realities of the modern world, this is ultimately a dispute with the type of thinking that feeds on the confusion of concepts, and as such, causes the faster and faster degradation of man, measured as something more than a fleeting manifestation of the expansion of protein forms – and finally the destruction of human civilization.

Again, we ask: does offering such an approach not simply fall within the modern supply of lifestyles, alongside other paths of engagement? To judge this, we should first establish at what level the premises of humanistic thinking are situated. Does it really go deeper than the (meta-) discourses that have dominated over the last few centuries? After all, how many times have fresh im-petuses been announced, citing inspirations that were distant in both time and space! Didn't the ideals of the *polis*, of Rome, of the Middle Ages, but also of the lamas, of yoginis, and of the man-darins of the East circulate? An indispensable step, then, is to de-fine the concept of "humanism" in relation to an opposing idea that would, as far as possible, contain all the meanders of the "program" of modernity. Such a concept, stubbornly reformu-lated and attacked by humanists, is "humanitarianism." Signifi-cantly, it is in itself a reaction to the frequent (possibly even the only contemporary) use of the word "humanism." Thus, accord-ing to Babbitt, *Gladstone speaks of the humanism of Auguste Comte, Professor Herford of the humanism of Rousseau, and the Germans in general of the humanism of Herder; whereas Comte, Rousseau, and Herder were all three not humanists, but humanitarian enthusiasts.*[34] What does this mean? What exactly is humanitarianism? Indeed, it must be a very absorbent concept, of primary importance, and having appeared prior to the innumerable mass of modern sign-boards and signposts, and yet one that is discursive for us. In any

33   Id., *Democracy and Leadership...*, pp. 221–22.
34   Id., *Literature and the American...*, p. 4.

case, if we want to seriously understand the "program" of humanism in its assumed distinctiveness, we have no choice but to consider the action of thoughts with an opposite vector.

III.

The word "humanitarianism" often appears in the humanists' texts. Its scope of meaning seems strongly context-dependent and is sometimes narrowed down to naively or falsely professed altruism. People usually talk a lot about the welfare of others – even that of the entire population of Earth – while simultaneously doing a lot to ensure concrete good for themselves. However, the real problem is not the difference, universal and irremovable, between the declared attitude and the actual attitude. On a side note, this difference can even be salutary – for example, when "human matter" resists the implementation of great ideological projects. From the humanist's point of view, the real problem lies in the first principles, or, which coincides in this case, with the approach to the ultimate questions. What end or goal is everything moving towards? People need to believe in something, take something on, seek something, rely on something. Humanitarianism is belief in humanity. This is a provisional formula because it requires that we first determine what "humanity" is and what this idea is based on – but we have to start somewhere. In Babbitt's view, *the great line that separates the new era from the old is (...) the idea of humanity and the cult of its collective achievements. With the decay of the traditional faith this cult of humanity is coming more and more to be our real religion.*[35] It becomes crucial to link the actual achievements of man – in fact, those of a few people who practice modern science – with their emotional reception, the shining hope that appears and grows upon the soil of waning traditions. The whole, as Foerster states in turn, is defined by two motifs: firstly, the "sympathy" found in oneself for all others, each of whom is "himself," i.e., a creation of nature, and should not be tormented

35 Ibid., pp. 34–35.

On the Mixing up and Explanation of Concepts

by the demand for spiritual development (do not do onto others ...); secondly, the orientation towards ensuring the constant improvement of living conditions in this, and not another world. *In place of a supernatural relations of souls, humanitarianism offered a natural relation of natural men. Christian love was metamorphosed into natural sympathy, and the old faith in personal immortality yielded to the new faith in social progress (...) in the new faith, a commiserating disposition was enough; God dropped out, or at most retained a faint and diminishing* Nachschein (we can understand this as an afterglow or simply a memory). *In the old faith, the essential virtue had been the humility of the spiritual man before God; in the new faith, it was the sympathy of the natural man for other men.*[36]

We can see from this that even a preliminary attempt at presenting humanitarianism leads to general religious reflection, or rather reflection on the fall of the old religion and a change in responding to religious needs. We can thus conclude that the term "humanitarianism" describes the specific social phenomena we mentioned earlier when we posed the question of whether humanism is a religion. Such a structure encourages the study of the disease symptoms – symptoms that recur with differing intensities and in different configurations. Someone could say that each generation finds its axis of observation, and so do we – if we have retained the ability to observe at all. The problem is how to go deeper, how to recognize an internal disease from blotches on the body, how to extract the basic principle of motion from an endless number of "engagements." It is particularly difficult to "descend" in the political dimension, where we necessarily act as adherents of a particular good – of our own country or of our own family. It is difficult to question the ideas which we think condition this good. Meanwhile, we should not assume that the disease is far away or that, for some reason, *we* are inoculated against it. Humanistic thinking is reflected in the reality of every modern state or nation while simultaneously creating – which we will consider separately – very deceptive aporias. The ideals of modern politics

---

36   N. Foerster, *The American State...*, p. 32.

are nothing but the ideals of the "new faith" in its subsequent versions, sanctioned by public opinion ("authorities"), as well as by state coercion. As Babbitt states: *democratic fraternity (...) and progress (...) are, however much they may clash at certain points, nevertheless only different aspects of the same naturalistic movement. This movement may be defined in its totality as humanitarianism.*[37]

In his first book, Babbitt proposed a clear outline of how humanitarianism became embedded in the history of ideas. This outline was seemingly unoriginal. As a starting point, we are to take the Copernican Revolution, which was followed by a change in perception of the relationship between man and nature. The English word "nature" in this context corresponds to the Polish word "przyroda"; what we are referring to, then, is physical nature, a set of things that – sooner or later, more easily or difficultly – can be touched and counted, or experienced and enjoyed. The rejection of the medieval vision of the order of creation, and especially the feeling of losing the intellectual guarantee for the regard that the Creator had for only man, not trees nor monkeys – all this gives rise to a fear that requires solace. With all its possible perturbations, this solace can only come from thought that assumes the unity of human nature and nature in general and ultimately offers us fulfillment in this unity. We are not privileged over all the rest, but we can settle ourselves in perfectly, being a conscious part of an infinite whole. To settle ourselves in – whether it be actively, undertaking the conquest of nature, which is possible thanks to a better and better knowledge of the laws to which we are subject; or passively, floating on the waves of natural instincts, which are located within us and constitute our emotions (feelings, sentiments). Both possibilities turn out to be grounded in the premises provided by naturalistic thinking, i.e., thinking that revolves around the hypothesis of the unity of man with nature or the completeness of humanity's natural image. Naturalism is, of course, not a modern phenomenon; according to Babbitt, it "coexisted" with humanism in antiquity and at the

---

37 I. Babbitt, *Democracy and Leadership...*, pp. 26–27.

On the Mixing up and Explanation of Concepts

dawn of the modern era. However, what is new – and precisely constitutive of modernity – is the transformation of naturalism into humanitarianism, of an intellectual attitude into a religious attitude (faith in humanity). *Naturalists then have evidently been divided into two great classes, according as the predominant temper has been sentimental or scientific, and corresponding closely to the two classes of naturalists have been the scientific and sentimental humanitarians. The positivist and utilitarian movements (...) have been inspired mainly by scientific humanitarianism, and sentimental naturalism again has been an important element, if not the most important element, in the so-called romantic movement.*[38]

Both the "scientific" and the "sentimental" option should be associated with the influence of two emblematic thinkers who broke with the past. These are the prophets of humanitarianism proper: Francis Bacon (first half of the 17th century) and Jean Jacques Rousseau (second half of the 18th century). In considering this point of Babbitt's outline, let us make two brief observations: first, it is not that those who follow the paths of this pair must directly admit their inheritance or affinity with them. However, such a relationship appears every time Bacon's faith in progress is strengthened or supplemented by Rousseau's faith in the liberation of the good man I am within. Man is liberated thanks to the "heart," which from the bottom-up exerts the pressure of "positive emotions." Second, we must realize that we cannot separate these surprising efflorescences of human thought from the specific needs of those who formulated them. Studying their biographies, we may quickly conclude that neither of them was a decent person. So just as flawed concepts favor flawed characters, so much the more flawed characters favor flawed concepts. People ruin words to justify their own conscious mistakes or weaknesses, to absolve themselves more or less literally.

In particular, Rousseau's "great" achievement is to make his own moral indolence a general human virtue. Connected with his trick is the concept of "primitivism," which – from the humanists'

38 Id., *Literature and the American...*, p. 33.

point of view – should be defined as a belief that we can fall back into the germ of our nature. Within each of us sits a "noble savage," innocently listening to the birds' trill and simultaneously demanding the restoration of freedoms taken away by civilization. The "primitivist dream," also present in ancient poetry, is taken very seriously in the current initiated by Rousseau in the fashion of true religion. It lies at the root of the mature, modern utopia. According to Babbitt, *the more or less innocent Arcadian dreamer is being transformed into the dangerous Utopist. He puts the blame of the conflict and the division of which he is conscious in himself upon the social conventions that set bounds to his temperament and impulses; once get rid of these purely artificial restrictions and he feels that he will again be at one with himself and "nature" (...) he is ready to shatter all the forms of civilized life in favor of something that never existed, of a state of nature that is only the projection of his own temperament and its dominant desires upon the void.*[39] However, whatever Rousseau comes up with – perhaps only to feel better about himself, in his own body – fits perfectly into the direction of modern thinking. This thinking requires the strengthening or supplementing of Bacon's prophecy about progress, while its religious dimension corresponds perfectly with the political dimension. The coming of a blessed transformation of humankind seems to depend upon the success of the new concept of rights. *Rousseau had many precursors (...) yet it was he who more than any other one person put behind the doctrine of the rights of man the imaginative and emotional driving power it still lacked, and at the same time supplied the missing elements to the religion of humanity.*[40] To understand the whole marriage that constitutes the "program" of humanitarianism, it is necessary to establish what connects the two trends at their foundation. Babbitt writes: *one can imagine the Rousseauist interrupting at this point to remark that one of his chief protests has always been against the mechanical and utilitarian and in general the scientific attitude towards life. This is true;* however, what turns out to be more important: *one can discern the cooperation of Baconian and Rousseauist from a*

39   Id., *Rousseau and Romanticism...*, p. 79.
40   Id., *Democracy and Leadership...*, p. 91.

On the Mixing up and Explanation of Concepts

very early stage of the great humanitarian movement in the midst of which we are still living. Both Baconian and Rousseauist are interested not in the struggle between good and evil in the breast of the individual, but in the progress of mankind as a whole. If the Rousseauist hopes to promote the progress of society by diffusing the spirit of brotherhood the Baconian or utilitarian hopes to achieve the same end by perfecting its machinery. It is scarcely necessary to add that these two main types of humanitarianism may be contained in almost any proportion in any particular person. By his worship of man in his future material advance, the Baconian betrays no less surely than the Rousseauist his faith in man's natural goodness.[41] In short, the key to both is their lack of humility. On the one hand, we can read this lack of humility as the absence or weakening of critical reflection on oneself, i.e., a deficit of character, and on the other hand, as a general abandonment of realism (in the assessment of human nature or nature in general) in favor of the realization of a utopia ("extracting" what is good from nature) and accepting the role of the modern prophet behind it. In both cases, the model figure of Prometheus comes to mind, who – it is worth remembering – is simultaneously the romantic incarnation of a rebel and a provider of goods in a material sense.

Something else also underlies all this, however – namely, "naturalistic fatalism." For one can argue that humanitarian optimism about the content of the human interior and the fate of humanity constitutes merely a particular phase of thought – or how this thought wishes to present itself – while fatalism is present in its deepest assumptions. Seen through the eyes of a naturalist, nature is an "empire of necessity." It does not matter whether we interpret "necessity" to ourselves based on the immutability of natural laws or fate or chance. The lion will not ask anyone – including itself – whether it should eat an antelope. It will just do what it is supposed to do – without thinking, without hesitating, without making decisions (in our human sense). But is our situation significantly different from that of the lion? Or is it that for us, too, things just happen, and what is supposedly above this natural

41 Id., *Rousseau and Romanticism...*, pp. 139, 137–38.

Humanism as Realism

flow is only a string of distortions caused by the burdensome social conventions and superstitions of the old civilization? After all, neither the energy resources that allow us to conquer the Universe nor the instincts that cause us to do what we do, come from us as agents consciously deciding for ourselves. Doesn't science itself prove that we are – like all the rest – determined? It is easy to guess that humanists object to such a perspective. What we wrote about earlier in the context of the rejection of historiosophical "narratives" (that there is a rational, necessary historical process within which we think not so much for ourselves as for our epoch) becomes, when supplemented, a clear premise for the critique of humanitarianism. However, the main object of this criticism is not the mental constructs isolated for analysis. Babbitt does not necessarily deal with the "technical" side of Bacon's or Rousseau's reasoning. However, the question of the effects of their writing keeps recurring. We can summarize this method by saying that, going down to the visceral level, we must keep in mind the blotches present on the body; or that a tree's fruit provides the best information about the root of the tree growing out of it. According to Babbitt, *the upshot of the whole* (Baconian-Rousseauist) *movement is to discredit moral effort on the part of the individual. Why should a man believe in the efficacy of this effort, why should he struggle to acquire character if he is convinced that he is being moulded like putty by influences beyond his control – the influence of climate, for example? Both science and romanticism have vied with one another in making of man a mere stop on which Nature may play what tune she will.*[42] Oh, how this omnipotent "Nature" fits the popular Freudian image of man as an innocent demoniac! Ultimately, there is probably no better illustration for the functioning of humanitarianism than the image of a modern, "educated" metropolis resident who seeks certainty and solace in a psychoanalyst's office.[43] And, honestly – what could be more degrading than falling victim to one's dreams?

---

42 Ibid., p. 163. Cf. ibid., especially pp. 187, 238, 300.
43 Cf. L. Kołakowski, *Psychoanalityczna teoria kultury* [in:] id., *Czy diabeł może...*, especially pp. 61–62.

On the Mixing up and Explanation of Concepts

Let's try to gather some findings. Humanitarian thinking means thinking about humanity in terms determined by philosophical naturalism, animated by a religious impulse, and producing overwhelming political (economic, cultural) effects. Thinking in this way, as we age with this thinking, we may be deeply disappointed, but we have no real alternative. There is only emotional drift ahead of us, with or without a smile. "Scientific" humanitarians will tell us about progress, development, economic growth, modernization, innovation, globalization and the like – thus accepting, into the depths of their faith and hope, as their first premise that change at the natural level is beneficial; that the winner is the one who best "gets along" with nature as an active part of that nature – even if this human part of us, through the naked force of its expansion – that is, the power to devour everything – turned out to be lethal to other particles in this system. On the other hand, "sentimental" humanitarians will create for us a language of cheap absolution or – more broadly – "natural" spiritual satisfaction, thanks to which we will finally be able to assume the pose of a noble savage, not giving up the gains of technology, but using them to indulge ourselves (as never before); the language of democracy, human rights, dialogue, multiculturalism (or monoculturalism, the melting into a particular, homogeneous community – a seemingly basic alternative, but only seeming), "authenticity," tolerance, emancipation, integration, "adrenaline," therapy, "positive emotions," not to mention "gender identity" and the art of love. Their fundamental premise also applies to the charity of expansion. It is only the accent, however clearly placed, that shifts from acquiring what is external to bringing out what is internal. However, the vector remains the same: towards expansion, opposed to concentration.

Moreover, abandoning the requirement of individual concentration is by no means balanced by taking advantage of the opportunities that life in the "global village" presents to us. On the contrary, the closer we get to one another – which is perfectly visible nowadays in the operation of the Internet or mass tourism – the more our life turns out to be false, lonely, and pointless. It is as if connecting on a global scale, we found ourselves in a void unknown to our poor ancestors, whose horizon was limited to the nearby church and tavern. In Babbitt's view, *a terrible danger lurks in the whole modern programme: it is a programme that makes for a formidable mechanical efficiency and so tends to bring into an ever closer material contact men who remain ethically centrifugal.*[44] In other words: we are less and less connected because there are no serious norms (statements about how to act, deduced from general concepts: good, justice, etc.) that all "contacts" would agree to. Such norms cannot be derived from individual self-expression or, say, from the expression of particular political entities, communities, or associations, or from "lifestyles" organized in some way or other. This experience of a "moral centrifuge" as a practical emanation of humanitarianism is undoubtedly crucial in the existential dimension and probably also – unfortunately – much more literally felt by us than by most people in More's and Babbitt's time.

It is also hard to deny that we have moved far away from the uncritical enthusiasm for the achievements of science and technology over the last century. Although the apocalyptic vision of machines rebelling dates back to at least the nineteenth century (More himself treats it quite seriously, albeit concisely, in his writings[45]), the food for our modern imagination in terms of modern "remorse" – from the dust of Hiroshima to the views of automated pigsties – nevertheless seems much more abundant. The more so because since the expeditions to the moon (several generations ago!), the romantic picture of penetrating unknown expanses of the Universe seems to have blurred a bit. Where are all those interplanetary cruisers, orbiting cities, teleportation devices? If you think about the quantity and quality of inventions disseminated during the time of the "Humanist Movement" (from airplanes to vacuum cleaners), these

---

44 I. Babbitt, *Rousseau and Romanticism...*, p. 331. Cf. ibid., pp. 156, 324.
45 Cf. P. E. More, *Samuel Butler of Erewhon* [in:] id., *A New England...*, pp. 193–94.

On the Mixing up and Explanation of Concepts

celebrated technological changes at the beginning of this century may seem almost bland; or to put it another way – oriented more towards the conquest of human nature (through the means of communication and control, this "ever closer material contact") than towards the conquest of nature as a whole. But faith in science is still the backbone of civilization as we know it. It accompanies us whenever we hand our bodies over to doctors, when we learn with hope about new ways to extend our lives, fight misfortune or discomfort, and in general in the sense of obviousness with which we eat the fruits of technological progress (even if they gained their fundamental shape many decades ago). Suppose there is more cynicism in us and less enthusiasm. In that case, it is all the more worth reaching for opinions from the times when the creed of science lacked the false note of ambivalence and contained more of the straightforward faith that did indeed change the material world.

Our need to invoke the humanitarian creed in pristine form perfectly accommodates the idol of scientific visionaries, Nikola Tesla. Let us cite one of his speeches, addressed in 1897 to the builders of a power plant in Niagara Falls. Bearing in mind the double outline of humanitarianism that we sketched following Babbitt, we face the purest – albeit philosophically inferior – formula of this way of thinking. Tesla states: *It was a happy day for the mass of humanity when the artist felt the desire of becoming a physician, an electrician, an engineer or mechanician or – whatnot – a mathematician or a financier; for it was he who wrought all these wonders and grandeur we are witnessing (...) let one concentrate all his energies in one single great effort, let him perceive a single truth, even though he be consumed by the sacred fire, then millions of less gifted men can easily follow.* It was this new artist of progress, *too, who awakened that broad philanthropic spirit which, even in old ages, shone in the teachings of noble reformers and philosophers.* There is no doubt that people are improving thanks to changes taking place on a global scale. Eternal peace – this is no longer a vague dream on the horizon of future achievements. A dozen or so years before the outbreak of World War I, Tesla dismissed the opinion that an armed clash of countries at the

HUMANISM AS REALISM

forefront of progress may occur one day. *The time will not be long in coming when those men who are turning their ingenuity to inventing quick-firing guns, torpedoes and other implements of destruction all the while assuring you that it is for the love and good of humanity will find no takers for their odious tools, and will realize that, had they used their inventive talent in other directions; they might have reaped a far better reward than the sestertia received.* By predicting the imminent end of wars between civilized nations, the speaker, in turn, foretells a different kind of "war" in which the enemy of humanity will be ... bacteria. Apart from the peculiarity of this juxtaposition itself – military conquests and successes in the development of medicine – it is hard not to think that someone who does not see the ironclad consistency in the attitude toward war has not understood much about human nature. Namely, since the dawn of political organization, people have been inclined to fight other people precisely because those others are similar to them in size and endowment; because they want to face them, gain an advantage, and rule. The humanist is aware of this and therefore knows that this game is not about peace but justice (in the form that those fighting understand it); we should keep this realistic motif in mind. However, let us return, to the record of the humanitarian's exposé. The event he is venerating on the road of progress *will stand out as designating a new and glorious epoch in the history of humanity – an epoch grander than that marked by the advent of the steam engine. We have many a monument of past ages: we have the palaces and pyramids, the temples of the Greeks and the cathedrals of Christendom. In them is exemplified the power of men, the greatness of nations, the love of art and religious devotion. But that monument at Niagara has something of its own, more in accord with our present thoughts and tendencies. It is a monument worthy of our scientific age, a true monument of enlightenment and of peace. It signifies the subjugation of natural forces to the service of man, the discontinuance of barbarous methods, the relieving of millions from want and suffering (...) if we want to reduce poverty and misery, if we want to give to every deserving individual what is needed for a safe existence of an intelligent being, we want to provide more machinery, more power (...) in the great enterprise at Niagara we see not only a bold engineering and*

On the Mixing up and Explanation of Concepts

commercial feat, but far more, a giant stride in the right direction as indicated both by exact science and philanthropy.[46]

If the above incantations sound foreign to us, this is because – in the overwhelming majority – we are not involved in the art of practicing modern science. We do not experience emotions related to the inventing and testing of "new solutions" and we know of laboratory experiments only from films. We are merely consumers of "new solutions" and at the same time – which is probably more difficult to accept – the broadly understood subjects upon which the "modern experiment" is being conducted. Foerster writes: *when the common man is reminded that this is the great age of science, he is reminded, primarily, that this is the age of the machine – of an endless flow of new and astonishing instruments of living. The power of which he is aware is the power of innumerable utilities. To the true scientist himself, this thirst for immediacy is always irritating.* A society built on the achievements of scientists will therefore not be a community of people facing the forces of nature, but a gigantic set of individuals hungry for material comfort, the conscious production of which is the result of the work of a few. In the political sense, it is nothing but a well-armed plutocracy (rule by the rich) because equal participation in consuming the fruits of progress is an obvious pipe dream. There are too many of us ... and we want too much. What we need to do, according to the logic of the "experiment," is to awaken our aspirations to make the most of the available resources of human energy. Contrary to what Tesla states, common folk do not so much follow the great artist of progress as they themselves become the material of progress, a contribution to the great mechanism of humanity's transformation, and finally – general processing waste. *What is wanted is a rugged individualism. The naked, abstract "natural man" of the eighteenth century is now clothed in the garments of the industrial age: he becomes the "economic man" in his first dress, he becomes the rugged individualist.*[47]

46 N. Tesla, *On Electricity* [in:] id., *The Nikola Tesla Treasury*, Radford, Virginia 2007, pp. 307–09, 312, 314.
47 N. Foerster, *The American State...*, pp. 52, 55.

The political sense of this "creation" will come up again later. For now, let's make the following observation. According to Foerster's approach, the indelible prestige of science is associated with the boon of technology, that is, with what science gives or promises to everyone. In other words, faith in humanity – apart from the fact that it feeds on enthusiasm, i.e., an irrational attitude (the very word "enthusiasm" comes from divine inspiration[48]), taken from the "old faith" and "invested" in "natural sympathy" – reaches deeper layers of faith in the beneficial power of expansion. As humanity, we reach further and further, acquire and take over progressively more, and we can prove it to ourselves! The proof of the proper course of affairs is the accumulation of achievements that supposedly improve life and make it a better expression of "oneself." In short, we derive our certainty – at least as long as we want and can think about it – from the fact that what is new turns out to be the most effective.[49] Thus, it would be appropriate to recognize – in reference to the material realm; we are leaving the spiritual realm aside – that with progress, nothing is lost. And yet, this is not true, and our actual understanding of how to deal with natural phenomena or techniques that in the past facilitated or diversified our lives with other people may even decrease. By nature, we are burdened with the disadvantage of forgetting. When the new comes, we lose sight of the old. We forget how this or that used to work, whether it was sometimes better for life and made it possible to express "yourself" more fully. However, this is a retrospective point of view. It is difficult to blame the thinkers who lived a hundred years ago – in the period of the greatest explosion of innovation, transformations of human needs, and living conditions – that this fundamental accumulation problem eluded them for the most part.

For a long time, we have focused on the "scientific" thread to immunize ourselves against associating the effects of humanitarianism only with the realm of "spiritual" grievances or emo-

48 Gr. $\dot{\varepsilon}v + \theta\varepsilon\acute{o}\varsigma + ov\sigma\acute{\iota}\alpha$.
49 Cf. I. Babbitt, *Rousseau and Romanticism...*, pp. 119, 148, 217–18, 363.

On the Mixing up and Explanation of Concepts

tions. These are not just "soft" issues; these are our cities, roads, and all the rest. Faith in humanity is embodied in every modern device, literally and figuratively. Indeed, we can repeat after Foerster that *what has actually happened (...) is that progress in power has been a substantial reality, while progress in service has been a chimera.*[50] However, let us quickly add, the intellectual front of humanism as a movement grows around this "chimera." This is evidenced by the number of pages written on "soft" topics, so the expected results of our "review of concepts" – if we wish to follow the paths of More and Babbitt – seem to be more about exposing the faith of "sentimental" than "scientific" humanitarians; more of a naive faith than one fortified with a string of impressive gains. Why, then, undertake a showdown with Romanticism (in one form or another) instead of attacking the foundations of Bacon's prophecy of progress? Babbitt's answer to this question may surprise you with its simplicity. According to him, *the devil, as is well known, is a comparatively harmless person unless he is allowed to disguise himself as an angel of light. An unvarnished materialism is in short less to be feared than sham spirituality.*[51] Developing this idea, it is easy to call the devil a devil when he has asbestos horns on his head and leaves carcinogenic fumes in his wake. It is easier to escape from a mechanical terminator (or a fuming boss demanding tangible results here and now) than to resist the ambiguous charms of the "flower children" (even the old ones). However, the choice between technocracy and counterculture is only seemingly a choice – and a real misfortune for thinking people who can grasp the shallowness and hopelessness of both primary forms of "engagement": a cog in a machine, on the one hand, an irresponsible madman on the other; for one loses true life and the other lives a false life. The most acute problem is the lack of an escape route from the laboratory of the modern world in which we are stuck; not only are we stuck not of our own volition, but we are also cleverly reared as

50 N. Foerster, *The American State...*, pp. 43–44.
51 I. Babbitt, *Democracy and Leaderhip...*, p. 308.

prisoners of the "centrifuge," who are allowed to live on the trough we are given, but on whom nothing depends.

Skepticism concerning further perspectives for the development of science and the corresponding political aspirations remain the most prominent motif of the humanist "program." In a 1924 book, Babbitt hits prophetic tones, writing: *the results of the material success and spiritual failure of the modern movement are before us. It is becoming obvious to everyone that the power of Occidental man has run very much ahead of his wisdom. The outlook might be more cheerful if there were any signs that Occidental man is seeking seriously to make up his deficiency on the side of wisdom. On the contrary, he is reaching out almost automatically for more and more power. If he succeeds in releasing the stores of energy that are locked up in the atom – and this seems to be the most recent ambition of our physicists – his final exploit may be to blow himself off the planet.*[52] Above all, we see in these words a poignant response to Tesla's imprudent cry cited earlier: "more power."

But, what of it? Elsewhere, Babbitt writes that *unethical science* (i.e., science that is not subjected to "truly humanistic or religious discipline") *is perhaps the worst monster that has yet been turned loose on the race (...) it would be possible to frame in the name of* insight (one of the key ideas in humanism) *an indictment against science that would make the indictment Rousseau has framed against it in the sense of instinct seem mild.*[53] Rightly so? In reinitiating the unfinished "service check of the vehicle of general concepts" after about a hundred years, should we not harshly evaluate what seems to be Babbitt's tactical retreat from the Baconian front? Let us leave this question unanswered for now. It is certain that if we want to propose an alternative to progressive modernity in its "scientific," utilitarian, or mechanical versions, then referring to the legacy of the Romantics, marked by the canon of "sham spirituality," for this purpose cannot be a good idea.

---

52 Ibid., p. 167. Cf. P. E. More, *Philosophy of War* [in:] id., *Aristocracy and Justice...*, pp. 223 ff.

53 I. Babbitt, *Rousseau and Romanticism...*, p. 383. Cf. id., *What I Believe...*, p. 237.

On the Mixing up and Explanation of Concepts

IV.

The concepts of "humanitarianism" and "humanism" appear less frequently in Paul Elmer More's writings than in Babbitt's. Here too, in the maze of studies concerning various philosophers' and poets' thought, it acquires a powerful connotation as an "overturned" form of religion, the clear foreshadowing of which lies in late antiquity, in the Gnostic reworking of the seeds of Christianity, if not deeper, among the meanderings of the Hellenistic spirit.[54] More, a true master of English prose, a prolific scholar, and an efficient "idea detective," operates on many levels and makes use of various contexts. All the greater is the weight of his criticism of modern thinking, thinking, which offers us a "simulacrum of happiness" through fleeting, illusory reconciliation with the material world, with a lack of the true gravity demanded by humanists.[55] Although a multitude of attitudes, "theories," and "worldviews" collide and reproduce on the surface of the intellectual corpus of modernity, at its core it turns out to be a monolith. In More's view, *to the superficial observer it might appear, in fact does appear, that the acknowledged distractions under which the artist, with the rest of us, suffers is the result of conflicting theories of life; but a closer study of the phenomena will show, I think, that we are rather under the sway of a single philosophy* (however, not in the sense of classical philosophy, but rather what is considered "philosophy" in the modern sense) *which bears in itself the inevitable seeds of contradiction. We subscribe indeed to innumerable isms, but they all go back to that ism of nature which was one of the peculiar products of the Renaissance, and which, for English readers, found its most eloquent advocate in Francis Bacon. We are all (...) seeking for liberty by submitting the mind to things; we*

54 Cf. P. E. More, *Property and Law* [in:] id., *Aristocracy and Justice...*, p. 135; id., *Tolstoy; or, the Ancient Feud Between Philosophy and Art* [in:] id.., *Shelburne Essays First Series*, New York–London 1904, p. 208; id., *Christ the Word*, Princeton 1927, p. 69; id., *William Beckford* [in:] id., *Shelburne Essays Eighth Series: The Drift of Romanticism*, New York–Boston 1913, pp. 20–23.

55 Cf. idem, *A Revival of Humanism...*, p. 19.

are set upon mastering nature by regarding ourselves as a part of nature. In Aristotle's thought, which was dominant immediately prior and which, at least in this respect – despite the flaws of scholasticism, against which the early modern thinkers rightly argued – corresponded to the best premises of classical thought, man *is both of nature and above nature; as an animal he belongs to the natural realm of unconscious ends, while as a human being he possesses in addition to his animal instincts the faculty of consciously directive purpose. Here, in this faculty of conscious purpose, begins the field of conduct, of ethics and statecraft and religion, wherein a man makes* of himself *by free choice, under certain limitations, that which he will; and here lies the field of art, wherein a man makes* for himself *that which he will. The recognition of this dualism of the natural and the supernatural in man (or of a higher and a lower nature, for the word "nature" is as unstable as the sea) is precisely the philosophy of humanism, as contrasted with the philosophy of naturalism, which denies that the distinctive mark of man is a consciously directive will.*[56]

After rejecting the old, bipartite concept of man on the basis of naturalism – this "ism of nature" – we are left with nothing to do but to take part in a performance based on the constant switching of two scenarios. In the first, we are fundamentally made cogs inside a "huge fatalistic machine." In the second, everything boils down to chance and arbitrary decisions. A possible rebellion – usually perceived as the prerogative of an artist who can "do more" (thus, in the eyes of the crowd, it is worth being an artist!) – against the ordered satrapy of natural phenomena thus leads, almost automatically, to a descent into the tyranny of nonsense. In short, into madness. *Some of the more courageous rebels have even sought a way of escape by claiming for the imagination a complete independence of the laws of life (…) but that is only to fall from one absolute into another, to exchange servitude for vacuity.*[57]

More's writing undoubtedly comes to the aid of all that we have tried to recreate thus far based on Babbitt's arguments. This

56   Id., *The Demon of The Absolute*..., pp. ix-x. Emphasis in original.
57   Ibid., p. xii.

On the Mixing up and Explanation of Concepts

should come as no surprise, as they were friends, discussing issues together and inspiring one another. At the same time, we can follow specific threads or accents in their texts, which help fill out our image of thought on the vector opposite to humanism. To begin, then, we have a fundamental dichotomy: that of "monism" and "dualism." The naturalistic position on which the humanitarian religion of humanity is based seems to be a version of monism, while humanism, in turn, requires dualism as its philosophical basis. Since we are not able to adequately address this issue here, it's important to emphasize one thing: we do not understand dualism as a thesis or a solution on an ontological level; it is not like the Cartesian division of substances or anything like that; it concerns a universal experience of self-awareness that is not mediated by discourse and is in this sense pre-philosophical; it is, in short, a dichotomy of purpose and lack of purpose; order and disorder; roads and swamps; shape and shapelessness. Secondly, according to More, the key event of the nineteenth century was the formulation of Darwin's theory of evolution, which, by its extraordinary reception, led to the *de facto* hegemony of naturalistic monism in the common understanding of human affairs. This theory very effectively injects into the mass imagination – and the political imagination, which, after all, eagerly feeds on some or other translation of the concept of "natural selection" into norms binding in society – a formula of law constituting a naturalistic substitute for divine rights. Namely, this is the "law of change," which betrays a general belief that change as such leads to good. More writes: *science and romanticism sprang up together and have grown side by side. In one respect they have embraced diverse, even hostile, temperaments – on this side the man who deals with facts and tends to a hard materialism or a dry intellectualism, on the other the man of sentiment who dreams and loses himself in futile revery. Yet it is a notorious, if paradoxical, fact that the effect of science on art and literature has been to reinforce a romantic impressionism* (that is, the tendency to admire change, to receive sensual impressions ecstatically and to "deeply" experience the fluctuation of one's mood), *and that the man of scientific training when he turns to the humanities is almost always an impressionist. The reason is plain: he simply carries into art the law of change with which he has dealt in his proper sphere, and acknowledges no principle of taste superior to the shifting pleasure of the individual. In this he is typical of the age, for if the particular causo-mechanical theory of evolution promulgated by Darwin has proved untenable, evolution itself has remained as almost, if not quite, the universal creed of those who believe that some such hypothesis will ultimately be found adequate to explain all the processes of life. Men of science are only servants of the law of change in their special field of material observation, and it is easy to trace the working of the same belief in other regions of contemporary thought.*[58] Therefore, thirdly, the intellectual investigation conducted by More directs our attention to the entanglement of thinking, at first homogeneous, in multiple discourses – those "isms" – that describe various areas of life (such as the economy or education) in seemingly various ways, but which in fact can be reduced to one mental wedge from which individual denominations of modern religion emerge like on the arms of a compass.

This same naturalistic "mental wedge" is by no means a result of the achievements of nineteenth-century experimental science or even of contemporary reflections on progress. Darwin's and Spencer's ideas only constitute a particular stage of the emergence of the new "philosophy," which we should associate not so much with the selfless search for truth as with the acceptance of some predetermined vision of reality that is satisfying for the modern mind. What is this vision? More's answer contains four points, each of which merits a separate elaboration. At this point, we can only list them, preferably using the words of the author himself: *a faith in drifting; a belief that things of themselves, by a kind of natural gravity of goodness in them, move always on and on in the right direction; a confiding trust in human nature as needing no restraint and compression, but rather full liberty to follow its own impulsive desires to expand; an inclination to take sides with the emotions in*

---

58 Id., *Victorian Literature (The Philosophy of Change)* [in:] id., *Shelburne Essays Seventh Series*, Boston–New York 1910, pp. 251–52.

their rebellion against the inhibitions of judgment (...) and [what is] *the goal of this drifting?* – asks More, moving at this point (and it is the year 1915) to the level of political reflection – *as I read history and see it now making, we have two clear warnings of what the end must be. Just as the sentimental philosophy of the eighteenth century preceded the Napoleonic wars, so our humanitarianism, our feminism, socialism, equalitarianism, pacifism – all our sentimental isms, are indeed not the direct cause of the present war, but have so prepared the material for it that a slight spark was sufficient to set the whole world aflame with the passions of suspicion, hatred, and revenge, and to arouse in the most scientific land of all a veritable mania of organized brutality. All this is not the end; it is an admonition to reconsider those ideas of justice and discipline and true government which we have so lightly thrust aside (...) will the warning be heeded when the peace of exhaustion has come, or shall we mistake fatigue for wisdom, and so drift on to the utter catastrophe?*[59] Let us pose our question right off the bat: would More consider the hecatomb of World War II such a catastrophe, or would the irreversible consequences of a nuclear explosion fit better, or is it not so much about a final conflict as the eternal agony of humankind in a state of what we could call biomass farming – who knows? In any case, it is difficult not to associate More's phrase concerning "fatigue" with "the end of the age of ideology" and the conviction that you can make a mockery of all old disputes by listening to good music in bed.

Time passes, and the immediate experiences of subsequent catastrophes – not only those of war – are forgotten. Living tissue naturally passes into record. What has been recorded from past experiences goes on to the storehouses of history, and each of its rooms is locked for ordinary mortals. We are not necessarily referring to classified archives or censorship – instead, it has to do with interpretative keys. Assigned to different "isms" (or "narratives"), we view the whole through one piece or another that has been in-

59   Id., *Aristocracy and Justice...*, pp. viii-x; cf. id., *The Quest of A Century* [in:] idem, *Shelburne Essays Third Series*, New York–London 1907, p. 254.

terpreted for us; we "catch" thoughts without thinking for ourselves. The disturbing image of "drifting" described by More can be read on many levels, beginning with a passively lived relationship with a mystical "absolute," the desire to "consume," which is perhaps the most profound reason for the modern transformation of ideals, the birth of a new "philosophy" or eschatology. We will leave the absolute aside for now. Far removed from the elation of mystics, ordinary people living from day to day, who do not think for themselves or control themselves; people carried with the flow of events, gliding here and there in networks woven from concepts that no one checks – on this plane, unfortunately, we can all meet at will. Having realized this – having acquired a healthy distance to the current divisions and "engagements" – we begin to see humanitarianism as the primary direction of thinking or vector of the human spirit that sets the boundaries of reflection and shapes individual ideologies, doctrines, programs (political, economic, cultural). The practical impact of humanitarianism – faith in humanity – permeates every aspect of modern society, including what we are used to considering a part of the private sphere (however unspecified!). In other words, the societies of not one country. This also does not only refer to Western countries, since we know very well that modernity has spread throughout the world, that the raison d'être of once separate great civilizations was to take on Western models and join the game – we can call it the game for humanity – initiated in modern Europe. A game in which the United States was the constant leader for a good century.

Of course, there is no reason to believe that our Polish experiences, somewhat peculiar against the backdrop of our neighbors' memories, have nothing to do with the humanitarian profession of faith. It is enough to recall the famous two coffins and two doctrines that clashed during the turbulent process of building a modern Polish Republic. To simplify somewhat, the Piłsudski doctrine has much in common with sentimental humanitarianism or romanticism, while that of the National Democrats – with scientific humanitarianism and social Darwinism. It seems that the critique of romanticism may be especially problematic for us since it is not conducted in the name of enlightenment or rationalism (colloquially: "hard facts," "numbers," and "concretes" pitted against "ideas," "wishes," "dreams of power," etc.), but in that of humanism. In a way, this critique expresses the first phase of the humanist attack on modernity, the meaning of which remains difficult for us to grasp. The accusation of romanticism encompasses figures as diverse as Friedrich Nietzsche and John Henry Newman. Romantic thinkers get carried away, surrender to their emotions, lose their sense of measure and purpose; they cease to be realists. Recognized masters of poetry are accused of feelings of exaltation or of being dreamy aesthetes and, ultimately, of promoting "sham spirituality." According to More, *our disease is chiefly of the imagination; we are poisoned by our poets.*[60] We may argue that this "sham spirituality" of narrow circles became a household commodity over subsequent decades; that the heirs of Rousseau now populate television screens and festival scenes; they flirt with each other in TV series or roll around in the mud. They are amorous and "authentic." But what does this world of mass culture idols have to do with the great museum statues that the outstanding artists of the Romantic era, our national artists, have become to us?

The problem is that, from our point of view, modern language has long ago hardened among the incomprehensible relics of antiquity. Not only is it difficult for us to understand what our ancestors broke with, but it is also difficult to imagine the break itself. What is classical, and what is modern? What is Christian, and what is humanitarian? The idea of the nation-state – in its welfare state version, with free education, pensions for everyone, and all the other particular policy solutions – seems to us as ancient and respectable as the idea of Christendom. It is even hard not to combine these paradigms, connecting Rome to Częstochowa, Częstochowa to the independent Republic of Poland. Unfortunately, a critical analysis of the process of including the peripheral Polish element in the framework of modernity – one

60 Id., *The Sceptical Approach...*, p. 55.

HUMANISM AS REALISM

based on humanistic reflection, not on any sort of renunciations – has yet to be written. The writings of American humanists cannot directly help us deal with our native pool of issues, and we can only signal this task in the present essay. Indeed, it is enough to think of the figures and ideas that the Age of Romanticism left in the Polish political imagination (such as the King-Spirit).

Before a future critic reaches for great, dusty volumes of literature, perhaps it would be good to recommend a particular exercise to him. Hristo Botev's 1875 poem *My Prayer*[61] can help with this exercise. It is an endearingly transparent attempt by an "engaged" poet to lay out a new, humanitarian eschatology. It is worth considering its stanzas and reflecting – *sine ira et studio*, with this concrete work in mind – how the universal religion of humanity, ascribed to every heart, becomes the spiritual basis for the building of the particular political creation that is the modern nation-state; in this case (highlighted only for the purposes of our critic's exercise) – the Bulgarian state.

Botev writes:

> Oh, you, my God, my fair God,
> who doesn't live in Heaven up,
> but you, who are in me, my God,
> into my soul and in my heart.
>
> Not you to whom the monks and priests
> make their bows and bend, not you
> whom all the orthodoxal beasts
> light up the sacred tapers to.
>
> Not you who made of mud and dirt
> the man, the woman, but forsakes
> the human being on the Earth
> to be its everlasting slave.
> Not you who's consecrated kings,

61 See H. Botev, *My Prayer*, trans. T. Marinova, https://liternet.bg/publish5/hbotev/poezia/moiata-molitva-en.htm. Accessed 19 Oct. 2021.

On the Mixing up and Explanation of Concepts

the patriarchs and every Pope,
not you who's left in misery
my poor brothers in the woe.

Not you, who teaches slaves to pray,
to cry for mercy and to bear
the suffering until the grave
with their hopes in vain to cherish.

Not you, oh, God of liars, who
has blessed dishonest tyrants all,
not you, an idol of the fools,
an idol of the human foes.

But you, oh, God of sense and mind,
oh, God, defender of the slaves,
whose day the people and mankind
are going soon to celebrate.

Inspire everyone, oh, God
with love alive for freedom, then
each one will struggle as he could
with all the enemies of men.

And at the end support my arms,
when rises the revolt of slaves,
in rows of their fight at last
to find also my only grave.

Don't let abroad this vigour heart
lost in youth cool down at present.
Don't let my voice unlikely pass
silently as through the desert.

What the poet's God is for him, what He is for each of us – that is
the question that the humanist must ask sooner or later. Even

though, as we know, he does not consider himself a theologian and does not intend to influence anyone else's relationship to the ultimate questions.

V.

The difficulty in understanding the meaning of "humanism" as a concept corresponds with the bizarre circumstance that one of the best contributions to humanistic reflection was written to depreciate humanism. That contribution is the text *Humanism and the Religious Attitude* by English poet and essayist Thomas Hulme (1883-1917), included in the posthumous (1924) collection *Speculations*. Hulme was an excellent personification of the verse: "The Spirit breatheth where he will" (John 3:8, Wycliffe Bible). He was not a scholar; he lived on the outskirts of the academic world. In fact, he never completed his many years of philosophical studies (begun at Cambridge), but he traveled the world extensively and won the favor of Henri Bergson himself – who at that time was considered to be perhaps the greatest living philosopher – only to become a fundamental critic of Bergson's after many years. He took important notes, which he did not have time to use, as he died on one of the fronts of the First World War. Undoubtedly a gentleman and an aesthete, he was simultaneously an enthusiast of military memorabilia and an almost fanatical eulogist of the military.[62] Feeling deeply dissatisfied with the direction in which modern thought was developing, he created the concept of breaking the fetters of modern thinking as a whole – and called this concept the "critique of satisfaction." His description of intellectual awakening is undoubtedly worth quoting: *I remember being completely overawed by the vocabulary and scientific method of the various philosophers of the Marburg School, and in particular by Herman Cohen's* Logik der reinen Erkenntniss ("the logic of pure knowledge"). *But one day, hearing Cohen lecture on religion, where his*

---

62 Cf. H. Read, *Introduction* [in:] T. E. Hulme, *Speculations: Essays on Humanism and the Philosophy of Art.*, ed. H. Read, London–New York 1936, pp. ix ff.

On the Mixing up and Explanation of Concepts

views are, as is well known, entirely sectarian, I realised very easily that the overwhelming and elaborate method only served to express a perfectly simple and fallible human attitude. This was very exhilarating and enlightening. One could at last stand free, disentangled from the influence of their paralysing and elaborate method. For what was true of their work in religion was also true elsewhere. It becomes possible to see a good deal of Cohen's work as the rigid, scientific expression of an attitude that is neither rigid nor scientific, but sometimes romantic, and always humanist (we'll discuss what Hulme means by the "humanistic attitude" in a moment). Explaining it by way of analogy, *a man might be clothed in armour so complicated and elaborate, that to an inhabitant of another planet who had never seen armour before, he might seem like some entirely impersonal and omnipotent mechanical force. But if he saw the armour running after a lady or eating tarts in the pantry, he would realise at once, that it was not a godlike or mechanical force, but an ordinary human being extraordinarily armed (...) when you have recovered from the precision and refinement of the* method *in such philosophers, you will be able to recognise the frequent vulgarity of their* conclusions. *It is possible to combine extreme subtlety in the one, with exceeding commonplaceness in the other.*[63] In a word, it turns out that the Emperor has no clothes.

Hulme's work, though only outlined here, may appear to be a small, but potent source of inspiration for serious critics of modernity – at least those who, having come to know the contemporary academic discourse, similarly feel the conceptual pressure concealing the confusion, emptiness, or mediocrity in the heads of "authorities." Could this work count on the approval of American humanists and on its being used to meet the needs of the movement they initiated? Well, not really. Indeed, we can find it in the broadly defined list of "humanistic" reading at the end of the book *Humanism and America* mentioned above. Eliot also alluded to the essay we quoted in his attack on Foerster and Babbitt.[64] However, there is a conceptual barrier between the writings

---

63 T. E. Hulme, *Humanism and the Religious Attitude* [in:] idem, *Speculations...*, pp. 19–20. Emphasis in original.
64 Cf. T. S. Eliot, *Second Thoughts...*, pp. 489–91.

of the humanists and that of Hulme. First, Hulme does not understand "philosophy" in the Socratic sense, as a life based on the love of wisdom, but – as a consequence of his enlightenment about the role of the "scientific method" – in an eminently technical sense, as a "pure philosophy" dealing with an almost mathematical investigation into *the relations between certain very abstract categories*. As such, he then separates it, unambiguously and indisputably, from the issue of worldview or professed values. Edmund Husserl and Bertrand Russell should be considered proper proponents of "pure philosophy." This does not mean that Hulme values their views. *While I entirely agree with what they say as to the possibility of a purely scientific philosophy and the necessity for a clear separation between that and a* Weltanschauung (a philosopher-thinker's worldview or world of values), *yet for the purpose of my argument in this Notebook I must lay emphasis on a different aspect of this separation (...) they want the* Weltanschauung *separated from philosophy because they think it* (Weltanschauung) *has often injuriously affected the scientific part of the subject. I, on the contrary, want it separated because I think it also forms part of a* separate *subject, which has in reality no connection with philosophy (...) while what they say is satisfactory in its description of the nature of a purely scientific philosophy, it is extremely unsatisfactory in what is has to say about the nature of a* Weltanschauung.[65] Here is where Hulme's attempt to outline this separate discipline of "worldview" begins. However, the price of this intellectual procedure is quite high, as the history of human thought begins to resemble a sequence (not necessarily a "rational" one) of "attitudes" demonstrated in turn, of which – as we shall see – two count: the modern attitude and the one replaced by the modern attitude. Thus, the ancient emphasis on the integrity of the philosophical life, the activity of the mind, and the exercise of character or cultivation of virtue were lost.

Though, as we have already observed, the word "philosophy" could appear in More in the sense of a professed doctrine ("theory"),

---

65 T. E. Hulme, *Humanism and the Religious...*, pp. 14, 29. Emphasis in original.

On the Mixing up and Explanation of Concepts

roughly corresponding to Hulme's "worldview," the classical understanding of philosophy – as we will see elsewhere – must be extracted and maintained on the grounds of humanism. And there is undoubtedly no praise for "purely scientific philosophy" or the results of a "strict" treatment of "certain very abstract categories." The humanistic "review of concepts" makes sense insofar as we move within the living tissue of human experiences and not in the field of reasoned abstractions. We can assume that this difference results from the young thinker's personal and perhaps not fully digested fascination with the mathematic nature of the logic developed at that time. Apparently, he did not read Babbitt's first book either, since – secondly – in aiming to expose modern people's true, fundamental attitude, he called that attitude humanism. According to Hulme, *an understanding of the religious philosophy* (not "scientific philosophy"), *which preceded the Renaissance makes the essential unity of all philosophy since seem at once obvious. It all rests on the same conception of the nature of man, and exhibits the same inability to realise the meaning of the dogma of Original Sin. Our difficulty now, of course, is that we are really incapable of understanding how any other view but the humanistic could be seriously held by intelligent and emancipated man; or that an intelligent man might not be a humanist.* And further: *I hold* – Hulme confesses – *the religious conception of ultimate values to be right, the humanist (...) I have none of the feelings of nostalgia, the reverence for tradition, the desire to recapture the sentiment of Fra Angelico, which seems to animate most modern defenders of religion. All that seems to me to be bosh. What is important, is what nobody seems to realise – the dogmas like that of Original Sin, which are the closest expression of the categories of the religious attitude. That man is in no sense perfect, but a wretched creature, who can yet apprehend perfection.*[66] Putting these minor reservations aside, we can say that Hulme's "humanism" is, in fact, humanitarianism.

Why, then, should the argument of someone who has made such a mess with his use of the concepts of "philosophy" and "humanism" be such an essential supplement for us to the barely touched-on views of Babbitt, More, and Foerster? We must keep

66 Ibid., pp. 12–13, 70–71. Emphasis in original.

in mind that what we are talking about here are notes edited and published after their author's death. In contrast, the humanists' texts were generally published during their lifetimes, most often in the form of systematized books, thus reflecting the advantages and disadvantages of consciously adopted rhetoric. If we filter some idiosyncrasies out of Hulme's text, it turns out to be very useful in correctly indicating modern thought's center of gravity; that is, on what level naturalism turns into humanitarianism and how to "feel out" this place by reaching for it with a thought that just risked freeing itself from the conceptual trap. The starting point for these findings is realizing the possibility of replacing what Hulme calls the "principle of continuity" – which was finally formulated in the nineteenth century – with the no less legitimate and opposite-oriented "principle of discontinuity." The former, *originally urged only by the few (...) has spread – implicit in the popular conception of evolution – till it has attained the status of a category. We now absorb it unconsciously from an environment already completely soaked in it; so that we regard it not as a principle in the light of which certain regions of fact can be conveniently ordered, but as an inevitable constituent of reality itself.* If something cannot be different than it is, that means that when it seems different – it only "seems" so; not being able to think of discontinuity as such, we are also unable to perceive – respectively – the phenomena to which it gives rise. *For an objective view of reality we must make use both of the categories of continuity and discontinuity. Our principal concern then at the present moment should be the re-establishment of the temper or disposition of mind which can look at a gap or chasm without shuddering.* It is on the bold treatment of the premises of thoughts that seem to have settled at the bottom of our perception that it depends whether we can *emancipate* [ourselves] (...) *from the influence of certain* pseudo-categories (concepts that are not obvious but are considered obvious). *We are all of us under the influence of a number of abstract ideas, of which we are as a matter of fact unconscious. We do not see them, but see other things through them.*[67]

67   Ibid., pp. 3–4, 37. Emphasis in original. Cf. ibid., pp. 65 ff.

On the Mixing up and Explanation of Concepts

Precisely! Concepts expressed and mutually relayed in a certain way turn out to constitute one large filter or lens – like a light-breaking mega-bubble inside which each of us lives separately and tries to think, leading to our thinking being looped.

According to Hulme, the knife to break this loop lies in the indicated confrontation of two "principles." Namely, despite the brakes implanted in us, we must consider the example of "absolute discontinuity" that imposes itself on us. Our thoughts concern three separate areas of reality: the "inorganic world" (which mathematics and physics deal with), the "organic world" (dealt with by biology, but also psychology and history), and the "world of ethical and religious values." The outermost regions contain areas of "absolute knowledge" (illustrated by the perfect shapes of geometric figures), while the central area is *a muddy mixed zone* [that] *lies between two absolutes;* however, just because something is "muddy" does not mean that it provides continuity. *There must be an* absolute *division between each of the three regions, a kind of* chasm. *There must be no continuity, no bridge leading from one to the other.* According to Hulme, the dynamic development of modern thought leads to recognizing the fundamental difference between what is inanimate and mechanical, on the one hand, and life, on the other. Nietzsche, Bergson, and Wilhelm Dilthey successfully challenged the earlier presumption of continuity. Having accepted the results of their critique of the scientific "worldview," life should be understood as a stream that flows through time and space. *But the same movement that recognises the existence of the first absolute chasm (between the physical and the vital), proceeds to ignore the second, that between biology and the ethical, religious values (...) it does not distinguish different levels of the non-material. All that is non-material, must it thinks be* vital. Based on these new assumptions, we should treat religion as the result of certain life processes (or, at least, intense human experiences). This would be in line with the general vector of "humanism," that is, a thought that has prevailed since the Renaissance, for which it is impossible that religion be the basis. *It is necessary to realise that there is an absolute, and not a relative, difference between humanism (...) and the religious*

HUMANISM AS REALISM

spirit. The divine *is not* life *at its intensest. It contains in a way an almost* anti-vital *element* – of course not in the sense in which bursts of lava burn the living organisms in their path or in which a black hole could absorb Earth's entire biosphere at once, humankind included. "The divine" expresses its own absolute – not below but above everything that lives below. When we pull different areas of reality together and try to explain each of their contents in the same way, the result is two types of erroneous thinking that enslave us. The first grave error is *the attempt to introduce the* absolute *of mathematical physics into the essentially relative middle zone of life,* which *leads to the* mechanistic *view of the world.* The second grave error is *the attempt to explain the* absolute *of religious and ethical values in terms of the categories appropriate to the essentially relative and non-absolute vital zone, leads to the misunderstanding of these values, and to the creation of a series of mixed or bastard phenomena,* such as *Romanticism in literature, Relativism in ethics, Idealism in philosophy and Modernism in religion* (...) *Romanticism, for example, confuses both human and divine things, by not clearly separating them. The main thing with which it can be reproached is that it blurs the clear outlines of human relations – whether in political thought or in the literary treatment of sex – by introducing in them the* Perfection *that properly belongs to the non-human.*[68]

The modern attitude towards reality, which Hulme describes as "humanistic," is based on the choice of a sense of satisfaction, which turns out to be most distinctly foreign to a religious attitude. The covering up of "discontinuities" makes it possible to build, with the full sanction of philosophy, images of the progress and improvement of the human race. Man's destiny and place in the world must be "satisfying"; they must satisfy whoever inherits an unshakable attachment to "continuity." The resulting "canons of satisfaction" are not consciously accepted; thinkers question the truthfulness of their findings but are unable to question the need to be "satisfied" by those findings. This is what Hulme wishes to subject to criticism, which – in his understanding – is neither

68 Ibid., pp. 6–8, 10–11. Emphasis in original.

On the Mixing up and Explanation of Concepts

philosophy nor psychology; what we are dealing with here is a *special region of knowledge (...) absolutely and entirely* misunderstood *by the moderns*. Thus, the "critique of satisfaction" requires an understanding of the religious attitude. We can understand this attitude as long as we recognize the "gap" between life and the absolute. What is perfect is always on the side of the absolute, never on the side of life. Hulme's translation is based on a very suggestive illustration: *imagine a man situated at a point in a plane, from which roads radiate in various directions. Let this be the plane of actual existence. We place* Perfection *where it should not be – on this human plane. As we are painfully aware that nothing* actual *can be* perfect, *we imagine the perfection to be not where we are, but some distance along one of the roads (...) most frequently, in literature, at any rate, we imagine an impossible perfection along the road of sex; but anyone can name the other roads for himself.* In this way, the essence of religious experience – "the divine" – is literally brought down to earth; religious needs are on the same plane as the need to consummate a sexual relationship; in the desired version ("we are working on it ..."), everyone gets their fulfillment; thus, claims of "something more" out there must be false. However, this is a premature decision inasmuch as we agree with Hulme that this picture does not suffice. *If we continue to look with satisfaction along these roads, we shall always be unable to understand the religious attitude.* We must force the mind *back on the centre*, push it to give up exploring the surrounding roads. The thought must enter our minds that finding "satisfaction" is impossible as long as we are moving on a horizontal plane. *The result is that which follows the snake eating its own tail, an* infinite *straight line* perpendicular *to the plane.*[69] Therefore, the religious attitude requires practice resulting from a particular way of thinking, which we can define as vertical thinking. Nothing is free, however. Whatever we may achieve comes with the discovery that none of the earthly paths promising us various moments of "satisfaction" is worth following. *For whosoever will save his life shall lose it: but whosoever will lose his life for my sake, the same*

69   Ibid., pp. 23, 33–34. Emphasis in original.

HUMANISM AS REALISM

shall save it (Luke 9:24). In this sense, life is tragic. The classic symbol of this state of affairs is the wheel, Hulme reminds us. The modern imagination calls for a spiral instead of a wheel; this signifies progress. However, it is difficult not to associate this thought substitute with the "moral centrifuge," with the constantly accelerating centrifugal motion of countless masses of people mechanically joined together.

What, then, is to be the proper center of gravity of modern thought? You could say that it is the place where horizontal thinking meets vertical thinking. While the former tends towards supernatural perfection, the latter is fulfilled in the continual penetration of natural phenomena. The first of necessity is closed to the plane from which it originates. The second necessarily moves flatly or horizontally. Being human, however, we feel – even if this "feeling," common to all of us, has been severely handicapped by beliefs based on corrupt concepts – that it is impossible to have everything, that there is always give and take, that – as Hulme wants – there is no necessary continuity, or any continuity, between what moves under the sun and what "speaks" to us as the immaculate Perfection in heaven. And the essence of humanitarianism is the denial of this state of affairs. Vertical thinking takes over the role of horizontal thinking. Concepts that make sense when describing "vertical" relationships are used to describe "horizontal" relationships. Our life is subordinated to the justification of a thought that cannot be justified because it has been deliberately misplaced. Not understanding the ultimate questions, we become believers in the "eschatology" of orgasms and all "eschatologies" in general, which convince us that our destination is the next experience, the next turn, the next project, the next position in bed, the next skydiving jump. The whole spectacle of quasi-fulfillment reveals its nothingness at the time of death, which is why each of us – even those who live longest – will get our chance to learn the truth. If this is the case, then the "religious conception of ultimate values" *finally* gains the upper hand. But does life have to consist in anticipating its end? Hulme referred to his own essay as "a prolegomena to the reading of

On the Mixing up and Explanation of Concepts

Pascal."[70] A particular passage of *Thoughts* especially, discussing recreation and killing time,[71] can help us "unclog" our heads. All of this so that we can again ask seriously about an alternative to the thinking that we have called "horizontal." Such an alternative is a religious attitude, properly understood. But what about humanism?

Since humanitarianism turns out to be a faith detached from vertical thinking, would the humanism confronting it also be a faith? Or perhaps – a strategy of defenders of the faith? Previously, we tried to show that the humanists of More's and Babbitt's circle did not think about building a new secular religion, but also did not necessarily want to defend the old non-secular religion. Their mixed attitude towards contemporary authorities invoking religious traditions should be associated with different views on effective methods of reaching young minds. On the other hand, after all these arguments have been presented, it will not surprise us to learn that the success of a humanistic "review of concepts" requires – above all – that those concepts whose original meaning is manifested within traditional religious attitudes be seriously dealt with. Humanism needs vertical thinking precisely to be able to judge horizontal thinking with its multiplicity and intensity of eschatological temptations. *This Earth –* More writes – *would be a sorry place were it not for the few men always in it, who, while living among the things of time, have their hearts set wholly on the things of eternity. We whose life must be regulated by the shifting law of humanism, have need of the saints.*[72] And which "shifting law" orders us to enjoy holiness without leading us to be saints?

VI.

The final step in our attempt to define "humanism" – an attempt at finding out the difference between a humanistic "review of

---

70 Cf. ibid., pp. 56–57, 22.
71 See B. Pascal, *Pensées and Other Writings*, trans. H. Levi, Oxford 1999, fragment 205(139), pp. 96–103. Cf. I. Babbitt, *Pascal* [in:] id., *Spanish Character*..., pp. 86–87.
72 P. E. More, *The Christ of the New*..., p. 140.

concepts" and an otherwise more famous and promoted intellectual enterprise – will be to show the relational nature of this concept. For this, we must first come back to the proper understanding of a naturalistic view of human affairs. This is necessary to avoid the very deceptive formula of opposing naturalism and humanism so that the position taken by the humanist would completely contradict the position of the naturalist. If this were the case, the humanistic "program" would be some bizarre "third way," proposed ad hoc by a handful of resolute Americans; it would be a way of thinking, as it were, that competed with science on the one hand and religion on the other; it would probably be an unfortunate *ersatz* Christianity, a long-outdated reaction to one of the many crises of the American spirit and American mores. This isn't the case. The problem with naturalism in the eyes of a humanist is not that it is false at its base; false supposedly because people are not beasts, because they sculpt statues, create symphonies, and generally have a rich inner life. People are beasts. Human nature is the nature of a beast. But such a beast that by itself cannot remain *only* a beast. According to Babbitt, *man is – as Nietzsche says – the being who must always surpass himself, but he has – and this is a point that Nietzsche did not sufficiently consider – a choice of direction in his everlasting pilgrimage.*[73] Bearing in mind the image drawn by Hulme, we can assume that this choice means: either upwards or sideways, back and forth; we either rise above the earth's paths like a rocket, or we furiously trample our own footsteps as long as we have enough life to trample constantly; either go straight to God or dance into nothingness. Does such a strongly formulated alternative – between a religious life and a wasted life – correspond to the humanistic postulates of basing the "review of concepts" on the "secular experience of both the East and the West"? Have we not sided with traditional-religious enthusiasts too hastily? Will we not be surrounded sooner or later by the sellers of devotional objects who accompany them? Will they not exploit our rebellion and make money

73   I. Babbitt, *Rousseau and Romanticism...*, pp. 245–246.

On the Mixing up and Explanation of Concepts

off of it? The "religious attitude" – is this not an empty phrase, some romantic rêverie, as well as food for fanatics? That could be the case. What gives a "natural" man a sense of fulfillment (and he knows no other) is a waste of time for a religious man. And the fact that the latter prays is a cause for the former's amusement.

It seems that to get out of the impasse surrounding the beast-man, we must ask about the conception of human nature. How does what is human compare with what is natural? What do humanists have to say about this? Based on the considerations presented thus far, we can see that the purely physical, "natural" approach will not be enough for them. There must be room for "something more" that does not follow from the mere fact of things happening; a place for the conscious act of transcending, a place for a purpose. There must be a deeply embedded ability to say "no," the ability to block the flow of impulses or instincts, or rather – to suspend an affirmative judgment about what "flows" in us. More and Babbitt devise specific terms for this ability: *inner check, will to refrain, frein vital*. Analyzing the use of these terms is a separate topic. At this point, let us simply note that the notion of "nature" is treated as highly problematic here. This word, to recall the phrase from More quoted earlier, turns out to be "as unstable as the sea." Such a perspective results not from basing humanism on "hard" anti-naturalistic metaphysics but from a skeptical assessment of the possibilities and limitations of metaphysical discourse. In short, the naturalist's problem is not that he cannot say enough about nature or that what he says does not seem to apply to man as a spiritual being. His problem is that he wants to say too much.

Humanists – especially More, who read Plato this way[74] – reject the possibility of metaphysics in the sense of a coherent, rationally proven view of reality. Much can be said about the universe, but it is not possible to say everything completely. In any

74 Cf. P.E. More, *Platonism*, Princeton–London 1917, especially pp. 262–69.

case, there is no indication that anyone could ever write down the last word for one particular part of the universe – human nature. There is no single formula by which we could set out all philosophical issues in a way that would explain the fullness of the human experience. In practice, this means stigmatizing the attitude of an intellectual or sophist convinced that they can sell the world a *de rerum natura* handbook that may be used as a reliable key to learning about moral (and political) issues. In More's view, *reason becomes metaphysical – or eristic, as Plato would have said – the moment it presumptuously disregards the dualism of consciousness and attempts by its own naked force to build up a theoretic world of abstract unity excluding multiplicity or of abstract multiplicity excluding unity. Morally expressed, it is equally the error of metaphysics to explain away the reality of evil in favour of some conception of infinite goodness and to deny the existence of the absolute Good in favour of some conception of infinite relativity.*[75] Each person potentially recognizes in himself and around him everything that constitutes the premises of the naturalistic approach, along with the optimism or pessimism in evaluating things that is built upon it. It's just that for that person – if he thinks for himself rather than putting forward some internalized formula – this "everything" never constitutes a whole. Yet true philosophy cannot stop at pronouncing a half-truth. Thus, a philosopher worthy of the name does not allow himself to simplify what he experiences as a human being dogmatically; he does not seek solace in a "worldview" arranged this way or other; he is open to what (seemingly?) does not fit into any intellectual puzzle; he separates what is visible from what only constitutes the fabric of opinions, even those expressed in a refined and abstract fashion, or those that impress with the severity of their attachment to the laws of nature. In light of this distinction between philosophy and "metaphysics," we begin to understand the proper role of the humanist. Babbitt explains it this way: *man is (...) a living paradox in that he holds with enthusiasm and conviction to the half-truth and yet becomes perfect only in proportion as he achieves the rounded view. The*

75   Ibid., p. 233; cf. id., *The Religion of Plato...,* p. 340.

essence of any true humanistic method is the mediation between extremes, a mediation that demands of course not only effective thinking but effective self-discipline; and that, no doubt, is why true humanists have always been so rare (...) The Truth (with a capital T) is of necessity infinite and so is not for any poor finite creature like man. The most any man can do is to tend toward the truth, but the portion of it he has achieved at any given moment will always, compared with what still remains, be a mere glimpse and an infinitesimal chapter. If he attempts to formulate this glimpse, the danger is that it will thus be frozen into a false finality. Anyone who thinks he has got the Truth finally tucked away in a set of formulae, is merely suffering, whether he call himself theologian, or scientist, or philosopher, from what may be termed the error of intellectualism or the metaphysical illusion.[76]

Naturalism – the philosophical basis of natural science – is thus part of the truth, however well it is understood and used. How great a part this is, there is no point in discussing. Indeed, the key issue for us concerns the outline of the sphere of the legitimacy of naturalistic judgments or the validity of "natural law." For the present discussion, suffice it to say that "natural law" is treated here as a convenient interpretation of cause-effect relationships discovered by the experimental sciences. Therefore, it has nothing to do with the "natural law" of the Stoics or Thomists. But next to this law, which can be called "the Law for Thing," we recognize norms appropriate to man, mediated by conventions (traditions, customs, laws in the positive sense), but preceding those conventions and conscious arrangements – norms not invented by us. Let this latter law then be called "the Law for Man."

Babbitt writes: *for the pure naturalist there is only one law, the law for thing. Now anyone who thus identifies man with phenomenal nature, whether scientifically or sentimentally, is almost inevitably led to value only the virtues of expansion; for according to natural law, to grow is to expand.* Meanwhile, according to the humanist, *if man as a natural phenomenon grows by expanding, man as man grows by concentrating.*

---

76 I. Babbitt, *The New Laokoon: An Essay on the Confusion of the Arts,* Boston–New York 1910, pp.189–97.

He proves that he is set above nature, not so much by his power to act, as by his power to refrain from acting.[77] Again, we should not take this as an anti-naturalistic preference for general inactivity (or even the choice of death) born out of resentment. It is not the breaking of our ties with matter that is at stake, but our control over that matter. After all, to effectively – *truly* effectively – control external matter, control nature, one must first control the matter in oneself (and we are referring more to the cerebral ganglia than to the intestines). To take control – that is, to say internally: not necessarily, wait a minute, let me check; that is – to ask yourself: what for? This is a critical moment, a moment of very-human concentration on the innumerable "flow" of impulses that make up the dynamics of our being here and now. For, while we cannot reject the "virtues of expansion" related to the struggle for existence and transience living in this world, the very core of civilization – which enables us to seek a *good* life, not just life in general – grows out of the ability to rule over oneself and out of the appropriate regulation of "traffic" on the roads of expansion. In More's view, the ancient Greeks understood this well and were willing to accept that *we have the two orders. The phenomenal world is a sphere of mechanical law established on the flux, but our place in this world is changed and determined by the gods in accordance with our conduct. The material world itself is heedless of our wants (...) but the Providence of the gods is just. There is the physical law of things and there is the moral law of souls, and these two laws, so far as our limited vision reaches, seem to run side by side without causal nexus or composition. So it is that, according as our interest and concern are set on one of these laws, the other law will appear to us as a sphere of unreality.*[78]

The sinking of "the Law for Man" norms into unreality can occur at the individual level, but also at the level of modern civilization as a whole, based on a humanitarian mixing up of concepts. A vision of the progress of all humankind is slowly taking the place of the hope of saving one's soul. *This progress* – Babbitt

77   Ibid., pp. 200–01.
78   P. E. More, *The Religion of Plato...*, pp. 102–03, note 11.

On the Mixing up and Explanation of Concepts

notes – *has been won by an almost tyrannical concentration on the facts of the natural law. Man's capacity for concentration is limited, so that the price he has paid for material progress has been an increasing inattention to facts of an entirely different order – those, namely, of the human law. The resulting spiritual blindness has been an invitation to Nemesis.*[79] The poetic name *Nemesis* signifies the painful realization of the real effects of the sanctions that fall on those who break the norms of "human law": internal and external disorder, incurable hopelessness, self-forgetfulness, dissolution into nothingness.

Having roughly grasped what the humanist critique of naturalistic metaphysics is all about, we may slowly begin to understand the previously troubling question of the "humility of common sense," which we cannot reduce to religious "spiritual humility." The point of departure here is not the humbling of man before God (we will leave aside the question of whether we can consider this to be the destination). For a humanist, "humility" constitutes not only a premise of healthy self-criticism or the individual reception of the "facts of the human law," but also – and perhaps above all – an expression of an attitude towards metaphysical abstractions, sophistry, vain intellectualism. So, on the one hand, we have a common-sense opposition to too far-reaching or "hassle-free" ideas of an individual about himself, and on the other hand, a critique of such ideas about man in general, about the entire human species. On both levels, plunging into intellectual expansion implies a certain level – key from a philosophical perspective – of surrendering to the general desire for expansion. Without self-control, we pour out, as it were; pouring out, we flood the world around us; we drown other people in this grist to the mill of our well-being – their experiences, their thoughts and, finally, maybe them, if we get the opportunity to transform our dreams of power into real means of building power.

There are a few caveats, however. First, the problem posed

79 I. Babbitt, *Democracy and Leadership...*, pp. 36–37.

this way concerns a certain category of people – the "restless"; potential philosophers and statesmen – not the "masses," "average Joes," for whom the best food is always what is at hand.[80] However, they are not the ones who changed the face of the Earth with a series of spiritual cuts. The legitimacy of modern "science" and "culture" – by way of the claim that never before have so many had so much of what they want – can only support a skeptical judgment of human nature. However, this does not change the fact that humanitarianism – in the eyes of a humanist – is not some necessary emanation of the desires of a simple man but the result of the conscious renunciation of humility by the most gifted and well-endowed: *corruptio optimi pessima*! It is precisely this kind of approach, linking the problem of leadership with the question of humility, that Babbitt found in classical Confucianism, essentially free from the anticipation of modern metaphysics.[81] Second, it is worth emphasizing that "humility of common sense" does not conflict with the intellectual radicalism that we previously ascribed to the protagonists of the "Humanist Movement." Their critical thinking does indeed lead to questioning all modern metaphysics at its base. In this sense, it is radical and even "transcendent" vis-à-vis various versions of naturalistic monism or humanitarianism. After all, the purpose of the "review of concepts" is to clarify them. It is not to create a new metaphysical structure, some new version of connecting everything with everything else; a system that would be – to use Hulme's phrase – "satisfactory." Third, we must pay attention to a problem plaguing many of those who try to point out the *differentia specifica* of classical thought with the help of a useful attribute that our distant ancestors had no reason to use. Namely, what does it mean for humility to be "commonsensical"?

The phrase *common sense* – especially on the grounds of humanism – turns out to be more than problematic in translation into Polish. It would be best to cut it off both from our everyday

---

80 Cf. id., *The New Laokoon...*, pp. 186–87.
81 Cf. id., *Democracy and Leadership...*, pp. 56–58, 188–90.

On the Mixing up and Explanation of Concepts

linguistic associations (where the Polish "zdrowy rozsądek" probably comes close in meaning to peasant cleverness) and from textbook presentations of philosophical discourse (e.g., Descartes' *sensus communis*). Indeed, *common sense* is neither common knowledge nor a set of verbal habits resulting from imperfect assimilation of particular sources of scientific knowledge and attachment to them. Of course, it would be ridiculous if thinkers who aspired to an essential exposition of Greek thought identified their philosophical criterion with some sort of simplified and shifting reflection of the current paradigms.[82] *Common sense* should also not be associated with "the opinion of the majority" or "the preferences of a broad audience." It seems that the most fruitful procedure may be the Polonization of this phrase as "czucie wspólne" [Eng. "what we (humans) feel or sense in common"]. In this way, we come closer to what could be called the pre-philosophical discovery of our humanity, or to a certain positive quality of the path of species identification, which begins with contact with one's loved ones and the threshold of a small political community. In other words, the point is to view the domains of human life or human affairs as a whole and, therefore, the limitations and costs of natural human expansion (*my* expansion), which is the basis of the concept of "humility": that nothing comes free, that there is always give and take, that whatever we do comes back to us with the force of "something more."[83] The moral consequence of this "shared feeling" will be a sense of responsibility for oneself – in relation to other people. As Babbitt writes: *the true opponent of both intellectualist and anti-intellectualist* (modern approaches to philosophy) *is the man of intuitive common sense. For common sense may not only rest upon intuition, but on a form of intuition that should be especially cultivated by those who wish to escape from the present naturalistic imbroglio (...) in contrast to this type of intuition which makes*

82 Cf. P. Świercz, *O sceptycznej krytyce etycznej części filozofii w świetle pism Sextusa Empiryka*, Kraków 2013, pp. 143–44.
83 Cf. L. Strauss, *Natural Right and History*, Chicago 1965, pp. 76 ff., 121–23.

HUMANISM AS REALISM

itself felt practically as vital impulse (...) I have distinguished another type of intuition – the perception, namely, on the part of the individual, of a something in himself that he possesses in common with other men,[84] which is practically manifested in the all-too-human ability to control himself. It seems reasonable to add that *common sense* can be significantly impaired or lost, like any other sense or way of feeling. Entangled in modern metaphysics – even at the level of the most "vulgar" opinions, simple formulas, ectypal "worldviews" – we cannot find our way in a discourse devoid of a monistic overlay on reality. Seen from this perspective, we can conclude that the humanistic "review of concepts" aims to renew the "shared feeling" or at least demonstrate that this "sense" can function effectively. For now, *common sense* remains more a hidden potential[85] for us than anything that produces universally tangible results. We differ in this from the ancient Greeks, who recognized this potential and built the achievements of their civilization on it, from the Delphic oracle through poetry to the findings of philosophers.

Another point seems to be just as important. "Human law," at least in its classical-Greek version, should contain norms concerning the weighing of arguments, the granting of proportions, and above all – the avoidance of extreme aspirations and emotions. Therefore, it is a "law of measure" most readily associated with Aristotle's concept of virtue as the "golden mean." Leaving aside a deeper analysis of the ancient context, we find the notion of "mediation" here, crucial for humanistic rhetoric. How should it be understood? Probably in the sense that it would be a "mediation" (i.e., a constantly renewed effort to reconcile or mediate) between the general, initial norm and the requirements of a specific situation. Hence, "human law" can be described as devoid

84 I. Babbitt, *The Modern Spirit and Dr. Spingarn,* "The Journal of Philosophy, Psychology and Scientific Methods," vol. 11, no. 8, April 9, 1914, p. 216.
85 Cf. G. B. Munson, *Our Critical Spokesmen* [in:] *Humanism and America...,* p. 237.

On the Mixing up and Explanation of Concepts

of a strict letter of the law, as variable. There is a problem here, however. It is easy to conclude that the mediation framework covers all ideas (programs, "worldviews"), whose implementation – or even confrontation with reality (how things are "here and now") – is a problem for all those moving from the thinking phase to action phase. Such an approach turns out to be unbearably formal and can lead to absurdity. Suppose it was, in principle, about mitigating the effects of enthusiasm or stubbornness. In that case, we might as well recognize that a Chekist or member of the SS who decided to temporarily moderate his methods (not "overkill" at a given moment) and kill fewer enemies of the people or subhumans would be a "humanist"; the same goes for someone who harms a small child, hesitates and wipes away the child's tears, and then calmly continues harming it. We are certainly not talking about such "humanists" or such "mediation." It is not the case that all general norms in the above sense – and we are taking into account the whole body of humanitarian thinking – could constitute an element of humanistic mediation or a reference point for the norms of "human law." According to Babbitt, *when first principles are involved the law of measure is no longer applicable. One should not be moderate in dealing with error.*[86] The "first principles" must be "sound," and a distinction between truth and error should precede "mediation" attempts. But what is truth? We know that a definitive and rational answer to this question is beyond our reach. Are we, then, allowed to leave the circle of formal verbosity? It seems so, as long as we keep in mind the simple image we picked up from Hulme. We live on a flat plane, and what is above us is calling us – at the cost of abandoning our earthly ways. Our position here on earth results from the natural necessity to which we are subject. We can, in a way, merge our thoughts with the demands of natural necessity, and thus – successfully or not – go back to the stage of the "unpretentious" beast, free from the cost of vertical thinking. If, however, what is

---

86   I. Babbitt, *Humanism: An Essay...*, p. 32. Cf. id., *Democracy and Leadership...*, pp. 46–47.

at stake is the preservation (or restoration) of civilization, then neither vertical nor horizontal thinking (used to describe our earthly ways) can gain (maintain) an absolute advantage. We "mediate" between holiness or perfection that ultimately transcends the limits of human nature and the necessity that itself makes nature inhuman.

What next? "Human law" – in times of impaired *common sense* – can be effective insofar as it distinguishes the concepts of "natural" and "religious" from one another and optimally juxtaposes them. This juxtaposition requires their explanation, i.e., the tearing apart of two layers: one of superficial and immediate ("vulgar") connotations, the other of more profound ("philosophical") errors and abuses. In regards to humanitarianism, this means bringing to light the most basic falsehood – the "naturalization" of religious concepts, that is, the chutzpah of placing what is vertical on the horizontal plane. Babbitt writes: *the chief adversary of the humanist at present is the humanitarian "idealist." Though this type of idealist often usurps (in the United States at least) the name of humanist, he is at bottom not so much pseudo-humanistic as pseudo-religious.*[87] Humanitarianism is thus characterized by a completely different account of religious concepts than humanism. Instead of constituting elements of mediation, humanitarianism views these concepts as resources that can contribute to the treasury of the "new faith." Earlier, to simplify the argument, we called this new faith "faith in humanity." What kind of humanity are we talking about – on the grounds of humanitarianism? It is, in short, a projection of a naturalistic image (part of the natural world), shown in the light of generally understood benefits of surrendering to the "power" of impulses or of trusting one's instincts onto the sphere of individual religious needs. We can also see it as "transplanting" the experience of an extreme situation (when "there's no time to think") into a set of notions on the ultimate questions. Anyway, inevitably, everything is flowing. The less you grapple with the beast, the less self-discipline you impose on

87   Id., *On Being Creative...*, p. xli.

On the Mixing up and Explanation of Concepts

yourself to reach a goal that is not and cannot be obvious, accessible on the spot, tangible (not just any goal, but precisely spiritual or eschatological ones) – the better. Therefore, humanity is defined via the lowest common denominator, which does not consider the vertical dimension of human aspirations, the desire for holiness or moral perfection, the reference to "something more." You either rape or get raped. We have already discussed the practical consequences of humanitarianism, which pose a danger to us and the planet as a whole. However, we must also realize – and this will be the subject of separate reflections – that there is another side to this issue.

There is no reason to believe that naturalistic monism – however perfidious and offensive to us it is in its simultaneous draining of human potential and placing it at the very bottom – is the only variant of monism ("metaphysical illusion"). There is also a spiritual monism for which everything earthly immediately loses its meaning, which therefore contradicts natural necessity and does not recognize any resistance to spirit. It may be possible to show how closely these two perspectives come together in the everyday "management" of the ultimate questions. At this stage, we want only to suggest that "pure" religion is incompatible with the existence of civilization. The world, simply put, cannot be made up of only monks and hermits. Someone has to seriously attend to what the monks do not attend to at all or do not attend to seriously. Someone has to beget children – if only so that they, in turn, can become monks and carry the yoke of holiness for years and epochs to come. Thus, not only does religion judge civilization, but civilization also judges religion since it is itself a test of the requirements of natural necessity. The humanistic "review of concepts" corresponds to a certain extent to this general need for judgment – in the particular circumstances of the modern world, when genuine religious experience is forgotten or "distorted." Thus, somewhat paradoxically, Babbitt's expression about the "secular experience of both the East and the West" turns out to be pointing, in a significant sense, to the experience of religion facing the tribunal of civilization; religion, without which the thinking that creates (or "assembles") civilization could not exist; a religion, however, that ought to take on such a form that humanity could bear.[88] If modernity relies on impulses, then, as such, an impulse to convert or return to traditional religiosity will easily be assigned to one of the rare – one might say, *premium* – options in a broad package of modern forms of consolation. The humanist attempt to take over the "modern experiment" also takes on meaning within the context of the deposit of faith's fate, if it is not to be left in the hands of humanitarians. What is needed here are people who think for themselves and control themselves. According to Babbitt, *the world (...) would have been a better place if more persons had made sure they were human before setting out to be superhuman; and this consideration would seem to apply with special force to a generation like the present that is wallowing in the trough of naturalism. After all to be a good humanist is merely to be moderate and sensible and decent. It is much easier for a man to deceive himself and others regarding his supernatural lights than it is regarding the degree to which he is moderate and sensible and decent.*[89] Now we are no longer fooled by the noble simplicity of the above characteristics. Moderation, common sense, and decency take on an essential meaning and become a serious or even salvific proposition for modern man insofar as they reflect the relationality contained in the very concept of "humanism." More and Babbitt redefined it in such a way that the desired opening of the modern mind could not be equal to opening a knife in one's pocket; so that no one else could attempt to save the world starting with – others.

At this point, it is appropriate to elaborate on the justification for our interpretation. As already mentioned, dualism is the key philosophical concept in More's writings.[90] In his most fundamen-

---

88 Cf. id., *Humanism: An Essay...*, pp. 41–42; id., *Democracy and Leadership...*, pp. 180–81, 184, 220.

89 Id., *Rousseau and Romanticism...*, p. xx; cf. ibid., p. 380 ff.

90 Cf. P. E. More, *Marginalia* [in:] *The Essential Paul Elmer More: A Selection of His Writings*, ed. B. C. Lambert, New Rochelle, New York 1972, pp. 37–38.

tal *modus operandi*, this thinker's attention is drawn to the collision of the *vita contemplativa*, the call to contemplation, with the demands of natural necessity. Dualism in the religious sense presupposes the existence of two eschatological perspectives: holiness and temporality (or perhaps "otherworldliness" and "intra-worldliness"). As early as 1897 – in the preface to his translation of Sanskrit epigrams (whose direct, named addressee is the young Babbitt) – More tries to explain the need to "fortify" the contemplative life, which he precedes with the finding that the ancient Hindu *moralists (...) speak of the three paths, pleasure, worldly wisdom, and renunciation; but in reality they recognized only two ideals, between which they could conceive no substantial ground of mediation.*[91]

From this perspective, the experience of humanism should be considered an ephemera: either-or. It becomes understandable only due to the self-limitation of the philosopher who considers his closest "ideal" of holiness. It contains – as an eschatological pole – uninterrupted peace of mind. This peace of mind, conditioned by self-denial, is presented as opposing the other pole, constituted by an equally evident desire to be carried on the waves of an earthly life. As More writes in a later text: *it is possible (...) to view the ceaseless intellectual fluctuations of mankind backward and forward as the varying fortunes of the contest between these two hostile members of our being – between the deep-lying principle that impels us to seek rest and the principle that drags us back into the region of change and motion and forever forbids us to acquiesce in what is found (...) the moral disposition of a nation or of an individual may be best characterized by the predominance of the one or the other of these two elements. We may find a people, such as the ancient Hindus, in whom the longing after peace was so intense as to make insignificant every other concern of life, and among whom the aim of saint and philosopher alike was to close the eyes upon the theatre of this world's shifting scenes and to look only upon that*

91 Id.., *To Irving Babbitt, Esq.* [in:] *A Century of Indian Epigrams: Chiefly from the Sanskrit of Bhartrihai*, transl./ed. id., London–New York 1899, p. 5.

changeless vision, which testifies to the achievement of peace of mind. According to More, in the eyes of the Hindu saint-philosopher, the scaffolding of civilization appears as a structure on which we can only base vain phantasmagories; everything important comes from internal experiences. In the Greeks, on the other hand, *the imperturbable stillness of the Orient and the restless activity of the Occident meet together in intimate union and produce that peculiar repose in action, that unity in variety, which we call harmony or beauty.* It is also a mature view of *common sense*, which is threatened by the intellectual expansion of "logicians" seeking to deny all movement and change through a desire for peace; or vice versa – to subordinate all thought, all of the soul's experiences, to the law of change. *The brood of Sophists, carrying this law into human consciousness, declaimed the possibility of truth altogether; and it is no wonder that Plato, while avoiding the other extreme of motionless pantheism, regarded the sophistic acceptance of this law of universal flux as the last irreconcilable enemy of philosophy and morality alike.*[92] Therefore, the pinnacle of the ancients' achievements seems to be the conceptualization of the highest intellectual or spiritual aspirations based on dualistic equilibrium. The further history of Western thought also revolves around problems resulting from subsequent attempts at upsetting and restoring this balance. This is likewise how we should interpret the disputes of medieval metaphysicians, from whom the nominalist school of the concrete emerges – an essential source of modernity. All this is, in fact, old news, and the moment of the triumph of the evolutionist glorifiers of progress falls on an age that recognizes only the pole of change, without understanding ancient aspirations for holiness or the desire for spiritual peace. In the end, More will write: *I am asserting that the Kantian metaphysic spells death to philosophy, and that the Lutheran theology spells death to religion.*[93] What remains, then?

All that is within the framework of humanitarianism, of course. For a clear description of the ensuing situation, we can again turn

92 Id., *The Quest of a Century...*, pp. 245–47.
93 Id., *The Christ of the New...*, p. 119.

On the Mixing up and Explanation of Concepts

to one of the testaments to the early stage of More's work – an epistolary novel he co-wrote titled *The Jessica Letters*. It is worth getting a taste of the literary bluntness of the judgments expressed in this work. Thus, we read: *thou shalt love God with all thy heart and thy neighbour as thyself, was the law of Christianity. We have forgotten God and the responsibility of the individual soul to its own divinity; we have made a fetish of our neighbour's earthly welfare. We are not Christians but humanitarians, followers of a maimed and materialistic faith (...) mankind (...) are divided into two pretty distinct classes: those to whom the visible world is real and the invisible world unreal or at best a shadow of the visible, and those to whom this visible realm with all its life is mere illusion whereas the spirit alone is the eternal reality. Faith is just this perception of the illusion enwrapping all these phenomena that to those without faith seem so real; faith is the voluntary turning away of the spirit from this illusion toward the infinite reality. It is because I find among men of to-day no perception of this illusion that I deny the existence of faith in the world. It is because men have utterly lost the sense of this illusion that religion has descended into this Simony of the humanitarians.*[94] In this approach – a literary approach, it should be emphasized – the most succinct justification of one of the critical theses of humanism comes to the forefront: to regain true faith – the pole of the spirit – humanitarianism must first be disarmed. Establishing the meaning of and relationship between concepts which, in their confusion, formed the basis for modern thinking should be seen as a necessary condition for regaining a live religious discourse. It was a peculiarly Western Christianity – starting with its Protestant branches – that became the vehicle for a humanitarian attitude rather than a response to the errors and threats of humanitarianism. *Worship in the temple* – More writes in a later essay on the humanitarian "new morality" – *is no longer a call to contrition and repentance, but an organized flattery of our human nature, and the theological seminary is fast becoming a special school for investigating poverty and spreading*

94 P. E. More, C. M. Harris, *The Jessica Letters, An Editor's Romance*, New York–London 1904, pp. 54, 190. "Simony" is referring to the figure of Simon Magus; cf. ibid., p. 104.

agnosticism (...) humanitarianism is no longer opposed by organized religion, but has itself usurped the place of the Church.[95]

Of course, we can argue about the general validity or timeliness of such assessments. Are we not speaking here again of the condition of American Protestantism over a hundred years ago? However, it seems that the processes highlighted in the last decades (especially since the 1960s) on the whole confirm More's hunch about the direction of change. We are dealing not only with the adaptation of forms of religious life to "current trends" but also with the orientation of their content so that they serve to justify modernity (democracy, prosperity, etc.). At the same time, the Roman Catholic Church of More's and Babbitt's time – the Church of the *Vaticanum Primum* and the "anti-modernist oath" – was quite different from the Church we know today. The former could be accused – rightly or wrongly – of intellectual fossilization and perhaps even desperate isolation from modernity. The present mode of church life should raise other objections. Are we not used to seeing the head of the Church as a harmless older man who pats the heads of little, innocent children? And isn't it the case that the Luther mentioned by More ceases to be a dark theologian for us, a renegade allying with power- and money-hungry princes of the Reich countries, and instead becomes a romantic rebel, a precursor of freedom of conscience, an invigorating sign? In any case, along with the establishment of changes usually referred to as societies' "secularization" or "laicization," humanitarianism's hegemony of thought was politically sealed. These changes mean that religious concepts lose what guarantees they had left in the public debate, so they may be played with at will within the confines, of course, of what is appropriate at the present stage of humanitarianism's emergence.

However, we may pose a different question. Isn't the modern "faith in humanity" itself the fruit of Christianity? Even were it given birth to in pain, should the child really be branded a

---

95   P. E. More, *The New Morality* [in:] id., *Aristocracy and Justice...*, p. 208. Cf. I. Babbitt, *Rousseau and Romanticism...*, p. 367.

On the Mixing up and Explanation of Concepts

bastard? Are those who teach us equality and tolerance not merely trying to express what Christ spoke of two thousand years ago in new ways? If we are all to love one another, then shouldn't we, to an even greater degree, "tolerate" one another and recognize each other's "rights"? If we follow this path and realize that the mainstream of modern thought contains at its core a mature desire to implement the "doctrine" of the Gospel, that despite its errors and turmoil, this thought marks the next stop on our way of becoming better people, then would it not follow that the humanism we are describing would boil down to nothing but a hiccup following an ancient pagan reaction? Doubts such as these necessarily revisit us and are difficult to dispel. Humanists patiently demonstrate that the problem of the soul – the most urgent and evident for ancient Christians and pagans – has been replaced by the moderns with the problem of humanity; that our most outstanding intellectual achievement may be to reverse this state of affairs. In the first published volume of More's essays (1904), we find a text titled *The Religious Ground of Humanitarianism*; it certainly does not offer a solution to the Christian question, but it does provide some clue where to begin. It is enough to compare the simple message of Christ's teachings with the most daring plans for social reforms to realize that the radicalism of the former destroys the latter. *The doctrines of Christ if accepted by the world in their integrity, – the virtues, that is, of humility, non-resistance, and poverty, – would not institute any such desired revolution in society; they would simply make an end of the whole social fabric; and if to these chastity be added, they would do away with human existence altogether* (because there would be no intimacy and children would cease to be born). *As a matter of fact, according to the overwhelming evidence of the Gospels, never for a moment contemplated the introduction of a religion which should rebuild society. His kingdom was not of this world, and there is every reason to believe that he looked to see only a few chosen souls follow in his footsteps.*[96] According to More, Christianity and

---

96 P. E. More, *The Religious Ground of Humanitarianism* [in:] id., *Shelburne Essays First Series...*, p. 243.

Buddhism reflect the superb results of the work of the "religious instinct." The latter includes, as extremes, spiritual aspirations to certain "states of mind" ("faith, hope and love"), on the one hand, and a "universal code of prohibition morality" (the Ten Commandments) on the other, which we can associate with the action of common sense that forces us to recognize bodily limitations (natural necessity). The above-mentioned religious virtues are, perhaps somewhat surprisingly, a special case of mediation. However, both in the Christian and Buddhist versions, they are addressed to those who renounce this world, so they do so effectively.

What is this world? A battlefield for existence and passing away. But there are also, thank God, certain rules on this field: first, the "prohibitive morality"; second, located above all else is *the guiding principle of character, corresponding to the aspiration of the spirit but concerned with that lower personality which buys and sells, marries and gives in marriage, and looks to earthly success as its reward. And this principle of character shows itself under three manifestations in the same way as the law of the spirit.* Thus, the figure of faith corresponds to prudence, "temporal wisdom," *sophia*; hope – to courage; love – to honor. All of this creates character or a person, this time – living in the world. Again, we are dealing with mediation: on the one hand, the ideal of living in the world, on the other, prohibitions resulting from recognizing natural necessity. In between the extremes are born *the social virtues of the secular life, which are curiously similar to the religious virtues, yet perfectly distinct from them.* The equivalent of humility is justice (let each one stick to his own and take care of it as best he can); non-opposition corresponds to pity or generosity towards those weaker than ourselves; poverty – to charity; chastity (innocence) – to faithfulness and self-restraint. As a result of cultivating these virtues, the law governing the material world (the norms flowing from natural necessity) is relaxed. However, appreciation of the role of these virtues must not be connected with a denial of the fact that they are religious virtues and the product of a "religious instinct." It is here that we get to the crux of the matter.

If you ask – More writes – *whence arises the widespread belief that the old order of things is to pass away and a new reign of humanitarianism to be introduced, the answer is ready at hand: it arises from that inexhaustible source of error, the failure to discern distinctions (...) the religious ground of humanitarianism is (...) a failure here to discriminate between the ideals of religion and the ideals of the world. To apply the laws of the spirit to the activities of this earth is at once a desecration and denial of religion and a bewildering and unsettling of the social order. To intrude the aspirations of faith and hope and the ethics of the golden rule of love into regions where prudence and courage and the dictates of honour are supreme, is a mischievous folly.* The state (society) belongs to Caesar, not to God. It has always been so. Nevertheless, when St. Francis of Assisi started on his way of renunciation, his choice was understandable and, in a sense, easy. We can assume that both eschatological orders existed side by side in his time, ensuring balance for the world: he knew what he had renounced; the world knew where he was headed along his individual path of holiness – different concepts corresponded to these different orders. *But in other days when faith grows a little dull and the all-levelling power of democracy has brought things spiritual and worldly to the same plane, – or so at least it looks to the eyes of men, – in such days the path of the individual is beset with difficulties.*[97] In short, the radical renewal of the concept of "humanism" stems from the need to respond to these difficulties.

VII.

What is humanism? According to Norman Foerster, *humanism is not a religion but a working philosophy, having for its object as a philosophy the clarification of human values, and for its object as a mode of working the realization of human values.*[98] Let us try to enrich this definition a bit, taking into account our previous considerations. In them, we wanted to show that "humanism" is a relational

---

97   Ibid., pp. 247–52.
98   N. Foerster, *Humanism and Religion...*, p. 147.

concept. In our understanding, a "relational concept" serves to represent the reality resulting from the relationship between two "objects"; it does not in itself constitute a separate or self-contained "object." The meaning of a "relational concept" thus depends on whether we view the "objects" "served" by it as distinct and whether we perceive the relationship between them as worthy of attention. Thus, for example, we can speak of marriage as "a union of two people." In the concept of "marriage," it is important to express what connects "those two." Of course, as "objects," "husband" and "wife" can be described separately, even with complete disregard for the effects of their relationship, which is not of interest to us. When we speak of "humanism," we move to a higher level of concept ordering. In fact, to the highest level, since the "objects" we are interested in here have a dimension belonging to the Ultimate, they relate separately to the ultimate questions, to the whole of reality. This means that each of these "objects" by itself is perfectly possessive of other "objects." Each of them absorbs the totality of our experience so that, on the one hand, we see only a goal appropriate to the spirit, and on the other – our fulfillment by meeting the requirements of natural necessity.

Analogously to the "art of living together" – which is probably the proper human content of the concept of "marriage" – we can define "humanism" as the *art of binding* what is both ultimate and disproportionate in *our* experience of all reality. And just as the value of marriage becomes the subject of intense thought when the marriage is in danger, so, too, does conscious reflection in defining the art of mediation and discovering the norms of "human law" follow when a threat is discovered at the level of the conditions for maintaining civilization or of the survival of the species. This danger becomes fully real insofar as the disappearance of vertical thinking accompanies the pursuit of "sanctifying" what is naturally necessary and "thought" horizontally. The political and legal seal of this change is only a final touch in the success of humanitarianism. Thus, we can say that humanitarianism is, in a way, a parody of the art of humanism – a bond

On the Mixing up and Explanation of Concepts

by way of annihilation – leading to the loss of both "objects": the natural world and the spiritual world.

Humanism, understood as above, as the art of being – fully – human, presupposes going through two stages of thinking. First, it is the separation of truth from error, that is, the restoration of the concepts that constitute the poles of mediation, and thus – the separation of the two orders or two eschatologies, verticality and horizontality. Then mediation within both orders occurs, wherein the virtues of the temporal order – those that ensure the endurance of civilization – are to be seen as a muddied reflection of religious virtues. For they do not come from the mere recognition of the requirements of natural necessity, but from setting these requirements in opposition to the works of the moral imagination – "the ideals of the world." For them, the ultimate justification is that they can constitute the framework of a true spiritual life or philosophy; in the end – to refer to our native [Polish] tidbits of *common sense* – "it is not saints who make pottery."[99] In practice, humanism signifies, above all, a realistic view of human nature. Seen through the eyes of a humanist, the greatness of man – like nothing else – may evoke admiration, but it is achieved rarely and with difficulty. True greatness is the fruit of deliberate mediation, known as "meditation" in the religious life. Being a human being is not so much guaranteed in advance as it is something that can be proven and is worth proving. It is not "human rights" we should be speaking of, but "righteousness."[100] While it is difficult to argue with someone who consciously insists on reducing our humanity to a bunch of impulses, the brown-nosing "flatterers of human nature"[101] – those who praise reason and those who melt

99 Pol. "Nie święci garnki lepią." The meaning of this saying is twofold. On the one hand, it suggests that one doesn't have to be an extraordinary human being to be able to get things done or to function. On the other, it may suggest that one should not expect extraordinary people to devote themselves to ordinary or mundane work (there must be potters for us to have saints).
100 Cf. I. Babbitt, *Democracy and Leadership*..., p. 272.
101 Cf. P. E. More, *A Revival of Humanism*..., especially p. 10.

HUMANISM AS REALISM

over the needs of the heart – will always be the practical opposition to the "Humanist Movement." There is no "praise" in humanist writing; what it does contain is an inquiry into the sickness of the soul; there is no faith that institutional solutions or mechanical social divisions (us-elite versus them-mob) can replace working on one's character and release us from the sense of responsibility for ourselves. No one who seriously reads the humanists can feel better in their own skin, especially if that would mean shifting the burden of one's life onto the level of humanity's overall struggle – and forgetting about oneself. For no meaningful thought about man can be born on grounds other than those of self-knowledge. After all, the disintegration of the *cosmos* is nothing but a function of the decomposition of an individual soul, *my* soul. In short, there is no support for the cynicism of superficially educated "intellectuals" in humanism. Thus, our "service check of the vehicle of general concepts" turns out to be an unusual task in modern thought since its goal is not, for instance, "customer satisfaction." Instead, the potential "client" of humanism is the one who *will, at any cost, strive to clear away the clouds of cant, and so open his mind to the dictates of the everlasting morality.*[102]

We can ask one more question. To what extent should the humanistic "review of concepts" be considered a closed chapter of the achievements of More, Babbitt, and other members of the "Humanist Movement" from the first half of the previous century, and to what extent is it a merely initiated and still open undertaking? It is impossible to overestimate the intellectual effort which these thinkers put into achieving the goals of humanism. Their thoughts, which have reached into the next century, are by no means a record of impressions of a bygone era. They are writings the likes of which people are *no longer* writing in our times due to a lack of proper preparation and perhaps a lack of courage on the part of the authors. However, it would completely contradict the humanists' intentions to treat their legacy as the textbook sum of knowledge about man. It's better to imagine a somewhat

102 Id., *The New Morality...*, p. 139.

On the Mixing up and Explanation of Concepts

cheerful picture of a ladder that has More and Babbitt to thank for securing the first rungs, but which we have to climb ourselves, carrying more boards on our backs for the next rungs. At the same time, let us emphasize that this climbing, progress, is a purely individual effort, though not without consequences for the world. When we think about the first levels – those we have inherited – they are indeed connected with showing the falsehood at the source of humanitarianism and the recovery of concepts such as "the good," "virtue," "happiness," and "justice." We must bear in mind the first especially, so as not to end up tramping in place despite our best intentions. As Babbitt notes (here, it just so happens to be within the context of the Hindu tradition), premodern thought *conceives (...) of the good not as we do in terms of expansion, but in terms of concentration.*[103] Another crucial concept is "life," which is discussed in a variety of ways, and each accepted discourse betrays attachment to a particular segment of experience: from that announced by Christ to "life" evaluated from the perspective of property owned ("that one is living the life ..."). Thus, *those who recognize the different types of experience that have been summed up in the varying meanings of the word "life" are less open to the charge of narrowness and dogmatism than those who still wear the blinders of a dogmatic naturalism and so recognize only one type of experience.*[104] Thus, while the practical opponent of the humanist is "the flatterer of human nature," the philosophical antipode of humanistic reflection invariably belongs to those who want to understand less to be able to say more.

The mixing up of concepts destroys both the experience of the divine and the orderliness of the man. But, as humans, we don't have much to lose – we can at least try to respond to the course of affairs that concern us – in this, as in any age. To respond, in turn, means *to answer action with action, to oppose to the welter of*

103 I. Babbitt, *Interpreting India to the West* [in:] id., *Spanish Character...*, p. 153.
104 Id., *Experience and Dogma*, "The Saturday Review of Literature," vol. 1, no. 15, November 1, 1930, p. 299.

circumstance the force of discrimination and selection, to direct the aim-less tide of change by reference to the co-existing law of the immutable fact, to carry the experience of the past into the diverse impulses of the present, and so to move forward in an orderly progression.[105] The art of humanism is not intended for those who somehow "get on," but for those with whom the world ultimately cannot cope.

105 P. E. More, *Victorian Literature...*, p. 268.

UN-ECONOMIC IDEALS

I.

"It's the economy, stupid!" – these are the simple words of a famous politician from the end of the last century. They had a noticeable effect on his presidential campaign and became a neat formula of what to think about politics, a summary of the most reasonable approach to the role of the state and the ruling elite. If you are not an incurable dreamer or an alienated weirdo, sooner or later, you will adjust your views and judgments to less noble realities. Ultimately, nothing matters in politics but creating and maintaining a strong economy. Politics depends, or should depend, on the state of the economy, not the other way around. One can understand the supposed common-sense primacy of economics over politics in two ways: in a more "everyday" way and in a more intellectual way.

In the first case, we're talking about a simple opinion shared by many people, especially those intolerant of the grand gestures and altered "narratives" portrayed in the media. Any genre scene can illustrate the nature of a simple opinion. For example, let's take the conversation of compatriots at a table. Sitting at this table, we find a realist and his idealist cousin. The idealist is very worried about how human rights are violated in various places, so she tries – over dinner – to summon the forces that will defend freedom and democracy. The realist opens his eyes wide – perhaps dimmed by drink – and asks passionately: do you really believe that? Just look around! "Human rights" and other lofty slogans serve to justify specific actions undertaken to pursue very mundane, even dirty, interests. Always and everywhere, we only take tangible benefits seriously. Where economics ends, manipulation or empty words begin. Do not be persuaded, naive cousin, that it is otherwise, that what this is really about is something other than oil deposits or, more generally, some kinds of agreements between the powerful of this world. *Money makes the world go 'round*. It's pointless to discuss equal opportunities and equal treatment. The stronger win. History demonstrates that. Is it so hard to accept that great fortunes come from armed robbery and exploitation? Is this not, to a great extent, what the Eastern European experience of political transformation at the end of the twentieth century boils down to? It is enough to think about the enfranchised oligarchs. And historically speaking, wasn't the world ruthlessly colonized, with lofty phrases on the colonizers' lips? *Et cetera*. The realist cousin has no problem cornering his idealist cousin. After all, it is impossible to deny the contemporary economization of politics, and it is hard to prove on the spot, sitting at the table, that we can and should understand politics in the light of the pursuit of a good that is not merely material itself or serving a material good.

The economization of politics means that we must understand its goal as an economic goal. Therefore, the entire political discourse makes sense only insofar as it translates into the excellent functioning of the economy. What or whom the economy is good *for* is another question. After all, it is not surprising that we use the available resources primarily for ourselves and our loved ones. Every realist knows that "near is my shirt, but nearer is my skin"; that – as the charming Malay proverb teaches – it is not time to feed the monkeys in the forest when your own child is starving.[1] For our children, we wish not only that they will not starve, but also that they will be able to afford "as much as possible" thanks

---

1   *Anak kera di hutan disusui, anak sendiri di rumah kebuluran* (Eng. "The child on the lap is set down, while the monkey from the forest is taken to the breast."). Cf. K. H. Lim, *Budi as the Malay Mind: A Philosophical Study of Malay Ways of Reasoning and Emotion in Peribahasa*, Hamburg 2003, p. 60.

Un-Economic Ideals

to us. The broader fight against poverty and exclusion, the fight for the right to life and the right to buy, may be profitable for us or not. However, considering the ruled's basic preferences, it is much more advantageous for an ordinary actor on the political scene to pose before his society, and even all of humanity, as a benefactor, altruist, philanthropist than as a robber or an exploiter. The practice of politics – that is, being a professional politician, an actor on the political scene, supported by the audience – should be seen in terms of providing certain services to the public. In a modern democracy, at least in Western countries, the public has the right to control and hold politicians accountable as the managers of their state.

Here, however, quite inevitably, an endless array of misunderstandings and disappointments opens up before us. How naive are those who wish to view modern democracy as on par with the Athenian *polis* or tribal rallies! When compared to premodern political communities, our society turns out to be an enormous collective bound by innumerable complex interpersonal relationships (even if all these relationships can eventually be reduced to economics – what an economic monstrosity this is compared to pre-industrial economies!). Our state, based on the operation of the bureaucratic apparatus, is a machine that is utterly incomprehensible to minds busied with other affairs on a day-to-day basis and moving around in different spheres of life. This is overlaid by the operation of technology in a strict sense, without which there would be no possibility of such effective organization on such a scale, but also no chance to involve the general public in the political game, to make citizens of people, to inform ("enlighten") them properly. But does it work like that? Are we, in the here and now, really citizens in the classical sense of the word, discerning in public matters and having a significant influence on these matters? Isn't it the reverse side of the "common-sense" economization of politics that we are presented with a media circus instead of true discourse? That the actors of the political scene are beginning to perform a real operetta in front of us (who can be more "emotional" in their speech, etc.), and that

HUMANISM AS REALISM

the services they provide should be reduced to entertainment services to some extent – alongside, say, sports and show business? It is easy to suspect that the puppets on our TV screens are not the people making the crucial decisions. The real decision-makers, avoiding the limelight, would use these figureheads of public life for their own purposes. They would uphold a semblance of democracy to avoid social unrest when what we'd be dealing with would be a form of oligarchy. In a system like that, in the conditions of modernity, the most important skill would be the art of behavior, that is – practically – generating impulses and playing on emotions to convince us, at the lowest possible cost, of our consent to the implementation of someone else's plans and interests.

This is not a new dilemma. The development of the modern state and society presents us with the painful observation that "real" democracy – in the sense of the power of a well-informed crowd – is simply impossible to build. The crowd ends up getting too large, and there is always a problem with information. Contrary to appearances, this is not changed by the twentieth-century eruption of new means of communication, leading to the ever-greater domination of visual images (in the cinema, television, internet). People's opinions and beliefs remain what they were; they do not become more rational, more independently formulated, or better thought out. Views and arguments, romantic declarations and claims to truth, shouts, and explanations – all this appears as one big mishmash that somehow needs to be sorted out. To help with this, we are forced to use learning aids – stereotypes – that others then recognize and use. Since it is difficult for us as consumers to determine the truth about eggs, for instance, whether they are healthy or unhealthy, we need an egg expert's opinion, as long as the egg industry or its competition does not corrupt it. Are we not, as citizens, equally at the mercy of experts in the field of management? Walter Lippmann first seriously considered the concept of a "stereotype" about a hundred years ago. He did so within the context of changing the understanding of the democratic system of government. In his view, *the practice of democracy*

Un-Economic Ideals

*has turned a corner. A revolution is taking place, infinitely more signif-
icant than any shifting of economic power. Within the life of the generation now* (in 1921) *in control of affairs, persuasion has become a
self-conscious art and a regular organ of popular government. None of
us begins to understand the consequences, but it is no daring prophecy
to say that the knowledge of how to create consent will alter every political calculation and modify every political premise. Under the impact of
propaganda, not necessarily in the sinister meaning of the word alone,
the old constants of our thinking have become variables. It is no longer
possible, for example, to believe in the original dogma of democracy; that
the knowledge needed for the management of human affairs comes up
spontaneously from the human heart.*[2] Lippmann's response lies in
the expectation of a professionalization of political discourse – in
short, in the power of experts. We need elites to watch over our
minds. It is necessary to educate people who – with the advance-
ment of knowledge about stereotypes and macro thinking – will
be ever more efficient in arranging the desired sequences of images in the minds of citizens who have neither the time nor the
ability to make independent analyses. The real science of politics
– and ultimately politics itself – comes down to "opinion management"; the future belongs to opinion managers. It is worth
noting that the essential function of political services in such an
arrangement is not to act for the material welfare of all, but to
achieve universal agreement. After all, it is not difficult to imagine
experts who do not so much work for us, as they "play for themselves" at our expense, creating conditions for achieving and
maintaining their supremacy and that of their loved ones (or hidden masters). Who will judge them and on what basis?

If we are somewhat surprised that American intellectuals of
the 1920s foresaw our problems with democracy in the "age of
the media," some reflection on the history of modern political science may show us how entangled we are in the reinterpretations
of old ideas. The discovery of the self-aware "art of persuasion,"
or, as we called it earlier, the art of behavior, is associated with

2   W. Lippmann, *Public Opinion*, New York 1997, p. 158.

the much older, 16th-century discovery of a "new moral continent" by Niccolo Machiavelli,[3] the patron of political realists and political researchers alike. Admittedly, we cannot connect his name directly with the issue of immediate interest to us, i.e., the economization of politics, as he did not descend to the level of uncritical enthusiasm around the idea of material progress or economic growth. As a teacher of virtue, he certainly valued masculine honor over feminine involvement in trade and the amassing of wealth. But what of it? The author of *The Prince* paved the way to a purely "self-interested" approach to political affairs, where virtue is nothing but a vehicle for efficient operation, and one can mold fellow human beings practically at will. Lippmann seems to be aware of this when he writes of Machiavelli: *but there have also been philosophers* (as opposed to the idealists striving for order and harmony) *who were bored by these schemes of rights and duties, took conflict for granted, and tried to see how their side might come out on top. They have always seemed more realistic, even when they seemed alarming, because all they had to do was to generalize the experience that nobody could escape. Machiavelli is the classic of this school, a man most mercilessly maligned, because he happened to be the first naturalist who used plain language in a field hitherto preempted by supernaturalists. He has a worse name and more disciples than any political thinker who ever lived.* His teachings are *cynical. But it is the cynicism of a man who saw truly without knowing quite why he saw what he saw (...) he would not indulge in fantasies, and he had not the materials for imagining a race of men that had learned how to correct their* (i.e., sixteenth-century Italians') *vision.*[4]

Ultimately, Lippmann may have considered himself the new Machiavelli.[5] The advances made in four centuries enabled him

---

3   Cf. L. Strauss, *What is Political Philosophy? And Other Studies*, Chicago 1988, pp. 91, 94–95; id., *Natural Right and History*, Chicago 1965, pp. 164 ff.

4   W. Lippmann, *Public Opinion...*, pp. 168–69.

5   Cf. P. V. Murphy, The New Era: American Thought and Culture in the 1920s, Lanham 2012, p. 159., *Public Opinion...*, pp. 168–69.

Un-Economic Ideals

to see things as they are more consciously than what he attributed to his predecessor. The American would be a "vision correction Machiavelli" – scientific, but also less disaffected with humanity; after all, his "philosophy" is considered "democratic." Seeing this difference, we may begin to suspect the modern fate of realistic thinking (in the version appropriate for experts and intellectuals) in advance, namely, that it strangely fits with the ideal that – due to presumed skepticism, cynicism, or sober distance should be opposed. For now, it is worth emphasizing the deeply embedded continuity in the understanding of politics from Machiavelli to modern opinion managers. It doesn't matter whether they want to call themselves propaganda, PR, or marketing people. This continuity shows us the consequences of thought that calls for universal enlightenment. Man must be enlightened to define his self-interest properly. Of course, enlightenment can be called "informing a citizen" and presented as a political discourse to which everyone born in a given territory is invited, for instance. However, most people are not philosophers hungering for discourse; at best, they may like or respect philosophers. What remains for the responsible ruling elite is to sanction certain opinions accepted on faith, and finally – the art of behavior.[6]

Everything we have said thus far illustrates the first way of expressing the primacy of economics over politics. This whole time we're bearing in mind the simple opinion that money rules the world, and any denial or limitation of the role of money only means that the interested parties are turning a blind eye. This opinion does not imply – though it also does not exclude – significant intellectual claims. The second method is different. In it, we are dealing with a belief in access to knowledge that has a value of certainty or even absoluteness, knowledge that ancient philosophers could only dream of. They were like children compared to us – with no chance of embracing the whole of reality; they didn't have our textbooks, encyclopedias; in fact, they didn't know history at all. For us, general history lessons are technically

6   Cf. L. Strauss, *Thoughts on Machiavelli*, Chicago–London 1958, p. 297.

readily available, but also easy to transform into metaphysical views.[7] Note that the opinion of a "simple" man – our realist cousin – concerns some of the matters he wants to talk about to support a judgment ("only money matters") and thus face the opposite judgment ("money isn't everything"). *Ultimately*, we can go this way or that. The intellectual, on the other hand, wants to see the whole and talk about the whole. His opinion takes on the features of a total narrative. It is not, then, that economics stands opposite to ideals (whether wisely or unwisely professed). Instead, all ideals – aspirations, interests – are contained in one and corroborate what we "know" (even if some are not yet able to use that "knowledge" consciously and consistently). The decent intellectual understands – and reasonably accepts – that there is no real tension in this world because all tension(s) has been lifted. Therefore, he will not participate in his idealist cousin's unpleasant discovery that it is the realist cousin who's dealing the cards at the table while she plunges into *wishful thinking*. For many "simple" people, adopting an opinion on the power of money may constitute a reason to confirm their maturity, that they won't let others push them around; others, however, may react at the level of childhood trauma connected to the revelation that Santa Claus doesn't exist. Expressing strong opinions is often accompanied by strong emotions. However, no one here is interested in overcoming the thought horizons of classical philosophy or gaining absolute insight into the history of humankind. Of course, the realist cousin may invoke reason to try to justify his opinion, so he can impose it on his idealist cousin as a rational solution – a key to understanding the things of this world. Nevertheless, it is hard to say that he was establishing a binding political discourse for all citizens. Rather, he remains an advocate of a particular view, one of the countless private "authorities" with perhaps some influence on family and friends, but none on all humankind. As everyone knows, intellectuals have more sway.

This is a critical issue in understanding the modern form of

---

7   Cf. id., *Natural Right...*, p. 27.

Un-Economic Ideals

political life and its humanist critique (which we will deal with later). Politics is, above all, an area in which particularist positions clash. The opinions we express may flow from various sources and concern ways of describing reality. As such, however, they are to serve our relatives and us or, more broadly, communities and organizations that ensure our well-being and our identity. If we say, for example, that Krakow is the most beautiful city in Poland, and Poland is a lovely country – we are expressing an opinion that we can probably justify in our group of interlocutors, but we do not expect it to become a universal truth shared by everyone, anywhere on Earth and – potentially – at any time in history. Opinions may or may not be true, but what matters is their effectiveness in strengthening what is ours or dear to us. The problem of intellectualism begins when an opinion assumes the place of a philosophy that comes to know the truth and a particular position becomes equivalent to a universal approach; when, in other words, a multitude of complicated ("scientific," "cultural") spells shields an individual's crude presumptuousness: I "know" it, so it must be true. Such a person is floating along on a wave of thought that someone has told him is winning. And the more deeply ingrained this thought is, the less clear the perfidious assumption that what wins, thus definitively confirms the relationship between its supposed truthfulness and its efficiency in mastering or establishing a discourse. From this perspective, Stalin must have been right since he was victorious. If, however, we decide too late that he lost, it remains for us to determine who defeated him – whose thought turned out to be more effective and therefore truer; that, e.g., the American economic model turned out to be truer than the Soviet one. Indeed, digging deeper, won't we get to the point where both models will turn out to be one? And the modern intellectual – always a winner?

For now, let's make one, seemingly banal, objection. We can see that our intellectual is not a person of flesh and blood. In reality, this type of person, saturated with "knowledge" and properly directed – sometimes simply having inherited his family's status and library – falls into cynicism, going through various stages of doubt and confirmation concerning his ideas, and in the end, placing his own interest over grand visions for humanity. However, we can expect that he suffers few doubts about himself in the course of his experiences; if he does suffer a little, he soon puts on a brave face. Real, natural attachment to the particular (what is close, one's own) does not weaken with the development of one's career; it is certainly not harmed by universal claims contained in the formula of the worldview itself. Meanwhile, masses of people with much worse attitudes are trying to become "authorities." Similarly educated, they consider themselves intellectually sophisticated, reasonable representatives of the intellectual class, in sum – serious participants of a real (i.e., currently victorious) political discourse. This is most often a liberal or "centrist" discourse, but these terms do not seem relevant in themselves (what do today's liberal, conservative or socialist have in common with their namesakes from two hundred, one hundred, or even fifty years ago?... and how do they differ here and now?). Let the point for this thread be the endearingly simple *dictum* of German-American political philosophy researcher Leo Strauss: *it is as absurd to expect members of philosophy departments to be philosophers as it is to expect members of art departments to be artists.*[8]

Since, as modern people – or modernly enlightened people – we entrust ourselves to academic "philosophers" and "authorities," drawing from the resources of absolute knowledge, we are coming very near to pathos. Not so long ago, in the mid-19th century, Norwid asked (in the poem *Marionettes*[9]): *How can one help being bored on so restricted | A stage, so amateurishly set, | Where mankind's each ideal has acted, | And life is the price of a seat...* This question is very ironic, but today we know that this kind of "boredom" will not get to us and we don't have to worry about paying with our lives – at least Meryl Streep doesn't. The American actress "engaged" safely, therefore, and wanting to teach on the go,

8   Id., *What is Liberal Education?* [in:] id., *Liberalism Ancient and Modern*, Ithaca – London 1989, p. 7.
9   Translated from the Polish by Christine Brooks-Rose.

takes the light of truth with her: *ex occidente lux*! Let us quote: *gentlemen, you are deceiving yourselves (...) look at the world and the direction it is evolving. Do you really think you can stop it?! The past is dying a painful death, and the old order won't give up without a fight. I understand this, but I am happy to tell you that you represent a lost cause. Equality is the great dream and future of this world. We are different – men and women, straight and gay, black and white – but we should all have equal opportunities to express ourselves and be ourselves. Equal opportunities in work, love, and your own path to happiness. Gentlemen, you are losing power, and your old principles are falling into oblivion. Goodbye!*[10] No, the point here is not what Ms. Streep believes. The point lies in how she describes and assesses political and social reality through the prism of a particular experience of modernity. A historical perspective invalidating all prior views – before it is popularized and internalized by true warriors of the discourse like Ms. Streep – is born in the minds of intellectuals within the forge of *les philosophes*, Darwin, Hegel, Marx, Freud, and many others. From their point of view, as Irving Babbitt notes (here, in reference to John Dewey's teachings), *the religious experience Dante has sought to convey in the* Divine Comedy, *inasmuch as it is not the kind that can be tested in a laboratory, is mere moonshine. The similar experience symbolized in a great cathedral must also be dismissed as moonshine. In fact, most of the great art and literature of the past, East and West, being primarily concerned, as this art and literature have been, with either humanistic or religious experience, must be dismissed as moonshine.*[11] In the same way, we can talk about conceptions of the system of government and patterns of individual life based on the classical understanding of philosophy and religion.

---

10 *Meryl Streep do posłów polskich: Panowie, tracicie władzę* (interview conducted by M. Zakowska), "Gazeta Wyborcza" [online], 22 January 2014 [accessed 13 January 2018]. Available online: <http://wyborcza.pl/1,75475,15318901,Meryl_Streep_do_poslow_polskich__Panowie__tracicie.html>. Translation from the Polish: L. Fretschel.

11 I. Babbitt, *Experience and Dogma*, "The Saturday Review of Literature," vol. 1, no. 15, November 1, 1930, p. 287.

Virtually everything that does not correspond to the naturalistic premises of humanitarianism – faith in humanity from which the mainstream of modern thought gushes forth – must either be forgotten or transformed based on victorious economic ideals.

Why do we suddenly declare that economic ideals are "victorious"? We want to be realistic, which means – to separate the grain from the chaff; the horizon of horizontal thought – from the bloated phraseology which merely pretends to raise the horizon; a man who trusts the earth – from one who lies that he sees heaven. The "truth" constitutive of our times – and, contrary to appearances, generally unchallenged – is contained in the "philosophical" opinion that, as humans, we have reached the point where we can focus on solving real economic problems rather than arguing about matters of the spirit. After all, man's destiny – his desired fate – is known to us: the conquest of the Universe and full self-realization. It is a rational choice, a choice that has already been made. Therefore, the further dispute does not concern the first principles or the question of how to live. To put it without any hint of exaltation: it is worth being full, refreshed, and generally – satisfied. We could say that the great competition in history's arena is won by the *petit-bourgeois* increasing credit scores and enriched with supplements of entertainment and "engagement."

Political life may be entertainment for the "victorious" variety of the little bourgeois, but politics necessarily retains its more serious dimension. This is mainly due to the previously mentioned need to manage large communities. The game is about ensuring the right amount of material goods and efficient opinion management. The sphere of the spirit must be appeased; there is a requirement of "correctness" so that no one feels offended or "excluded," because this introduces a disturbance and even fosters the renewal of old diseases or anxieties of the spirit. With successful pacification, we can focus on disputes over the redistribution of goods: what to do to keep all citizens satisfied or make them *believe* that they are satisfied. Against this background, the issue of the legitimization (proper validation) of the

Un-Economic Ideals

political system arises. For example, someone may be surprised by the durability of political forms in modern China or Vietnam, where the rulers seem to shamelessly, or perhaps submissively, draw on compromised doctrines and symbols. But this whole Marxist-Leninist staffage should instead be seen as a superstructure of frameworks to carry out the "modern experiment" in a given area, whose practical achievement – and basis of social support – is constituted by a growing sense of wealth or material power.

Viewed from the perspective of the most recent political history, the "modern experiment" turns out to be a series of attempts aimed at the best possible – that is, "true" – implementation of the modern (humanitarian) model of the state and society. In 1935, Joseph Stalin addressed the assembled representatives of the Stakhanov movement with these simple words: *Life has improved, comrades. Life has become more joyous. And when life is joyous, work goes well.*[12] Of course, we know that he spoke these words in the very brief interlude between the Great Famine and Great Terror; that they came from the mouth of a figure who could serve as a model tyrant-oppressor; that therefore no one in their right mind would want to live in his country because life there could not be light or happy, and whatever could pass as a source of satisfaction, was soon to fall into ruins as a result of the invasion of his neighbor Adolf who, incidentally, prided himself on his economic success. The shocking magnitude of the crime is not something that can be forgiven – or explained away – in the name of "truth." Years after millions of human lives had again been used to rebuild the "homeland of the proletariat" after the conflagration of war, many allegedly competent people were eager to believe that the future belonged to this state and its political system. They believed that in the end, despite the constant "temporary difficulties," it would turn out to be a more effective ("true") system – that is, more focused on the ruthless exploitation of human nature

12 Cf. J. Stalin, *Speech at the First All-Union Conference of Stakhanovites*, 17 November 1935, [in:] *Problems of Leninism*, p. 531.

(and nature in general) and more consistent in this effort, more progressive, more modern. Of course, the "hard" intellectual fascination with Stalinism, with its inherent topos of "forced industrialization," had to die away quickly. However, were they not turning away from the crude, ineffective techniques used to manage the Soviet juggernaut rather than from justifications of the direction in which the juggernaut was apparently headed? Have great "philosophical" searches not been launched to offer the world a better version of the humanitarian utopia? Have there not been attempts at expressing the "truth" of the new epoch in a somewhat more attractive way, say, than that of the old Suslov-type apparatchiks? Attractive – especially for the intellectuals themselves? On the other hand, does the great debate on the separate paths of different countries' modernization, the convergence theories created on this occasion, and the topos of "globalization" not reveal a deep attachment to the same "truth" whose light filled the minds of the conspirators at the head of the Bolshevik tyranny?

There is no doubt that this harsh perspective, which reduces the intellectual biographies of many individuals to the single phenomenon of intellectualism, also has its drawbacks and dangers. The mechanical condemnation of the erring is sometimes a testament to a mutual error. *He that is without sin among you, let him first cast a stone at her* (John 8:7). However, it is impossible to understand the reasons for establishing the primacy of economics over politics, or the victory of economic ideals, without first showing the peculiarities of thinking that seem to dominate the political discourse completely – starting with those whose task and privilege is to educate the elite. This peculiarity of modern "authorities'" thinking, their "metaphysicality" from a humanistic point of view, can remain almost elusive to us, who are generally unfamiliar with anything else. We become all the more confused by the practical consequences of modern metaphysics, with the effects of identifying particular opinions with universal truth, confusing the order of inquiry with the order of effective action. One needs courageous insight to calmly consider such a

Un-Economic Ideals

strange-sounding statement as this, that – perhaps – *the objectives of Lenin's revolution never materialized in Russia but they are all about us here in bourgeois America*.[13]

Though unable to outline a complete, up-to-date diagnosis of the modern model's American version here, it's worth drawing attention to the interesting phenomenon of the revival of normative reflection on politics or the "philosophy of politics" at local universities in the second half of the twentieth century. Texts in this field seem to enliven the intellectual landscape. Contrary to political science, which we roughly take to contain "scientific" – objective, allegedly impartial, avoiding value judgments – descriptions of the political processes, the philosophy of politics promises to focus on how things should be or what we should aspire to. Second, academic "philosophers" remind us more of the great works of the past than do "political scientists," creating the impression of a "conversation" of great minds. However, this is done within a particular scope and based on a general interpretation, the aim of which is a better "justification by understanding" of the modern model. In short, we are dealing with a defense of modernity in its Anglo-Saxon version (liberal democracy) under pressure from "continental" modernity (of the "masters of suspicion," the Frankfurt School). The main issue concerns – which is easy to guess – the relationship between the state and the economy, thus how to secure the implementation of economic ideals, not their externally evaluated validity or legitimacy. The contemporary American philosophical and political debate began with the publication (in 1971) of *A Theory of Justice* by John Rawls. This work is a highly refined apology of the twentieth-century welfare state (the achievements of which include, for example, universal health care or pension systems). On the one hand, the response to this was spearheaded by libertarians led by Robert Nozick and his *Anarchy, State, and*

13   S. Bellow, "Writers, Intellectuals, Politics: Mainly Reminiscence." *The National Interest*, no. 31, 1993, pp. 124–34. *JSTOR*, www.jstor.org/stable/42894864. Accessed 6 Sept. 2021. (quote on p. 132).

Utopia (1974), which created a strong current within the entire liberal-democratic discourse demanding a fundamental reduction of the ineffective state apparatus; on the other – by the communitarians, who bolster appreciation for particular social contexts, especially local *communities*, including within the context of better need satisfaction. In all – Canadian author Will Kymlicka declares – *the recent emphasis has been on the ideals of justice, freedom, and community* (moved from findings on the subjects of *power, sovereignty, or of the nature of law*) *which are invoked when evaluating political institutions and policies* (...) *whereas the traditional view tells us that the fundamental argument in political theory is whether to accept equality as a value, this revised view tells us that the fundamental argument is not whether to accept equality, but how best to interpret it. And that means people would be arguing on the same wavelength, so to speak, even those who do not fit on the traditional left-right continuum.*[14] What is striking in the above approach is not so much the view of the overriding importance of equality, but the underlying belief in the progress made as a result of the "disputants" adopting a single "frequency" of thought expression. Is it not a "frequency" of faith – a mature faith – in the economic ideals of modernity? Faith that subordinating one's thinking to the realization of economic ideals makes this thinking truer, better? Since these ideals, after centuries of wandering about, after dispelling all illusions, turn out to be... everything? But then we don't think seriously anymore because there is no point in doing so. After all, the fact that a recognized thinker uses the works of Plato and Aristotle does not mean that he is a decent, critical exegete or, even more so, a worthy continuator. The association with a discount in the supermarket seems a bit more appropriate here.

The best-known conception of absolute exhaustion and the overcoming of old political discourses in modern thought is called the "end of history." For us, it is a slogan that gained

14 W. Kymlicka, *Contemporary Political Philosophy. An Introduction*, Oxford 2002, pp. 2, 4.

Un-Economic Ideals

popularity in the early 1990s, after the publication in the United States of a book by the same name authored by political scientist Francis Fukuyama.[15] The reception was broad but generally superficial: the gist of it is more or less that after the collapse of the Soviet Union, the only model of the political (and economic) system that counts is the American model, called liberal democracy, which everyone begins to implement, thanks to which we find ourselves on the threshold of a new era: one of everlasting prosperity and earthly peace. Thus, Fukuyama's name was associated, perhaps wrongly, with a wave of thoughtless optimism after the end of the Cold War. After all, every television viewer could see history march on before their eyes – from the untimely war in former Yugoslavia, through the attacks of September 11, to subsequent crises and conflicts. If, however, the "simple" man can be right to turn his nose up at the intellectual allure of "the end of history," since there is no end to conflicts or poverty, then from the point of view of our critique of modern (humanitarian) intellectualism, the problem lies elsewhere. Indeed, speaking of the "end of history" results from the adoption – more or less directly – of Hegel's philosophy of history, which serves to justify the whole of modernity or the modern direction of thinking about the state and society. Within the framework of this overall vision, the history of human thought appears to be something of a math problem; its solution depends on our applying the correct method, which is dialectics. Concentrated dialectical effort makes us sages, recognizing in advance the outcome of all possible actions – i.e., what humanity is heading towards.[16] Alexandre Kojève was one such self-aware "sage" (from whom the unfortunate Fukuyama, among others, drew handfuls) in the previous century. A Russian aristocrat in exile in Paris, he organized an extremely influential seminar devoted to the ideas of Hegel, and

15 See F. Fukuyama, *The End of History and The Last Man*, New York 1992.
16 Cf. G. W. F. Hegel, *The Philosophy of History*, trans. J. Sibree, New York 1956, p. 16.

after World War II, he became one of the leading constructors of the Western European model of integration. Kojève's teachings,[17] painfully abstract from the outside, contain a very suggestive development of the thesis that intellectual history (the history of seeking universal truth) fully corresponds to political history (the history of acting on behalf of the particular), even identifying itself with political history. Absolutely everything that concerns man can be explained from the perspective of the struggle for recognition, described by Hegel's concept of a dialectical clash between "Master" and "Slave." The history of humankind is the history of desired desires.[18] In other words, everyone – in every place and time – will say to everyone else: I want you to recognize me as your equal – this is how the engine of universal history worked; worked – in the past tense, because this "history of desired desires" ended with Napoleon's triumph at Jena, the meaning of which Georg Wilhelm Friedrich Hegel came to understand, reaching absolute wisdom by way of his dialectic; then, after the "end of history" (in 1806), there was a post-historic discourse within the framework of which Kojève operates. This discourse finds its political embodiment in the final (victorious, "true") political model, which he calls the "universal and homogeneous state." Little by little, thanks to the guarantees of reason, and despite all mundane perturbations, this "state's" power extends to all nations.

To be able to present an opinion as truth, you must change your opinion about truth. According to Kojève, *if Being creates itself ("becomes") in the course of history, it is not by isolating oneself from history that one can reveal it (transform it by discourse into* Truth *that man possesses in the form of* Wisdom*). To do this the philosopher must, on the contrary, participate in history, and then one cannot see why he ought not participate in it actively, for example by giving advice to the tyrant, given that he is, as a philosopher, more able to govern than*

17 Cf. S. Rosen, *Hermeneutics as Politics*, Oxford 1987, pp. 124–44.
18 Cf. A. Kojève, *Introduction to the Reading of Hegel: Lectures on the Phenomenology of Spirit*, Ithaca 1980, especially pp. 12 ff.

any "uninitiate."[19] This peculiar jargon expresses the idea that truth is not immutable, independent of the circumstances, or waiting to be discovered. It is revealed through the effects of political actions, through the cooperation of hands and minds. It is hard to find a better excuse for turning a philosopher into an intellectual. The latter, in turn, can do nothing but support with his engagement the – necessarily laborious – construction of the "universal and homogeneous state." This state – being the rational culmination of the historical process, that is, giving meaning to the fight for recognition – ensures its "citizens" are equally "recognized" regardless of their traits or origin.

Kojève's attitude towards the "end of history" was perhaps somewhat sarcastic, as he wrote about the "American animal" and the "Japanese snob" as products of a historical process guaranteed by reason.[20] Other less complicated souls would be inclined to recognize this nascent world (supposedly) without wars; a world where we all ultimately think (or profess) the same things; a world where we can all believe that our needs are being met – to recognize such a world as good, to put it simply. What great fortune we have to be able to live at the dawn of a good world! It may not be undisturbed happiness, but the thought of it does instill a sense of confidence. Yes, many of us are ready to frown at this, saying: no one here has been talking about the end of history for a long time! What we do have is a "clash of civilizations" – Europe threatened by Muslims, etc. The catch is still that we are unwittingly expressing essentially incommensurable opinions stemming from different levels of reflection. However one views its roots and spiritual "legitimacy," the great "modern experiment" is taking place on a global scale and has been for some time; "just any" crisis that produces victims does not constitute a change in direction. One might think that the expansive residents

---

19 Id., *Tyranny and Wisdom* [in:] L. Strauss, *On Tyranny. Revised and Expanded Edition, Including the Strauss – Kojève* Correspondence, Chicago 2000, p. 152. Emphasis in original.
20 Cf. A. Kojève, *Introduction to the Reading...*, pp. 454–56, note 1.

of the Middle East are eager to go back to the Middle Ages now. But does this supposedly religious reaction of Islamic societies to Western modernity not betray, above, all a desire to take the place of the West? For several centuries, this West has set the standards of universal expansion, and today seems to be equally immersed in apathy and mindless debauchery? One can also ask brutally: have Islamic fundamentalists not successfully demonstrated their ability to use modern means of communication, from the Internet to airplanes? In turn, the likely weakening of America's superpower role or the often articulated "increase in China's power" does not signify the abandonment of the modern model of the state and society (that is, the "universal and homogeneous state" that leaves everyone satisfied). For over the last two centuries, this model has absorbed, practically without exception, minds looking for political solutions (including the heirs of civilizations much older than the American or Anglo-Saxon), thus becoming a universal model.

As we can see, the intellectual way of expressing the primacy of economics over politics leads us to the relationship between politics and philosophy, or between political action (which, by definition, ends in compulsion) and critical thinking. Following this path, we come to a point when it is no longer possible to hide the totalitarian inclinations of power, which sees itself as a power in the final state, after which – and over which – there can be nothing. This is disturbingly consistent with what we wrote earlier on the art of behavior and opinion management. The final state's desired feature turns out to be its egalitarian unanimity (for the disciples of Hegel and Marx, this is a necessary feature). "Citizens" must believe that they are faring well; they should also be able to properly justify this faith within the framework of the current discourse. However, this means, *de facto* or *de jure*, the end of philosophical investigations. *Libertas philosophandi*, the freedom to philosophize – or, if you prefer, the freedom of speech – after all, it does not consist in the fact that everyone can say something, but in the fact that different people can say different things! What would be the use of a billion voice recorders if all the voices

Un-Economic Ideals

sounded the same? Perhaps Leo Strauss expressed this problem best and most vividly (in a polemic with Kojève): *the Chief of the universal and homogeneous state, or the Universal and Final Tyrant will be (...) forced to suppress every activity which might lead people into doubt of the essential soundness of the universal and homogeneous state: he must suppress philosophy as an attempt to corrupt the young. In particular he must in the interest of the homogeneity* (i.e., uniform consistency) *of his universal state forbid every teaching, every suggestion, that there are politically relevant natural differences among men which cannot be abolished or neutralized by progressing scientific technology. He must command his biologists to prove that every human being has, or will acquire, the capacity of becoming a philosopher or tyrant (...) from the Universal Tyrant, however, there is no escape. Thanks to the conquest of nature and to the completely unabashed substitution of suspicion and terror for law, the Universal and Final Tyrant has at his disposal practically unlimited means for ferreting out, and for extinguishing, the most modest efforts in the direction of thought (...) the coming of the universal and homogeneous state will be the end of philosophy on earth.*[21]

In turn, another voice will help us, summing up, to bring down to earth the reflections on the "end of history" and ultimately any image of a humanitarian utopia – no matter who implements it or by what means: whether under the banner of consumption on the free market, under that of government, of the continuation of development or of revolution. Friedrich Nietzsche put these words into the mouth of the prophetic Zarathustra almost a century and a half ago: *still is his soil rich enough for it. But that soil will one day be poor and exhausted, and no lofty tree will any longer be able to grow thereon. Alas! There cometh the time when man will no longer launch the arrow of his longing beyond man – and the string of his bow will have unlearned to whizz! (...) lo! I show you* the last man. *"What is love? What is creation? What is longing? What is a star?" – so asketh the last man and blinketh. The earth hath then*

21 L. Strauss, *Restatement on Xenophon's Hiero* [in:] id., *On Tyranny...*, p. 226.

HUMANISM AS REALISM

become small, and on it there hoppeth the last man who maketh every-
thing small. His species is ineradicable like that of the ground-flea; the
last man liveth longest. "We have discovered happiness" – say the last
men, and blink thereby. They have left the regions where it is hard to
live; for they need warmth. One still loveth one's neighbour and rubbeth
against him; for one needeth warmth. Turning ill and being distrustful,
they consider sinful: they walk warily (...) a little poison now and then:
that maketh pleasant dreams. And much poison at last for a pleasant
death. One still worketh, for work is pastime. But one is careful lest the
pastime should hurt one. One no longer becometh poor or rich; both are
too burdensome. Who still wanteth to rule? Who still wanteth to obey?
Both are too burdensome. No shepherd, and one herd! Everyone wanteth
the same; everyone is equal: he who hath other sentiments goeth volun-
tarily into the madhouse. "Formerly all the world was insane," – say
the subtlest of them, and blink thereby. They are clever and know all that
hath happened: so there is no end to their raillery. People still fall out,
but are soon reconciled – otherwise it spoileth their stomachs. They have
their little pleasures for the day, and their little pleasures for the night,
but they have a regard for health.[22]

We have devoted a lot of space to a conception whose roots
and fruits perfectly illustrate the problem posed by a "philosophical" faith in modernity. Of course, not all intellectuals – or intellectual humanitarians – are followers of Hegel or Marx; not all,
then, have to confront the Nietzschean parody of the "end of history," this wonderfully poetic vision of bestialization by gratification. Instead of citing a nominal philosophy of history, the
professional defenders of the humanitarian vector of history will
happily appear as practical and reasonable people for whom the
experience of the successes of modern science and education remains an important horizon of reference. The authority of the
masters ("classics") of natural science is considered inescapable
in the field of truth, despite various reservations and doubts born
in the previous century. Hence, we like to check what, say, Albert

22 F. Nietzsche, *Thus Spake Zarathustra*, trans. Th. Common, New York
1917, pp. 11–12. Emphasis in original.

Un-Economic Ideals

Einstein had to say about religion or politics. Furthermore, we use the rich resources of life science, biology (and the biologically-oriented human sciences) to learn the truth about our structure and destiny and, oddly enough, to learn about the prognosis for the development of our species. Seen from this perspective, the emergence of the theory of evolution in the nineteenth century along with the set of its "philosophical" or para-scientific off-shoots is a significant event. When we fill our imagination with the vision of an endless, benevolent transformation of the world we know (from "the simplest forms" to ...), we find ourselves – potentially – further than the "end of history" theorists. At stake for us may be the literal assumption of the role of Creator – that is, the ability to accelerate or redirect the natural evolutionary processes to which we are subject as beings of flesh and blood. Wouldn't it be nice – knowing the scale of suffering and humiliation that has existed in the bosom of nature up to this point – to create a new species, free from the diseases of the body and soul? For now, let's try to focus on economic ideals, which allegedly correspond to the least dangerous human instincts (let's say that I do less harm by eating my fill than by proselytizing my neighbors) and are oriented towards development or expansion. After all, our experiments require funding and access to experimental materials.

This is what the field of humanitarian hope – religious at its base – looks like in its purest form; for modern intellectuals, this is above all the hope of finding and solidifying themselves in the role of experts, "authorities," reformers, or management specialists. Again, this is not a new issue. Over 100 years ago, Louis Trenchard More (Paul Elmer's brother) wrote about the then-very-current projects of social transformation through eugenics and the "scientific ethicists" who undertook them, playing the role of *the arbiters of right and wrong*; ultimately, *the object is to mold the whole human race, with its immensely complex and diversified desires and actions, its egotisms and its sympathies, into a homogeneous society which shall progress toward a standard, previously determined, of a noble and god-like humanity. The reward to be expected by the individual who is born and lives well is that intense feeling of satisfaction he will have that the race as a whole has been carried a little closer to a distant and vague goal of perfection because of his submission to the laws of eugenical righteousness.*[23] Well, it is a miserable substitute for philosophical happiness and religious salvation. But isn't eugenics essentially passé – since it was associated with German crimes of the Second World War? We do have an interesting example here of the stigmatization of one of the most influential "scientific" approaches and the depreciation of its name. However, the problem resulting from the well-established hegemony of the humanitarian direction of thinking has not disappeared, quite the contrary. As Fukuyama notes, having escaped the Hegelian context: *if we look back at the tools of the past century's social engineers and utopian planners, they seem unbelievably crude and unscientific (...) all of these were techniques for pounding the square peg of human nature into the round hole of social planning. None of them were based on knowledge of the neurological structure or biochemical basis of the brain; none understood the genetic sources of behavior, or if they did, none could do anything to affect them. All of this may change in the next generation or two. We do not have to posit a return of state-sponsored eugenics or widespread genetic engineering (...) as we discover not just correlations but actual molecular pathways between genes and traits like intelligence, aggression, sexual identity, criminality, alcoholism, and the like, it will inevitably occur to people that they can make use of this knowledge for particular social ends (...) if wealthy parents suddenly have open to them the opportunity to increase the intelligence of their children as well as that of all their subsequent descendants, then we have the makings not just of a moral dilemma but of a full-scale class war.*[24] It is probably not the time to declare this kind of war. Still, the threat of man's total dependence on biotechnology – in the face of deeply entrenched belief in the economic ideals of modernity – is by no means abstract. Because don't people in our time – both

23 L. T. More, *The Limitations of Science*, New York 1915, p. 246.
24 F. Fukuyama, *Our Posthuman Future. Consequences of the Biotechnology Revolution*, New York 2002, pp. 15-16.

Un-Economic Ideals

young and old – pay dearly for various drugs, legal or not, that make them feel better? To experience, in other words, a simulacrum of happiness or perfect satisfaction? Do they not become weaker in the political dimension, that is, more susceptible to manipulation or, more broadly, to being formed by the managerial elite? Doesn't the natural inclination to invest in one's offspring also become a prerequisite for degeneration in so far as it focuses on achieving the "scientifically" approved, ultimate, universal model of physical perfection? It is worth adding that the now lesser-known and handy concept of "euthenics" appears next to the notion of "eugenics" at the same stage of the development of intellectual humanitarianism. It was supposed to be a science on how to "live well," but in the understanding of optimal living conditions, and thus complementary to eugenics. It was supposed to include a continuation of the "properly" programmed birth. The overall picture of human farming that emerges from this prompts us, once again, to associate ourselves with the totalitarian power, which seems to be a shadow that constantly accompanies the maturing of modern thought.

Meanwhile, it does not seem that adopting far-reaching visions or utopias is necessary for the profession of economic ideals by a "simple" man. Leaving aside the question of how this "simplicity" actually mixes with acquired intellectualism today, we must constantly bear in mind the classic distinction between opinion and knowledge. The usual course of events is that opinions change under the influence of what is considered knowledge. In other historical circumstances, Ms. Streep, quoted above, might praise the Puritan virtues or the unshakable patriarchy. Raised in the spirit of a religion that replaced the faith of her ancestors, the description of the experience of modernity that, roughly speaking, combines the thought of all humanitarian intellectuals resonates. Our cousins at the table do the same thing, and we can find precisely the same thing in the virtual world. On the one hand, we are aware of the requirements of natural necessity, no matter how hidden or subdued they are – that you can't make an omelet without breaking a few eggs and that once you've made your bed, you will have to lie in it; on the other hand, we are looking for a horizon of certainty. For many of us, this horizon is still tied to the authority of Revelation, however reinterpreted. Others directly face modernity's grand "narratives," and thus – the intellectual justification of the primacy of economics over politics. It does not matter whether modern "authorities" sail on the sea of political discourse under the banner of Hegelianism, Darwinism, pragmatism, or something else.

However, there is a confident, seemingly decisive alternative. It is necessary to distinguish between (1) situations in which we are all to be beneficiaries of general gratification or general satisfaction according to the pattern adopted for all humankind, and (2) situations in which what counts is only – or above all – the satisfaction of special needs resulting from the desire for material goods or recognition in others' eyes. The former signifies an outbreak of a modern utopia and can be challenged in the name of a realistic view of human nature (at least as long as we retain the essential features of *Homo sapiens*). The latter means nothing other than the substantive acceptance of the priority of economic ideals, and subsequently, the statement that all important norms of social life, especially those relating to the political system, must be based on the expression – or presumption – of agreement that, as a state or society, we want to implement the economic ideals that unite us (to a certain particular extent); that religious or humanistic ideals that could divide us would not fulfill such a function. If – in the first case – the imposed utopia quickly meets the definition of totalitarianism, this does not mean that – in the second case – the practice of a "realistic" regime will not bring about similar threats over time. Due to their size and complexity, modern political creations will never become like communities of philosophers devoted to rational debate. Agreement is possible thanks to opinion management, the supply of stereotypes (lifestyles, etc.), and influencing emotions. In short, successful expansion requires effective profiling of human behavior, aspirations, and thoughts. However, the most important thing is that we are driven by faith in the beneficial power of expansion in both cases, and the difference lies in

Un-Economic Ideals

naming or not naming the perfect end of this expansion. But should we believe in such an implied good? From a humanistic point of view – not necessarily. While the fact that we struggle with each other, err, and stumble over our limitations is a testimony to our submission to natural necessity, the fundamental direction we give to our life, our political community, and our entire civilization is outside the sphere of necessity.

Can humanists say more about these things? Will they show us how non-economic ideals – those related to "humanistic or religious experience," with a value that cannot be translated into money and universal agreement unmeasured in an individual – can be made at least a part, but a significant part, of the criterion for the evaluation of political actions without immediately weaponizing them politically? Can humanism, in the sense of a potentially "resurrectable" movement here and now, significantly impact politics? Can it do so without sharing and strengthening the modern belief in the good revealed by human expansion, from which the modern understanding of economics' primacy results, and by not forcing serious people to contradict themselves and compete in a tournament with professional "mess-with-your-head"s? We know from the first sentences of Babbitt's meaningfully titled book *Democracy and Leadership* that *when studied with any degree of thoroughness, the economic problem will be found to run into the political problem, the political problem in turn into the philosophical problem, and the philosophical problem itself to be almost indissolubly bound up at last with the religious problem.*[25] This is undoubtedly a neat and thought-provoking formula. We understand little of the seriousness of our situation if we do not delve deep into the very foundations of modern political discourse. For now, however, let us not rush to call for final matters. After all, it is time for us – intending to check the credibility of their general diagnosis – to find out a bit about how Babbitt and More relate to contemporary phenomena and political processes. Do their statements from a hundred years ago still hold any relevance?

25 I. Babbitt, *Democracy and Leadership*, Indianapolis 1979, p. 23.

Let us make one remark beforehand against such doubts. One of the compelling reasons why Humanism – as the historic movement at the top of American society in the first half of the twentieth century ("New Humanism") – was almost completely forgotten after World War II was the conviction that a new category of unique experiences had been discovered related to the disclosure and "working through" of totalitarianism's crimes; experiences that may have been thought to be, if not too difficult or elusive to earlier minds, then simply too distant from More's and Babbitt's description of reality. Leo Strauss, quoted by us, Voegelin, Hannah Arendt, and others – all of them had the advantage over the humanists that their critical reflection, which arose out of the subtleties of German science, seemed to be a reflection of living witnesses rather than parlor theorists.[26] When (in 1953) Russell Kirk presented a suggestive and influential dissertation on outstanding examples of the "conservative mentality," both humanists were like the links of a great tradition for him, connecting the Puritan religious ethos with the permanent foundation within Edmund Burke's intellectual legacy.[27] Thus, they were appreciated as noble defenders of order, at the cost of being locked into the cupboard of the history of ideas amidst equally noble and ancient writing trinkets. Meanwhile, one cannot fruitfully face the radical consequences of modern thought without mental radicalism. There is a need for inner boldness and distance. It is possible that only by using today's perspective can we properly understand the considerations of the humanists, experience their depth and "transcendence." As for the specter of totalitarian power, we must ask ourselves one simple question: is it still circulating? Are those who associate totalitarianism with the inhuman brutality of known twentieth-century regimes, which we know fortunately lost, correct in doing so? Or is it

26 Cf. G. H. Nash, *The Conservative Intellectual Movement in America (Since 1945)*, New York 1976, especially p. 78.
27 See R. Kirk, *The Conservative Mind: From Burke to Santayana*, Chicago 1953, especially pp. 362–86.

something other than the – however commendable – reflecting on past crimes and victims? In short, if the threat of totalitarianism emerges from the very core of modernity's humanitarian assumptions, which we recognize with remarkable acuteness from reading More's and Babbitt's texts, we would expect that they understood the threat no worse than we did.

II.

If we were interested in the number of words the humanists dedicated to various topics in their written works, we would be forced to admit that political matters were not a priority for them. They wrote mainly about literature and education, philosophy and religion (the latter is especially true of More). Thus, in the opinion of those later researchers who developed the intellectual biographies of both thinkers, the question of the relation of their thoughts to politics or the political system, while perhaps not considered entirely trivial, is generally viewed as secondary.[28] This approach is a misunderstanding, as the whole enterprise of humanism seems to contain an implicit political project – and it is only from the perspective of political theory that it becomes understandable to us. This becomes visible when we pick up Babbitt's work *Democracy and Leadership* (from 1924), mentioned above, which constitutes a detailed theological and political treatise and is simultaneously the most complete – though not necessarily the best written – formulation of this author's thoughts.[29] At the very beginning, he characterizes the reality of his times as shaped by "visionaries," which are indistinguishable in a democracy from "men of vision." *This distinction acquires its full importance only when related to the question of leadership. A main purpose of my present argument is to show that genuine leaders, good or bad,*

28 Cf. J. D. Hoeveler, Jr., *The New Humanism: A Critique of Modern America 1900–1940*, Charlottesville 1977, pp. 125 ff.
29 Cf. A. H. Dakin, *Paul Elmer More*, Princeton, New Jersey 1960, p. 222, note 62.

HUMANISM AS REALISM

there will always be, and that democracy becomes a menace to civiliza-
tion when it seeks to evade this truth (...) the worst difficulties of the
present time arise (...) even less from lack of vision than from sham vi-
sion. Otherwise stated, what is disquieting about the time is not so much
its open and avowed materialism as what it takes to be its spirituality.
Developing this idea relating to the infection of minds in the first
half of the twentieth century with the religion of humanitarianism, Babbitt addresses his readers solemnly: *in general I commit*
myself to the position that we are living in a world that in certain im-
portant respects has gone wrong on first principles; which will be found
to be only another way of saying that we are living in a world that has
been betrayed by its leaders. On the appearance of leaders who have re-
covered in some form the truths of the inner life and repudiated the errors
of naturalism may depend the very survival of Western civilization.[30]

Therefore, we can say that the threat to civilization identified
by Babbitt results from the errors of modern thought or modern
naturalism. Secondly, an appropriate response to this threat
should include an attempt to educate a particular type of leader.
This requires us to raise the question of "genuine" leadership, a
topic not generally favored by the usual political discourse that
prevails in a modern democracy. Where do we go from here? The
immediate consideration of replacing "first principles" at the
dawn of modernity makes it possible to simply formulate the negative difference between political leadership in past conditions
and political leadership in the present. *The leaders of the past have*
most frequently been bad in violation of the principles they professed,
whereas it is when a Robespierre or a Lenin sets out to apply his princi-
ples that the man who is interested in the survival of civilization has
reason to tremble.[31] We are certainly not being encouraged to long
for the political reality of pre-modern times, for Caligula and Vlad
the Impaler. Babbitt's primary reflections concern what should be
defined as the eschatological horizon determining the nature of
one's "inner life," in relation to which political or "external" life,

30   I. Babbitt, *Democracy and Leadership...*, pp. 38, 47–48.
31   Ibid., p. 292.

116

Un-Economic Ideals

with all the norms appropriate to it, is something secondary. If we are dealing with a false ("sham") image of the ultimate questions from the start, it would be better if the thinking and acting born of it would not come to fruition. There is no unerring Lenin. Bolshevism – and other "isms" –cannot be corrected from within.

If the world is in danger from people who want to apply the prevailing principles of the discourse ("freedom, equality, fraternity") as effectively as possible, then, politically, the "modern experiment" has simply failed. Having found the failure of the intellectual struggle so far, we must raise the question of modern people's imagination and thus enter the area common to politics and religion. At the dawn of political reality as we know it, opposition to authority becomes evident – both from without, personified by church institutions, and from within the world, embodied in the rule of monarchs and aristocrats; opposition tied to the promise that a critical dissection of what is extant will open up prospects for both moral and civilization progress. Thus, the social sciences (i.e., scientific opinion management, in a way, aside from logistical issues) should have repeated the success of the natural sciences. However, this did not happen. While we do not agree to understand truth through the prism of effectiveness in mastering or establishing a discourse, we obviously will not say that our life – that of people living in a modern state – is truer than that of people in earlier types of communities; here, "truer" could mean: not drawing from opinions, but from knowledge about oneself; one lived more fully and more deeply, more in keeping with the destiny of a rational and mortal being, closer to the perfect harmony of the human interior and the world as a whole. It seems to be quite the opposite. As a general rule, we live haphazard and not very serious lives. How many of us, looking in the mirror, will see a sacrifice offered to God or the dignity of a Roman senator, and how many – the careless features of "the last man"? And if this is the "true truth" about man – if knowledge is limited to knowing the path on which we achieve our economic ideals – then how can we explain those old manifestations of greatness, the fact that we were not always "the last"? What remains is to close your eyes and not think about it. Humanists, as you know, don't close their eyes, but they are also not interested in seeking refuge or solace among the stunted structures and confused heirs of the Christian (or any other) religion. As a result of their boldness, they have to face a challenging question: is it possible to propose the "ideal of the world" after the collapse of the "religious ideal"? Or more politically: is it possible to make the modern leader a gentleman (*spoudaios*) again without a living religion supporting his mind?

In Babbitt's view, it is about finding an "equivalent for grace."[32] In the Western tradition – formed by the Middle Ages – God's grace was like a vehicle that lifted human thought to a level higher than biological survival and satisfaction. We can understand it thus: the eyes of a potential leader looked, on the one hand, to the plane of expansion, where the possibilities of conquering the world and fulfilling ambitions or goals born of the natural *libido dominandi* appeared; and on the other hand, to the models of holiness present in the world, whose holders testified to the incomprehensible but real happiness that was connected with the rejection of commonly desired goods and direction of oneself "upwards" towards supernatural unity with the Creator and Savior. One look – at a swift horse; a second – at a praying monk. This fundamental tension of the imagination guaranteed the sense and durability of moral attitudes. Therefore, the chances of effectively influencing the character of people called to decide about other people's lives. The political ("world") reflex or equivalent of the world's religious renunciation would be *veto power*, that is, the ability to say "no,"[33] the consistent practice of the *inner check*, conscious recognition of the requirements of *common sense*; in other words – the ability to control oneself, find humility, control one's passions, self-limitation, concentration. Only when we manage to rethink this understanding of the relationship between "grace" and leadership can we correctly –

32 Cf. Ibid., p. 209.
33 Cf. Ibid., pp. 27–28.

Un-Economic Ideals

without the usual clichés about a conservative love of tradition – read the theological and political message of *Democracy and Leadership*. As Babbitt writes, our *modern problem (...) is to secure leaders with an allegiance to standards, now that the traditional order with which Burke associated his standards and leadership has been so seriously shaken.*[34]

The reference to Burke is, of course, not a vain nod at a monument to conservatism. For the humanist, Burke turns out to be, above all, a thinker who presents his notion of "moral imagination" against the notion of "idyllic imagination," the rules of which Rousseau had – how effectively! – imposed earlier. The significance of Rousseau is that he was able to meet the needs of the human imagination far better than any other exponent or apologist of modern naturalism. Well, the imagination requires certain conclusions of a dual nature – conclusions corresponding to the nature of consciousness or our individual experience of the basics of conscious life; experience that should be regarded as indefeasible and "untranscendable." And this is what Rousseau provides us with. We get a "new dualism" of associations preceding the discourse. The *conflict of good and evil in the individual's breast* is replaced by the conflict of a good individual and a bad society (or the new man and the old order). According to Babbitt, *Rousseau gave to naturalism the driving power it still lacked. It thus became possible to develop it into a new evangel that seemed to culminate, like the old Evangel, in love. This conception of love in terms of expansive emotion is (...) a sort of parody of Christian charity.*[35]

Compared to the fugitive from Geneva, Burke did not show the same hellish talent for creating or processing religious symbols. From his writings alone, it is impossible to obtain a timeless, philosophical antidote to the virus of humanitarianism. Nevertheless, he was the one among the non-revolutionary modern

---

34 Ibid., p. 284.
35 Ibid., pp. 99, 98. Cf. P. E. More, *Rousseau* [in:] id., *Shelburne Essays Sixth Series: Studies of Religious Dualism*, New York–London 1909, especially pp. 223–28.

thinkers to grasp "the supreme role of the imagination" and *saw how much of the wisdom of life consists in an imaginative assumption of the experience of the past in such fashion as to bring it to bear as a living force upon the present.*[36] Moreover, it is precisely Burke's words that we can use to tie a conceptual knot that – according to our interpretation – binds humanistic reflection on religious and moral issues with the domain of political thought. In his famous *Reflections*, we read: *nothing is more certain, than that our manners, our civilization, and all the good things which are connected with manners and with civilization have, in this European world of ours, depended for ages upon two principles; and were indeed the result of both combined; I mean the spirit of a gentleman, and the spirit of religion.*[37] Referring to this quote in a separate essay, Babbitt firstly states that the figure of a gentleman – especially based on the "fullest fall" of traditional patterns of behavior, i.e., in America – is perceived by association with the awkwardness of a cultural person (because you should push your elbows out, without paying much attention to manners), and at the same time, on the level of ideas, as "something slightly satanic" (because, doesn't the devil usually appear to us as polite and elegant?). Secondly, when it comes to (humanitarian) religion, we are dealing with a peculiar paradox. While observing the extraordinary effectiveness of actions aimed at conquering nature and material transformation of the world, we also notice a fundamental weakness of achievements on the part of the spirit. While the "utilitarian" version of humanitarianism prompts genuine efforts to gain earthly riches, "emotional" humanitarianism – built on promises of "the highest spiritual benefits" achieved without any effort in working on oneself or constant, persistent self-correction – only creates the appearance of changing or improving humanity. In short, there is no "equivalent to grace." On the "sham spirituality" of Rousseau and the romantics, suffice it to say that it is nothing but a "subrational

36 I. Babbitt, *Democracy and Leadership...*, pp. 127–28.
37 E. Burke, *Reflections on the Revolution in France*, ed. by H. P. Adams, London 1910, p. 18.

Un-Economic Ideals

parody of grace"[38] replacing what is divine (incomprehensible to reason) with what is instinctive (preceding reason). The effects of this on an individual level make up the well-known picture of a mediocre, deceived, simply wasted life in the most crucial respect. The effects at the political level need to be grasped in a slightly different way.

According to Babbitt, *the crucial question is whether one is safe in assuming that the immense machinery of power that has resulted from activity of the utilitarian type can be made, on anything like present lines, to serve disinterested ends; whether it will not rather minister to the egoistic aims either of national groups or individuals (...), there has been an ever-growing body of evidence from the eighteenth century to the Great War* (i.e., to WWI) *that in the natural man, as he exists in the real world and not in some romantic dreamland, the will to power is, on the whole, more than a match for the will to service.*[39] Without hesitation, we can add sardonically that the next hundred years provided a whole lot of the best evidence by far to support this opinion. And even if the current dramas do not affect us directly, we still live in the shadow of new forms of conflict and new types of weapons, with a nuclear apocalypse in the background. This means that we need to understand the threat to our civilization quite literally. We have no "grace equivalent" nor gentlemen in power; we have technology. The schema seems very simple, but one thing is worth emphasizing: while the disorder of an individual – an average Joe, one of the countless victims of a false, "subrational" spirituality – means a poor end for the individual himself, it most often leaves the world indifferent and intact. But when we move to the political level and start talking about the disorder of civilization (which for us takes the shape of the modern state and society), we face the

---

38 Cf. I. Babbitt, *On Being Creative and Other Essays*, New York 1968, p. xx.
39 Id., *What I Believe: Rousseau and Religion* [in:] id., *Spanish Character and Other Essays*, eds. F. Manchester, F. Giese, W. F. Giese, Boston – New York 1940, pp. 231–32. Cf. id., *Democracy and Leadership...*, pp. 219, 341; id., *On Being Creative...*, p. xxv.

prospect of the end of the world. Thus, from a political point of view, the most urgent matter would be to depart from vain intellectualism, to break through discourses based on the humanitarian distribution of the imagination, to show the role of those we call here – following Lippmann – opinion managers, and finally – to select a new category of leaders, unconnected with the current mode of conducting the "modern experiment," and able – through self-control – to control its further course. We need "spiritual athletes" to replace irresponsible visionaries, "cosmic vagabonds." We need real statesmen who, having taken control of Bacon's "machinery," will not give it back to the children of Rousseau. We need a humanistic invasion of the proper centers (or networks) of power. We need to be saved from self-destruction.[40]

The entire apocalyptic dilemma of the modern state and society stems from the entrenched domination, or even exclusivity, of one of the three "types of political thinking." This would, of course, be the naturalistic type, the mutation of which we owe to the present formula of the primacy of economics over politics. Next to this type, in Babbitt's interpretation, religious thinking and humanistic thinking occur in history. In the case of religious thinking, the matter seems simple again. Perhaps all political regimes up to modern times, including the *polis* of ancient philosophers, form various types of theocracies, or at least succumb to the overwhelming influence of religious claims and testimonies, peculiarly using the image of top-down sanctions for wrongdoing against one's political community. Against this background, humanistic thinking turns out to be almost ephemeral. Just as it would be difficult to talk about a humanistic doctrine, epoch, or faith, so too does it not make sense to define the system this way (in its particular version here or there). If we recognize, following Babbitt, that humanistic political thinking appears most fully in Aristotle's work, then it's important to note that he was

40 Cf. id., *Democracy and Leadership...*, pp. 248, 156; id., *The Political Influence of Rousseau*, "The Nation," vol. 104, no. 2690, January 18, 1917, pp. 70, 72.

Un-Economic Ideals

an excellent scholar more so than an effective legislator (unless we count the direction of young Alexander, whose final achievements may appear to be somewhat problematic in a humanist's eyes). Outside the European context, we can reflect on the humanistic embedding of the Confucian model in ancient China (leaving details aside) and on the political consequences of the Buddhist proclamation of the "middle way" (which does exclude later Buddhist practices, especially Tibetan Lamaism); the emblematic figure of a good ruler would be the third century BCE Emperor Ashoka.[41] As we can see, these threads are very distant from the mainstream of modern Western political thought. This is because the mainstream – from Machiavelli through Hobbes to Rousseau – is characterized by translating and designing transformations of social reality based on naturalism. It is also characterized by a departure from the universalist vision of Christendom in favor of sovereign particularisms from which modern nation-states emerge – part of the legacy of the Protestant revolution. Naturalistic thinking about politics culminates in doctrines that justify relinquishing man to full natural expansion. This is what new political creations and ideas serve to do. *According to the new ethics, virtue is not restrictive* (i.e., limiting the "spilling out" of the soul due to the urge to satisfy its instincts) *but expansive, a sentiment and even an intoxication.*[42]

In practice, we are dealing with an incessant charge of students of the school of "imperialism." For a humanist, this expression combines an approach to the most important political phenomena or processes, observed at least since Napoleonic times, i.e., politics revolving around economic ideals, with a judgment of individual characters. The imperialism of an individual

---

41 Cf. id., *Interpreting India to the West* [in:] id., *Spanish Character...*, pp. 160–62 and: id., *Buddha and the Occident (Part I)*, "The American Review," vol. 6, no. 5, March 1936, p. 543; id., *Buddha and the Occident (Part II)*, "The American Review," vol. 7, No. 1, April 1936, pp. 85–86. Cf. P. E. More, *The Catholic Faith*, Princeton 1931, p. 38.

42 I. Babbitt, *Democracy and Leadership...*, p. 143.

– the potential leader of a party or enterprise – is expressed in his desire for domination, his craving for luxury or broadly understood pleasures, and his willingness to make final decisions about everything to have the "last word." On a political level, there is the prospect of constant war, exploitation, and lies. How can "imperialism" be defined most concisely? It would be an emanation of modern naturalism through the false notions of the ultimate questions created as a result of living with the humanitarian faith in what is natural; an emanation in the *real* field of political leadership. Interestingly, Babbitt's (and More's) intention is not to condemn or question the political form of empire. Hence, he qualifies his statement: "irrational" or "decadent" imperialism; the associations with ancient Greece and Rome's fall are not accidental here.[43] These attributes – irrationality and decadence – can be clarified by using another word from the repository of humanist concepts: *eleutheromania*; this, in turn, signifies *the instinct to throw off not simply outer and artificial limitations, but all limitations whatsoever (...) Tolstoy (...) is an eleutheromaniac in his notion of sympathy; Nietzsche, in his notion of liberty. These two men (...) stand at what I have defined as the opposite poles of Rousseauism (...) for over a century the world has been fed on a steady diet of revolt. Everybody is becoming tinged with eleutheromania, taken up with his rights rather than with his duties, more and more unwilling to accept limitations.*[44] The imperialist, by definition, knows no borders. He chooses a place for himself beyond the order promulgated by reason and the laws of civilization. While, from the point of view of political science, one can imagine a geographically vast empire *not* ruled by *eleutheromaniacs*, their reign over any political creation is an inevitable source of misfortune and possible annihilation – and each modern

43 Cf. id., *The Breakdown of Internationalism (Part II)*, "The Nation," vol. 100, no. 2608, June 24, 1915, p. 704; id., *Democracy and Leadership...*, pp. 39–41.
44 Id., *The New Laokoon: An Essay on the Confusion of the Arts*, Boston–New York 1910, pp. 196–97. Cf. P. E. More, *The Lust of Empire* [in:] A. H. Dakin, *A Paul Elmer More Miscellany*, Portland, Maine 1950, pp. 58–61.

Un-Economic Ideals

nation-state determines, as we know, a previously unknown level of power.

Again, it is a kind of anecdote that we owe a quite helpful summary of the issue of imperialism in Babbitt's thought to someone who tried to demonstrate the absurdity of Babbitt's views. One of the co-authors of the polemical volume *The Critique of Humanism* (1930), C. Hartley Grattan, criticized the alleged lack of understanding in humanists of the pains of the modern world and the need for economic and social reforms. According to him, Babbitt tried to "curb Caesar," spreading the umbrella of humanism's influence over him while leaving a *carte blanche* as to the methods of dealing with "slaves." *We find him criticizing imperialists not because of the damage they do to the people they subject to their rule; not for their wasteful exploitative methods; not because they endanger the peace of the world; but because they do not exercise the will to refrain, the inner check which is to keep man firmly at his own business, the business of being saved!*[45] This description is based on a serious distortion of Babbitt's statements but highlights the correct intuition concerning the essence of the humanistic position. Everything comes back to the problem of finding the limits of expansion within oneself and shaping a character that respects these limits for its own benefit. It is not flawed institutions that give rise to imperialist leadership – it is imperialist leaders who do evil at an institutional level.

If we were to understand "psychology" as the science of the soul, we could say that the reflection proper to humanism invariably tends towards psychological investigations, and all solutions concerning the political system have a "psychological and political" dimension. In turn, by wanting to present our situation, that of people living in a modern state and society, in a "psychological" fashion, without being entangled in some metaphysical constructs, we can define ourselves as those for whom the humanitarian

45 C. H. Grattan, *The New Humanism and the Scientific Attitude* [in:] *The Critique of Humanism: A Symposium*, ed. id., New York 1930, pp. 12–13.

parody of mediation has become normalized. As we tried to clarify in the essay on concepts, humanist mediation occurs between the demands of natural necessity and a religious ideal or "ideal of the world." Both the natural and the supernatural (or extraordinary, outstanding, sublime) are blurred and distorted, even forgotten and falsified in the humanitarian version. Ultimately, we get a mediation between the two poles of belief in humanity: sentimentality, romance, counterculture on the one hand, and technology (and technocracy), economic and social development – on the other. The desired result is a man-beast, a modern hybrid – half self-absorbed artist, half cunning businessman. His inner life fully meets the needs of material expansion. He is an "efficient megalomaniac," a "little Napoleon," in Babbitt's terms; a man able to effectively develop and achieve his visions while simultaneously not demonstrating the ability to control himself, not applying the norms of the "law of man," thus causing catastrophes; one who feels like a fish out of water in war, politics, and trade. The answer to this harvest of humanitarianism, expressed in *Democracy and Leadership*, also contains the essence of a humanist understanding of order: *a man needs to look, not down, but up to standards set so much above his ordinary self as to make him feel that he is himself spiritually the underdog. The man who thus looks up is becoming worthy to be looked up to in turn, and, to this extent, qualifying for leadership. Leadership of this type (...) may prove to be, in the long run, the only effectual counterpoise to that of the imperialistic superman.*[46]

It is easy to see that the concept outlined above cannot be reconciled with a naive notion of the advantages of democracy, with the conviction that the more people can do more, the better. Anyone who observes the public activity of the protagonists of the Humanist Movement, even without investigating the deeper motives of this activity, will have to place them on the side of staunch critics of the democratization of social, cultural, and especially academic life. According to Babbitt, higher education should exist within the framework of the modern state or society *not to encourage the democratic*

---

46   I. Babbitt, *Democracy and Leadership...*, p. 283; cf. ibid., p. 163.

spirit, but on the contrary to check the drift toward a pure democracy, promoting aristocratic discipline of the spirit.[47] In the context of the leadership problem, and as a result of modern hegemony of the "naturalistic" type, direct references to democratic principles can be somewhat misleading and harmful. *If we are to judge by history, however* – Babbitt notes – *what supervenes upon the decline of standards and the disappearance of leaders who embody them is not some equalitarian paradise, but inferior types of leadership (...) the question of leadership is not primarily biological, but moral. Leaders may vary in quality from the man who is so loyal to sound standards that he inspires right conduct in others by the sheer rightness of his example, to the man who stands for nothing higher than the law of cunning and the law of force, and so is (...) imperialistic. If democracy means simply the attempt to eliminate the qualitative and selective principle in favor of some general will, based in turn on a theory of natural rights, it may prove to be only a form of the vertigo of the abyss.*[48] Belief in democracy – that is, majority rule linked to individual rights – as part of modern belief in humanity is part of Rousseau's religious or mythological legacy. The vision of a sovereign people belongs to it as much as the vision of a noble savage, on the principle of a game or exercise of the imagination. However, the effects are tangible. According to Babbitt, *the king, if not responsible to what is below him, is at least responsible to what is above him – to God. But the sovereign people is responsible to no one. It is God. The contract that it makes is with itself, like that which, according to the old theologians, was made in the council chamber of the Trinity (...) the notion of a general will in virtue of which Rousseau grants to the people a place that was formerly reserved for God Almighty is in itself only an Arcadian fiction (...) the general drift (...) is towards a more and more radical interpretation of sovereignty; it can be neither delegated nor divided; government, we feel, can scarcely be too responsive to the immediate impact of the popular will. (Hence the initiative, referendum, recall, etc.) We are developing a truly Rousseauistic distrust of the representative principle (...) the ordinary*

47 Id., *Literature and the American College: Essays in Defense of the Humanities*, Boston – New York 1908, p.80.
48 I. Babbitt, *Democracy and Leadership...*, pp. 270–71.

citizen is called upon to vote on the spur of the moment on a multitude of men and measures of which he is equally ignorant. The theory is that from a majority of these ignorant votes will emerge a general will, a sort of composite judgment, that will be sounder than can be had in any other way. The Rousseauist hopes to find a substitute for quality, which in this case means responsible leadership, in a sort of quantitative impressionism.[49]

The most important thing in all this is not the presence in modern conditions of the old curse of ignorance and deception of the masses. It does not boil down to dependence on the results of the polls and manipulation of the polls, that is, to the usual "diseases of democracy." What determines the shape and fate of the modern state is, on the one hand, its "absolute" legitimization by means of intellectual or "spiritual" tools (naturalistic metaphysics, ideologies), and, on the other hand, the incredible appreciation of the manifestations of emotional engagement in various particular organizations and projects, with perhaps the strongest particularisms that condition the existence of nation-states at the forefront. Let us pause for a moment over these emotions. You can love humanity "in theory," but in practice, this love of ours is – by the power of natural necessity – limited to our relatives, family, and circle of friends. Similarly, you can hate the whole world, but the purpose of this hatred needs to be clear; the enemy is usually a stranger (but a recognizable one!) and somehow gets in our way from a distance. Meanwhile, in Europe and America, we have long cultivated the view that every person is invited to participate in politics. However, when it comes to emotions – which always accompany the opinions that make up political reality – there is no way to get along with everyone, your circle and strangers. To put it even more bluntly, democracy (granted to everyone) and universalism (in the sense of serene cosmopolitanism or internationalist harmony) are fairy tales for well-behaved children. It is possible to use the slogans of the common good in its maximalist version, but it is impossible to "intoxicate" oneself with a good the possession of which does not distinguish

49   Id., *The Political Influence...*, pp. 68–69.

Un-Economic Ideals

us from others. Hence, as has been observed more than once, the most principled humanitarians (often describing themselves as the left) feel best in their own milieu, in a familiar cafe or college classroom, where they can easily take on the position of the rational avant-garde amid an ocean of ignorance. Such intellectual avant-garde movements can be extremely dangerous, as history from Lenin to Pol Pot shows. Nevertheless, yet another kind of "intoxication" plays a more significant overall role in recent history, and its critique may turn out to be much more ungrateful than a critique of the ideological folly rooted in Marxism or Freudism. Babbitt doesn't hesitate. In his take (from 1919), *if conscience is merely an emotion there is a cult that makes a more potent appeal to conscience than the cult of humanity itself and that is the cult of country. One is here at the root of the most dangerous of all the sham religions of the modern age – the religion of country, the frenzied nationalism that is now threatening to make an end of civilization itself. Both emotional nationalism and emotional internationalism go back to Rousseau, but in his final emphasis he is an emotional nationalist; and that is because he saw that patriotic "virtue" is a more potent intoxicant than the love of humanity. The demonstration came in the French Revolution which began as a great international movement on emotional lines and ended in imperialism and Napoleon Bonaparte.*[50]

What follows from this? Undoubtedly, we can say that the key feature of a modern state is its expansiveness. Someone may say that this is nothing new; politics is always about expansiveness, or at the very least agreeing to become greater or gain more through control of one's own state. However, it may be more significant to understand this undeniable inclination towards expansion thusly: here, we are dealing with the expansion of the particular, with reference to the universal. This would be, for instance, the expansion of the French element – in the name of

---

50   Id., *Rousseau and Romanticism*, Boston – New York 1919, pp. 345–46; cf. id., *Democracy and Leadership...*, pp. 143 ff.; and: id., *The Breakdown of Internationalism (Part I)*, "The Nation," vol. 100, no. 2607, June 17, 1915, p. 679.

republicanism and human rights; the German element – in the name of *Kultur* and racial purity (then likely multiculturalism and "Europeanness"); the Russian element – in the name of communism and what is not rotten (while in the West everything is rotten); the Anglo-Saxon element – in the name of "free trade" and democracy. And so on. If what is universal is no longer related to the order of vertical thinking (i.e., to the religious life and humanism), if the most distant goals lie on the plane of natural desires or instincts, if it is the strength of emotional involvement combined with technical prowess that decides in the end – things become dangerous, and familiar. The priests of the "religion of the state" have at their disposal an organized apparatus of violence; they can pursue and kill under a law whose sole source is the "sovereign" that they, in fact, control.

Referencing the name of Rousseau within this context as the cause of our problems requires at least two related caveats. First, as humanists know very well, Rousseau was not a one-dimensional thinker. There is an obvious paradox in the main thread of his teaching. Our imagination is ignited by the clash of the natural human innocent with civilization, remaining inside of which is equivalent to expulsion from paradise and life in the bondage of sin. Later, however, having become accustomed to the image of man as a pump installed in a well of feelings – my own, the only, *contra mundum* – we are to transform this new dualism, far more gracious than the dualism of Christians, into a permanent building block of a political community; a community reaching the foundations of newly discovered humanity and in the end, taking on the form of a republic which effectively absorbs us and fully manages our emotions thanks to good legislation. Navigating this mythological and eschatological whole is not a simple task. Moreover, we may suspect that Rousseau himself viewed his stories from a different perspective than did the much more naive worshipers of nature who followed him, that perhaps one should speak of his conscious grounding in the Socratic tradition. In Babbitt's view, *the great distinction of Rousseau in the history of thought (...) is that he gave the wrong answers to the right questions.*

It is no small distinction even to have asked the right questions.[51] However, in the eyes of the humanist, it is the Genevan's religious vision – a great work of transforming the imagination – that should be subjected to a full and fundamental critique before we immerse ourselves in analyzing the intentions or deeper connotations of his thought; a critique – on account of its fruits. Secondly, concerning these fruits, one should not, of course, place Rousseau in the role of the alpha and omega of modernity. He was a first-rate writer and, in a sense, a prophet (of "sham spirituality"), a patron of both rebels and dreamy aesthetes, but not the Creator of a new world. It is difficult to say to what extent his writings literally influenced the events of the French Revolution (which he did not live to see break out). We also cannot forget *the industrial revolution, compared with which the French Revolution is only a melodramatic incident*[52] – the former was conceived from humanitarianism but in the Baconian, utilitarian spirit. Simply put, our economic ideals have more to do with the smoking chimneys of factories than with the whistling of guillotines. As Babbitt describes it, the imperialism of modern leaders, whether of states or private corporations won over in various ways, draws from the *quasi*-religious appreciation of emotions, but is a threat to the world insofar as it has the means of material expansion. Rousseau's responsibility is also not entirely an intellectual responsibility because, from a philosophical point of view, he is not creating new concepts when he asks questions. As Paul Elmer More notes: *the ideas themselves – liberty and progress and natural religion and innate goodness – were in no wise original with him. If, indeed, disregarding the complexities of a civilisation and obscurer influences, we undertake to analyse the revolution of the eighteenth century, we shall find that the guiding principles and the original dynamic impulse of the age came from England, that the translation of these into a homogeneous social law was the work of France,*

---

51 Id., *Democracy and Leadership...*, p. 24; cf. ibid., pp. 108–09; id., *What I Believe...*, pp. 226–27.
52 Id., *Democracy and Leadership...*, p. 138.

HUMANISM AS REALISM

and that their conversion into a metaphysical formula was finally accomplished by Germany.[53]

But let's move away from what was history for Babbitt and More. Staying with the texts of the first of our protagonists, let us again ask about his view of the current political phenomena of his time. Of course, it is hard to doubt that the most important event or series of events among these phenomena was the First World War. For the humanist, it was a time when the humanitarian discourses were completely discredited: faith in progress, pacifist declarations and social reforms; socialists, liberals, democrats – hand-in-hand with the nationalist right – virtually all ready to shed their masks of noble savages and become real savages; imperialism, then, turned out to be a key word in describing what seemed to be the greatest possible turning point in Western civilization. At this point, many concerned and frightened observers probably believed that the lesson of war gases would completely transform the way of thinking in the West (which then meant – on Earth). Meanwhile, according to More's and Babbitt's diagnosis, the humanitarian discourses were not exceeded. On the contrary, they became radicalized: on the one hand, they fixated on economic development, and on the other hand, they tended towards irrational and decadent experiences. An emblematic figure during that period – or maybe since then? – was President *Woodrow Wilson, who, more than any other recent American, sought to extend our idealism beyond our national frontiers. In the pursuit of his scheme for world service, he was led to make light of the constitutional checks on his authority and to reach out almost automatically for unlimited power. If we refused to take his humanitarian crusading seriously we were warned that we should "break the heart of the world" (...) this language, at once abstract and sentimental, reveals a temper at the opposite pole from that of the genuine statesman.*[54] In Babbitt's eyes, the Wilsonian project of the League of Nations is a "humanitarian chimera"; we should evaluate the alleged progress in establishing

53 P. E. More, *Rousseau...*, p. 215.
54 I. Babbitt, *Democracy and Leadership...*, p. 314.

international order despite verbal mirages, with awareness of the "psychological" realities. It is clear, however, that the prospect of directing a political entity of the size and importance of the United States is equivalent to freedom of expansion – from military means to the economy as a whole, to the power to establish a hegemonic discourse on a global scale – that no one else has. But what about the rest of the world? In short, it races along to the best of its ability. In the 1920s, this was true for both Soviet Russia and Germany (which should not be confused with the suggestion that life under Lenin's rule was as light as life under Wilson's), but most of all, the situation in Asian countries changed. As Babbitt writes: *a type of nationalistic self-assertion is beginning to appear in various Oriental lands that is only too familiar to us in the West. Japan in particular has been disposing of her Buddhas as curios and turning her attention to battleships. The lust of domination which is almost the ultimate fact of human nature, has been so armed in the Occident with the machinery of scientific efficiency that the Orient seems to have no alternative save to become efficient in the same way or be reduced to economic and political vassalage. This alternative has been pressing with special acuteness on China, the pivotal country of the Far East. Under the impact of the West an ethos that has endured for thousands of years has been crumbling amid a growing spiritual bewilderment. In short the Orient itself is losing its orientation.*[55]

Risking a necessary simplification, let us note that the image of political reality that emerges from Babbitt's observation is an image of the forging of the world as we know it. Subsequent crises did indeed follow. The dimensions of the crime – for which the imperialist lust for domination is invariably to blame, domination tamed by a belief in the benevolent power of expansion and sanctified by humanitarian utopias – exceeded anything that had ever happened before. It is also a distant story for us. What

---

55 I. Babbitt, *Buddha and the Occident (Part I)...*, p. 517; cf. id., *Democracy and Leadership...*, pp. 177–79; and: id., *Humanistic Education in China and the West*, "The Chinese Students' Monthly," vol. 17, no. 2, December 1921, pp. 85–91.

do we have today? Rousseau's children unite and self-actualize by joining successive subcultures, niches, "targets" within a standardized mass culture that provides horizons for the imagination of both "simple" people, as well as crowd leaders and managers, together with our "authorities." Bacon's progeny focuses on achieving economic ideals per se, looking for (physically) distant goals less than in the past and instead focusing more on exploiting the resources we have at hand, that is, above all, ourselves. All of this, in general, fits together perfectly; both tribes rejoice at the effects of their mutual coexistence; both have no one but themselves. In the East, cities and roads are emerging that cannot be found in the West, but they are the same cities and roads. Malays, like the English and Poles, play rock music. They are all connected to the Internet. We have a "global village" – with many conflicts, with layers of envy and resentment, with areas of chronic poverty and hopelessness ... but we have one. What can we do when this "village" founded on economic ideals turns out to be a place where particular aspirations and interests can only be covered up by words (or images) of universal ideas, but not limited in any significant way by the "narratives" inherited from the prophets and acolytes of humanitarianism? The modern religion of humankind seems to persist on the principle of inertia, to the rhythm of "classic" hits (*imagine* ...), and clever priests earn more than ever. Babbitt might say: I told you so. Breaking through the existing layers of concepts and ceremonies belonging to the religion of modernity is as easy today as finding a real gentleman at the helm of government.

A lousy reality begets a desire to escape. We can, however, expect from the humanists that their response to the "post-imperialist" world will have nothing to do with evacuating inward into dreamland. That would not be unvirtuous. According to Babbitt, what we need is "healthy cynicism," that is, the ability to deal with evil. This is also why – from a political point of view –classical thought differs from modern thought; the former seriously considers the occurrence of evil *in us* and connects it with the inertia written into the patterns of human nature. We, too, are confronted with immeasurable indifference to our thinking and desires beyond what is available on the market. We cannot see good where it is not, in a life subject to instincts or emotions. Oddly enough, we should not think that providing material or mental comfort to as many people as possible will make this world a better place. Nor, on a different note, that whoever is trying to do so is acting in the interest of humankind, that he feels responsible for billions of lives, including ours; that – appealing to our Polish imaginations – someone somewhere far away (e.g., in Washington) loves us and wants the best for us. *We shall escape from the imperialistic madness (and we should remember that the pure commercialist is only the advance agent of imperialism) not by "idealism" of the "uplift" type, but by the sternest realism; but realism according to the human and not according to the natural law*[56] (here, we should treat "natural law" as the body of laws of nature with a particular emphasis on the biological law of selection). "Realism according to the human law" is "moral realism," the realism of humanist mediation; it requires independent thought and working on oneself. Babbitt writes: *the moral realist will not allow himself to be whisked off into any cloud-cuckoo-land in the name of the ideal. He will pay no more attention to the fine phrases in which an ideal of this kind is clothed than he would to the whistling of the wind around a corner. The idealist will, therefore, denounce him as "hard." His hardness is in any case quite unlike that of the Machiavellian realist. If the moral realist seems hard to the idealist, this is because of his refusal to shift, in the name of sympathy or social justice or on any other ground, the struggle between good and evil from the individual to society.*[57]

The clash of the humanist with Machiavelli is an intriguing tagline to Babbitt's theological and political reflection. It is impossible to deny the crucial role of the author of *The Prince* as the "programmer" of modern political thought. This thought breaks with the religious, otherworldly ideal of Christianity, which is subse-

56 Id., *The Political Influence...*, p. 72; cf. id., *Democracy and Leadership...*, pp. 300–02.
57 Ibid., pp. 315–316.

quently associated with the inability to be translated into political life (who will meet the requirements set by priests?) and, even more so, with the distortion and blunting of human aspirations (because how can one be a wholly earthly manager when one is a subject of the Lord in heaven?). Secondly, however, Machiavelli's thought marks a break with the humanistic ideal of civilization and the art of discovering order. By the same token, *one cannot grant that either Machiavelli or his spiritual descendants, the* Realpolitiker, *are thoroughgoing realists. The Nemesis, or divine judgment, or whatever one may term it, that sooner or later overtakes those who transgress the moral law, is not something that one has to take on authority, either Greek or Hebraic; it is a matter of keen observation (…) to be merely a naturalistic realist, to combine, that is, a clear perception of the facts of the material order with spiritual blindness, leads practically to imperialistic dreaming.*[58] Let us note that an imperialist can be – and sometimes is – any human being moderately endowed by nature, with so much as an average IQ. From this point of view, the practical difference between Machiavelli's appreciation of reality and Rousseau's appreciation of emotions turns out to be relative. The more profound alternative, in turn, can be expressed as Babbitt does: *the main preoccupation of thinkers like Plato and Aristotle (…) is with this very problem that Rousseau evades. Leadership of some kind Plato and Aristotle felt there must be, so that everything in the art of government hinges on getting the right quality of leadership. The total tendency of what they urge is to restrain the passions and appetites of the most intelligent members of a community, the tendency of what Rousseau urges is to inflame the passions and appetites of its least intelligent members.*[59] The advantage of the classics, assessed through the prism of humanism, is related to the fact that they recognize the primacy of civilization – that is, nobly understood politics over economics. Because, and this is Babbitt's ultimate message in *Democracy and Leadership, civilization is something that must be deliberately willed.*[60]

58 Ibid., pp. 62–63.
59 Id., *The Political Influence...*, p. 69.
60 Id., *Democracy and Leadership...*, p. 254.

III.

Our considerations thus far allow us to formulate the seemingly perverse thesis that humanists don't want to negate economic ideals. Instead, they strive to subject them to realistic evaluation from the outside by breaking the metaphysical vaults of modern naturalism and exposing the falsehood of spiritual claims and dogmas of the humanitarian faith. In this way, the door opens to rethinking the pre-modern philosophical and political tradition and trying to demonstrate the proper domain of non-economic ideals – ideals that are not an eruption of "sham spirituality" under the sign of Rousseau. In opposition to the prophets of modernity, the spirit of Socrates permeates the entire legacy of Paul Elmer More. In his *Definitions of Dualism* (from 1913), a stylized "scientific" collection of aphorisms created during his study of the Platonic dialogues,[61] we can find a kind of humanistic formula for the desired political system: *society for its preservation organizes the external checks in the form of government. A perfect government would be neither a crushing despotism nor an unrestrained license; its aim would be to bring the character of the few to bear in some effective way upon the impulses of the many; it would be an aristocracy of justice (…) were all men free in themselves, the perfect form of government would be an absolute anarchy. As the world is, the freeist society is that in which custom and law impose the least restraint upon the man who is self-governed, and the greatest restraint upon the man who is not self-governed.*[62] The proper title to exercise power, then, is the aristocratic capacity for self-governance, that is, self-control and the management of one's own life. It is this capacity that makes a person free. However, an impulsive person, whose behavior is determined by the intensity of the stimulus he is subject to at a given moment, is not free. A perfect aristocrat would be a master at practicing the suspension of judgment, the *inner check*; he

61 Cf. P. E. More, *Platonism*, Princeton–London1917, pp. viii-ix.
62 Id., *Definitions of Dualism* [in:] id., *Shelburne Essays Eighth Series: The Drift of Romanticism*, New York–Boston 1913, pp. 282–84.

would be a self-sufficient island in a sea of desires and emotions. Unfortunately, the masses do not care about the soul. Hence – More writes – *as the common disposition of mankind is lacking in character, the will to refrain needs to be, and largely is, reinforced from without by the restraining influence of public opinion, fear of punishment, education, and mythology.*[63]

The collection of essays titled *Aristocracy and Justice* (published in 1915) may be considered the most political of More's publications. The title itself seems to correspond with the later naming of Babbitt's book: *Democracy and Leadership* (intended initially as *Democracy and Imperialism*[64]). Undoubtedly, both authors agree on the critical diagnosis of modern humanitarianism. They also share the premise that *there could be no civilized society were it not that deep in our hearts, beneath all the turbulences of greed and vanity, abides the Instinct of obedience to what is noble and of good repute. It awaits only the clear call from above.*[65] Such a "call" should be the arrival of real ("natural") aristocrats. But this true aristocracy must not be confused with the "hereditary oligarchy" represented by those simply fortunate enough to be the child (or great-grandchild) of a Count rather than a shoemaker. The expectation of a "call from above" is not meant to be a claim to superiority rooted only in the family tree. Nothing from good ancestors is worth much when one's soul is neglected. We already know that the historical project of humanism was not tailored to the claims of the *ancien regime's* heirs. To put it another way, good governance or a good system of government – constitutive of "civilized society" – demands philosophical justification. Such justification must not only tie into the particular, that is, the history of one's own country or family, but also contain a universal dimension; it must be justification based on real insight and an understanding of human nature. Thus, while Burke's role as a teacher of imagination is

63 Ibid., p. 279.
64 Cf. I. Babbitt, *Rousseau and Romanticism...*, p. 345, note 2.
65 P. E. More, *Natural Aristocracy* [in:] id., *Shelburne Essays Ninth Series: Aristocracy and Justice*, Boston–New York 1915, p. 38.

Un-Economic Ideals

undeniable and *his pages are an inexhaustible storehouse of inspiration and wisdom,* it is necessary to face the assessment that *his ideas never quite freed themselves from their matrix, and that in his arguments the essential is involved in the contingent (...) as a consequence the problem of government for us to-day in its fundamental aspects is really closer to the exposition of the Greek philosopher two thousand years ago than to that of the modern English statesman.* The latter turns out to be *thus debarred from belief in a true philosophy by his experience of the false,* that is, the Enlightenment intellectualism of *les philosophes.*[66] The need, then, to transcend Burke's position on the issue of aristocracy leads us to the work of the political philosopher *par excellence* – Plato.

Plato's works have been interpreted in myriad ways throughout the centuries.[67] Some might see him as a mad visionary, others – a defender of the old order or a spiritual despot. One of the most influential positions in the political discourse of the second half of the twentieth century, Karl Popper's *The Open Society and Its Enemies* (1945), makes Plato out to be the forefather of totalitarian regimes, a proto-Hegelian, and patron of social engineering. More's reflection, which is not difficult to predict, follows an entirely different path. First of all, Plato, in his view, is not the "metaphysical" Plato. In fact, attempting to have the "last word" based on a reconstruction of the Platonic "system" means replacing the Greek's thought with modern "Teutonic" (Kantian or Hegelian) intellectual constructs.[68] Moreover, Plato, when read by a humanist, does not, in principle, appear to be the designer of the ideal state. Instead, he is a skeptical investigator of the human interior, a "psychologist," a master of character analysis. The mere linking of the problems of the soul and the state – the internal order with the political

---

66 Ibid., pp. 21, 11–12. Cf. I. Babbitt, *Democracy and Leadership*..., pp. 125– 26, 130.

67 Cf. P. E. More, *Platonism*..., pp. 270 ff.

68 Cf. id., *The Final Word on Plato's Philosophy* (a review of Constantine Ritter's *The Essence of Plato's Philosophy*), "The Saturday Review," vol. 11, no. 7, September 1, 1934, p. 82.

order – should not surprise anyone familiar with the texts of ancient philosophers. The classics of political philosophy remind us that our public institutions, however formally organized, reflect our private aspirations, advantages, and disadvantages in a crucial sense. *Or do you suppose* – Plato's Socrates asks rhetorically – *that the regimes arise "from an oak or rocks" and not from the dispositions of the men in the cities, which, tipping the scale as it were, draw the rest along with them?*[69] We can assert that the state – the political community, *polis* – is equivalent to man "on a macro scale." What we cannot perceive and organize while diagnosing ourselves as individuals will become more visible and easier to grasp using the peculiar magnifying glass that is the state. As More reads it, Plato's famous story about the emergence and fall of successive forms of political regimes does not anticipate the nineteenth-century philosophy of history, nor is it preparation for the gospel of the brave new world. Instead, the story results from the adopted method of self-knowledge. In learning from the philosophers, *we recognize immediately the man whose faculties are each, so to speak, attending to its own business – the man who is wise by the due exercise of reason, temperate by the proper control of his appetites, brave and self-respecting by the measured activity of the* thymos (passion, a drive for distinction); *and who deals with the world as he deals with himself. And we know equally well the flimsy creature who is tossed about from one unstable passion to another, until he sinks to the still lower stage, when out of the conflict of unguarded desires one master-passion arises, like the criminal tyrant in a lawless State, to enslave the man's soul and drive him furiously across the rights of others.*[70] So we have two extreme models – positive and negative, aristocratic and tyrannical – between which, as it were, the scale of justice extends. And it is precisely justice – the order of what is human in relation to what is divine[71] – that should be considered the proper subject of philosophical and political investiga-

---

69 Plato, *The Republic*, trans. A. Bloom, New York 1991, 544 D-E, p. 222.
70 P. E. More, *Platonism*, Princeton–London 1917, p. 73; cf. ibid., pp. 60 ff.
71 Cf. id., *The Religion of Plato*, Princeton–London 1921, pp. 37 ff.

Un-Economic Ideals

tions. These inquiries, however, did not serve – and were never intended – to directly impose an "applicable" vision of the political order. The Platonic model of the self-ruling aristocrat, being the universal point of reference for our present search for true leadership in place of "demagogues and flatterers," does not, therefore, imply the proposal of a "government of philosophers" as, say, an isolated clique of intellectuals.[72]

In every place and time, people are born who have a natural ability to be leaders, to lead their own and other people's lives. Who they become and what they demonstrate to the world depends above all on the education they acquire and how respected it is by the masses. The issue of education in a strict sense falls within the scope of one of the humanists' favorite subjects, namely the transformation of the imagination. This approach is not surprising as long as we remember the dilemma of the modern state and society as described previously. Nevertheless, to someone who thinks he is down-to-earth – to the one we introduced at the beginning as the realist cousin – this perception of the role of school and university may seem pretentious. We are used to linking educational needs with the needs of the labor market, the direction of a child's education (and even more so a young adult's) – with the prospect of a professional career. When we think about the successful life of our offspring, we first consider its material foundations. After all, no one will question the relationship between an affluent wallet or stable income and an individual's sense of satisfaction and achieving their desired social status. Nobody will condemn their child to read Shakespeare after many years spent hungry. And why bring any "ideologies" into it? ... Well, no. It is necessary to understand that this is a false lead in realistic thinking. Nature abhors a vacuum, so the place once occupied by the "products" of the religious and humanist imagination, by religious lessons and Latin lessons, is infiltrated by contents straight from modern utopias and by motives that completely disregard intellectual work.

72 Cf. id., *Natural Aristocracy...*, pp. 5, 8–10.

The concept of "imagination" More writes about expresses the ability to explain – using a "single firm vision" – *the long course of human history and of distinguishing what is essential therein from what is ephemeral.* Meanwhile, *the enormous preponderance of studies that deal with the immediate questions of economics and government inevitably results in isolating the student from the great inheritance of the past; the frequent habit of dragging him through the slums of sociology, instead of making him at home in the society of the noble dead, debauches his mind with a flabby, or inflames it with a fanatic, humanitarianism.*[73] In practice, the *nouveau intellectuel* type becomes dominant – an equivalent of a nouveau riche, without proper formation, dependent on fashion and novelty; trained to rent; in short – superficially educated. At best, we are dealing with a business "aristocrat" who knows his job, is technically efficient, and is resistant to stress. However, he has more in common with an old merchant or craftsman than with a philosopher or even a politician. His knowledge is "knowledge" according to the economic ideals he professes. His imagination reaches what is close by – both in space-time and spiritually. His acquired ability to engage with scientific experiments only enhances his latent idiocy, since detached from specific numbers and graphs, it loses clarity and coherence of thought.[74] In short, the higher education of professionals, i.e., professional managers and contractors, is as credible as the "ideological neutrality" of the rulers and authorities of the modern nation-state. Thus, More states that it is necessary to *distrust the present huge overgrowth of courses in government and sociology, which send men into the world skilled in the machinery of statecraft and with minds sharpened to the immediate demands of special groups, but with no understanding of the longer problems of humanity.*[75]

Indeed, these are not nice words to hear for contemporary sociologists, political scientists, and more generally, for specialists in the

---

73 Ibid., pp. 36–37.
74 Cf. P. E. More, *Academic Leadership* [in:] id., *Aristocracy and Justice...*, p. 47.
75 Ibid., p.59.

Un-Economic Ideals

field of the social sciences. Their methods and techniques for studying reality may be considered questionable. Their negative influence on the soul formation of potential leaders seems to be beyond doubt. All of them – irrespective of how necessary they consider themselves and whether they practice their discipline seriously, believing in its benefits – work on explaining how young people are to meet the expectations of the state and society. The welfare of the soul is not part of their specialty. However, in that case, it is difficult to admire knowledge that only has an instrumental value. Each of us has to start all over again. Before we can ask "which way?" it is worth asking – "where to?" Any form of commitment, self-realization, or life arrangement – what we call our goal or value hierarchy – must be justified: is it worth being a politician? Or a businessman? Or perhaps a scientist, a writer, or an artist? But on a deeper level as well, taking into account the humanists' findings: do I have to accept being a part of the equation of humanitarian thought, whose assumptions do not come from me? Do I have to be modern and "go with the flow" in a modern way? According to More, an answer to this challenge of the soul is possible within the framework of modern education with the maintenance and revival of humanities studies, with Latin and Greek courses that *possess a specific power of correction for the more disintegrating tendencies of the age* if only through developing the habit of disciplined intellectual work and practicing concentration. However, the most important thing is to encourage self-knowledge and self-improvement, which entitle one to exercise power and constitute the measure of aristocratic leadership. *If a single word were used to describe the character and state of life upheld by Plato and Aristotle, as spokesmen of their people, it would be* eleutheria, *liberty: the freedom to cultivate the higher part of a man's nature – his intellectual prerogative, his desire of truth, his refinements of taste – and to hold the baser part of himself in subjection; the freedom also, for its own perfection, and indeed for its very existence, to impose an outer conformity to, or at least respect for, the laws of this inner government on others who are of themselves ungoverned.*[76]

76   Ibid., pp. 52, 61–62.

This is not the first time that the Greek word *eleutheria* has appeared in our essay. Earlier, we saw how Babbitt denoted a human type that does not recognize the limits of its expansion (*eleutheromaniac*), that is, something like the substrate of an imperialistic human being. More, citing the classics, now shows us a completely different path to understanding "freedom."[77] This fundamental difference is summed up in the adoption of either a horizontal or a vertical concept of the soul. In the first case, the further we successfully reach out, without encountering resistance or withstanding resistance, the freer we are. In the second case, freedom results from the conscious submission of what is lower to what is higher, thus freeing oneself – as much as possible – from the tyranny of impulses or passions and ensuring the political advantage of people who rule themselves "internally" – or, in Platonic terms, of the righteous – over the impulsive masses.

More's proposal to encourage young people to read the ancient classics rather than "dragging [them] through the slums of sociology" also includes the problematic aspect of choosing a humanistic legacy, in the school sense, at the expense of other sources of civilization's identity and beacons for spiritual aspirations. In short, we put the achievements of the pagan Greeks and Romans above the biblical themes of the Christian Middle Ages. More calls their erstwhile interdependence, of which Tomaszów's synthesis remains the most splendid intellectual testimony, "the Oxford paradox." *In place of the secular tradition of the classics we have turned to science, and in place of obedience to the will of God we are seeking for salvation in humanitarian sympathy with our brother men (...) there is a great lack in our life to-day, which we feel and secretly acknowledge to ourselves, despite much bragging of progress and much outward scorn of the things we have cast away (...) for those who feel the lack, there is urgent need to consider the means at our disposal for restoring some part of what has been lost. And first of all there can be no sound restoration unless we can escape that paradox of civilization*

---

77 Cf. id., *Religion and Social Discontent* [in:] id., *On Being Human* (*New Shelburne Essays III*), Princeton–London 1936, pp. 127–34.

symbolized by the stones of Oxford.[78] And we need to escape, because the medieval tradition has long appeared dead, and at the same time – looking from the perspective of the current "need of this world" – is distracting the attention of young people. This is how More expresses his position in *Aristocracy and Justice*, the most pragmatic position possible, which was to be subject to a very significant correction (we will discuss this elsewhere). At this stage, it was necessary to outline the original relationship of the "secular tradition" and the religious life – one whose consequences would not be inferior to the spiritual fruits of the subsequent marriage of Athens and Jerusalem. More writes: *The true humanism, which speaks in the stones of the Parthenon, does not possess authority and saving power because the human is there regarded as excluding the divine, but the very contrary (...) if we forget this composite meaning of humanism* (on the one hand preaching the political doctrine of the "golden mean," on the other hand – granting the primacy of the philosophical contemplation of God), *we shall confuse if either with the formalism of the pseudoclassics* (i.e., works imitating the classical form, though not sharing the advantages of the ancients' imaginations), *or with the sentiment of modern humanitarianism.*[79]

The aristocratic "narrative" surrounding education can act as a red rag on a bull on the average defender of modernity. Nevertheless, who would take the requirement of caring for the soul seriously? It was not critical words about schools, habits, or a new type of social science that people best remembered from More's book. The actual rock of offense is found in a painfully provocative expression adorning the essay *Property and Law*. In it, we read: *after all, life is a very primitive thing. Nearly all that makes it more significant to us than to the beast is associated with our possessions – with property, all the way from the food we share with the beasts, to the most refined products of the human imagination. To the civilized man,* the rights of property are more important than the right to life. And

---

78 Id., *The Paradox of Oxford* [in:] idem, *Aristocracy and Justice...*, pp. 85–86.
79 Ibid., pp. 99–100.

a bit further: *in face of all appeals of sentiment and all reasonings of abstract justice, society must learn again to-day that it cannot legislate contrary to the decrees of Fate. In this way, looking at the larger good of society, we may say that rightly understood the dollar is more than the man, and that* law is concerned primarily with the rights of property.[80]

How can that be? Humanism exposed? "The dollar is more than the man" – can you imagine a more unequivocal call for the absolute primacy of economics in political or social life? At first glance, we should probably not be surprised that More's statements were taken as the profession of capitalism's creed through the mouth of a lazy rentier, grotesque in form and absurd in content.[81] This is what it looks like when taken out of context. In fact, this statement contains an accurate blow to the very heart of modernity's political dogma, which tells us to treat economic ideals as the only true and acceptable ideals. It is a question of understanding justice. The crucial question is: *what is the true aim of society? Does justice consist primarily in levelling the distribution of powers and benefits, or in proportioning them to the scale of character and intelligence? Is the main purpose of the machinery of government to raise the material welfare of the masses, or to create advantages for the upward striving of the exceptional?*[82] Any attempt at describing a just political order leads to findings concerning the fair distribution of goods, that is, of what is due to whom. Do we have a model at our disposal that we can refer to when proposing these findings? It seems – this is the dominant conviction in modern thought, according to More – that a universal model should be sought after within nature, which, after all, includes the human race. Our reason prompts us to do so; our feelings rebel against it. Emotional opposition comes from realizing the inexorable rules

---

80 Id., *Property and Law* [in:] id., *Aristocracy and Justice...*, pp. 136, 140–41. Emphasis in original.

81 Cf. id., *The Demon of The Absolute* (*New Shelburne Essays I*), Princeton 1928, pp. vii-viii.

82 Id., *Natural Aristocracy...*, pp. 30–31.

Un-Economic Ideals

of the struggle for existence. In the animal world, no one pities the weaker. If you can't cope – you'll be pecked to death. One may wonder whether the effects of natural selection seem satisfactory from the point of view of a rational external evaluation, whether better and stronger forms really prevail and what the role of blind luck or unplanned perversion is in all this. However, when we consider "our most instinctual feelings," we face a vacuum. *The fact is: the very idea of justice or injustice has no real application to Nature. She proceeds by a law and for a purpose of her own, and to judge her by our human standard, as we inevitably do if we judge her at all, is a pure fallacy. Our approval will not influence her a whit; not all our clamours will move her to relent. She will continue to warm us at the fires of life to-day, and to-morrow will ravage our cities with earthquake and conflagration. She moves on her way, impassionate and unconcerned, with sublime indifference to our creeds.*[83]

Let us dwell on this image for a moment – that of the inhuman Mother Nature. The fallacy that More writes about, which he sometimes refers to unoriginally as the "pathetic fallacy,"[84] constitutes an integral part of the mental puzzle of modern naturalism. To fully connect man, with his inherent need for eschatology, with nature, it is necessary to deny the fundamental premises of self-awareness and reject the hopeless distance between us and all other living organisms. There must be some emotional connection, compassion, unity in the face of harm caused by fate, or a community of affirmation of the Universe. Nature laughs and cries with us to the rhythm of the appropriate stimuli; at the moment of fulfillment, nature absorbs my soul – or vice versa, it makes no difference. They say nature is beautiful, but beauty, as we know, can be lethal, and more often, it is dulling. Of course, there is no reason to attribute the propensity for the "pathetic fallacy" solely to professional dreamy aesthetes. Much below the pantheistic subtleties, in the field of everyday observation, we

---

83 Id., *Justice* [in:] id., *Aristocracy and Justice...*, p. 108.
84 The Polish *patetycz*ny and English *pathetic* come from the Greek πάθος.

find numerous examples of how people invest feelings in personal relationships with animals, plants, with all living things. We also encounter sentimental, naive assessments of the general state of these relationships. Within this category, we have a lady who loves her dog like a baby – one which will not enter into any discourse, will not surprise anyone with its thoughts, but looks at you with such wise eyes. We have also got an entire gamut of attitudes and statements from advocates of "animal rights," advocates of a "return to nature," people sometimes rightly concerned about the cost of economic development and agitated by new reports of misuse of the planet's resources. However, concern about the fate of our species and the preservation of civilization – undoubtedly shown by the humanists – is one thing, and the expectation of the commensurability of human goals, at best born of humanist mediation, and the paths of nature is quite another. They constitute two disjoint measures and, as such, are confined to two dissimilar realms: the norms of "the Law for Thing" on the one hand and "the Law for Man" on the other. Nothing that comes from a beloved doggie or kitten can change the truth as understood by reason. But what of it? *The point is that the hearts of men are never very brave before the truth, or what they deem the truth, when their own deeper desires are thwarted.*[85]

This kind of erroneous but well-received response to the indifference of nature leads to a depreciation of reason, seen from that point on primarily as a tool for improving one's fate. At the same time, we should note that these dissimilar domains – the two "Laws" – do indeed meet on the grounds of the relationships that make up society, for there is no society without feelings. And feelings do not make sense until they come into contact with reason or the power of judgment. In the order of human affairs, a "pure," unjudged feeling would be something as inapplicable (or inappropriate) as volcanic murmurs. This is perhaps modern

---

85 P. E. More, *Evolution and the Other World* [in:] id., *Shelburne Essays Eleventh Series: A New England Group and Others*, Boston–New York 1921, p. 146. Cf. id., *Definitions of Dualism...*, pp. 261–62.

Un-Economic Ideals

man's greatest pain: that the more emotional freedom in life, that is, the freedom to let loose and indulge ourselves, the less real meaning. On the other hand, we have a classical solution, which consists in discovering the soul as a real "space" of a just life. While nature may unknowingly distance itself from our judgments, we may consciously distance ourselves from nature (in its foreign, inhuman dimension). Justice, then, means a harmonious balance achieved within ourselves through rational control over the sphere of feelings and desires; therefore, it signifies the separation of the dominion of human nature from nature in general – not by any act of redefinition, but – inasmuch as we can have (immediate) knowledge of ourselves – in accordance with the conditions of our self-knowledge. This self-knowledge leads us to discover individual happiness, which we must distinguish from pleasure as a non-accidental, established state of the soul. This is the shortest possible explanation of the noble teaching of the classics. The trouble is in transferring these findings to the political dimension. For *society is something more than the spontaneous association of free units; it is an organization with traditions and government, necessary to it for the reason that it is made up of individuals who, not being infallibly just and wise, must be guided and constrained by a conventional code of relations (...) manifestly, the problem here is far more complicated than when it is isolated in the individual soul,*[86] and being political beings, we have to face it. Whether we like it or not, we are returning to the natural model. According to More, modern thought is always drawn toward extremes: on the one hand, we have Nietzsche's fascination with the law of the stronger (in the name of progress), on the other – democratic egalitarianism, referring only to feelings; although the first variant should meet the requirements of rationality (what is better or more capable of happiness wins), it targets the layers of *libido dominandi*; therefore, it gives individuals with tyrannical tendencies an advantage, not those who should be considered natural aristocrats. How can we get out of this impasse? What is political

86   Id., *Justice...*, pp. 116–17.

HUMANISM AS REALISM

justice? *It is such a distribution of power and privilege, and of property as the symbol and instrument of these* – More writes – *as at once will satisfy the distinctions of reason among the superior, and will not outrage the feelings of the inferior (...) society (...) shares both the character of the individual soul, as being composed of souls, and the character of nature, as being fundamentally not a unit but a collection of units. The constitution of a just society, therefore, will inevitably have this double aspect: it will correspond to what is justice in the individual soul, and at the same time it will disturb us by admitting elements of that seeming oppression which we are wont to call injustice in the procedure of evolution, but which is really the fatal inhuman law of things. In other words, in aiming at a just State we must always, while men are men, act in such a way as will seem unjust to those who, judging for themselves, judge by the feelings alone.*[87] The task of the legislator, but also the teacher and "moralist," is to act by mediating. The practice of mediation relative to society as a whole forces a "disciplining of the heart." Nation-states are compromises with nature.

Having gone through these arguments, we surely understand that according to More, the political order grows out of irrational feelings and aspirations – mine, yours, of the masses. It is a reality that contains and reflects everything naturally necessary and not necessarily good and beautiful. However, it seems improbable that one could flog people on this basis with the claim that their "right to life" meant little in the face of "property rights" and that "the dollar is more than the man." What could the goal of this obnoxious rhetoric be? To capture the author's intention, it is necessary to refer to the figure of Rousseau again. We know that this prophet of humanitarianism performs a historic procedure on the imagination, sanctifying, in a way, the temptation to associate happiness with the mythical state of innocence of a savage. This savage is not subject to pressure from anyone and does not create any pressure himself, but lives simply, in a world free from barriers, because it is free from the consequences of dividing and possessing. More writes: *Rousseau, by inflaming the passions of men*

87   Ibid., pp. 120–21.

against the wrongs of society which by his own hypothesis are inevitable, was, and still is, the father of frightful confusions and catastrophes; but he performed a real service to philosophy by stating so sharply the bare truth that property is the basis of civilization.[88] Standing out among the escapee from Geneva's spiritual offspring were the socialists who preached the need to replace capitalist divisions with a community of goods, which would allegedly bring both moral progress and further economic benefits. Both had to turn out to be pipe dreams (looking at this from our perspective, this is hard to doubt). The most important thing is to realize that *the real strength of socialism, the force that some think is driving us along the Edge of revolution, is in no sense a reasoned conviction that public ownership is better than private ownership, but rather a profound emotional protest against the inequalities of ownership. The serious question is not in regard to the importance of property, but in regard to the justice of its present distribution. Despite all the chatter about the economic interpretation of history, we are to-day driven along by a sentiment, and by no consideration of economics.*[89]

Succumbing to sentiment should not be considered a virtue of the legislator. Meanwhile, in the conditions of the modern transformation of the imagination, the fundamental vision of law, the enacting of which is subject to the demands of justice arising as a result of emotional expansion, also changes. Sure, when I see the rich profiting from their wealth unworthily, and even more so in the face of the undeserved poverty of a hungry child, my heart cries out – enough of these wrongs! And it is precisely between the heart's cry and reason's findings that there is no mediation. Paradoxically, we want to achieve naturalistically defined political goals – corresponding to our economic ideals – not by compromising with nature but by contradicting natural necessity. In the classical tradition solidified by Roman lawyers, *it is not we who create laws; we are rather finders and interpreters of laws registered in a court beyond our control, and our decrees are merely the application of*

88 Id., *Property and Law...*, p. 133. Emphasis in original.
89 Ibid., pp. 134–35.

HUMANISM AS REALISM

our knowledge, or ignorance, of the law to particular conditions.[90] Hence we have the concept of natural law, *ius naturale*, that More ascribed to the Stoics. However, its postulate of living in accordance with nature is replete with ambivalence resulting from the understanding of "nature" as a particular ideal of humanity (the Stoic sage) and, at the same time, true behavioral norms mediated by conventions. In practice, a dangerous tension arises between the overly optimistic judgment of individual moral predispositions and the actual state of interpersonal relations. In short, the legislator cannot assume the realization of standards unattainable here and now among people who strive for holiness. In doing so, he would plunge into the fumes of *wishful thinking* – he becomes the legislator of this or that version of the humanitarian utopia. Inequalities in access to material goods are nothing good per se. Instead, they have a lot to do with robbery and exploitation. We need understanding, not delight: civilized theft is better than outright lawlessness. In general, it is better to accept the "cruelty factor" within civilization while retaining the chances of individual improvement in the sphere of religion or philosophy (i.e., where a rational soul can overcome nature) than to kill an imperfect civilization.

In More's view, *as the rights of property do not involve the economic interpretation of history* (because they remain irrelevant to a life based on religious or philosophical experience, visibly lived during history and giving rise to significant effects), *so neither do they result in materialism. The very contrary. For in this matter, as in all other questions of human conduct and natural forces, you may to a certain degree control a fact, but if you deny a fact it will control you.*[91] For example, feminism provides an analogy. In what is probably the most obvious version, this peculiar fraction of the humanitarian mindset seeks to deny the distinctive features of women, which, from the perspective of the exclusivity of economic ideals, constitute regrettable limits or burdens. As a result, we see countless examples of the ill-fated obsession with one's body conditions, the mania

90   Ibid., p. 137.
91   Ibid., pp. 142-43.

Un-Economic Ideals

surrounding strength demonstrations, and the affirmation of feelings of equality. The consequences of the romantic exaltation of love, the idealization of the sexual act, or the purely sentimental interpretation of marriage seem no less eloquent. It all ends in "morbid eroticism," the more or less serious adoption of an orgasmic eschatology. The effects of pacifism are similar; the good-natured struggle for peace turns into a hotbed of rape. In sum, beautiful slogans and gestures hide an abundance of stupidity and villainy. Again, we can add that the observations made during the last hundred years do not refute this skeptical diagnosis.

Though tainted with injustice, harmful divisions, and even cruelty, a stable political system can safeguard civilized life forms or a barrier to material bestialization. If this is the case, it is because a given state recognizes the privileges resulting from property rights. Simply put, man – as a creature of flesh and blood, not some angel – needs peace and security to deal with the things of the spirit seriously. When our stomach growls loudly, it impairs our thinking. However, when something further happens, when we are afraid of losing everything at a moment's notice and when the fruits of our work mean nothing to people obsessed with a vision of the imminent transformation of everyday life into prosperity – then we are dealing with a catastrophe. We must defend ourselves against that catastrophe. As More notes, if the situation of a person who pursues non-economic ideals in his life *is dependent on the rights of property, and these rights are denied or belittled in the name of some impossible ideal, it follows that the demands of intellectual leisure will be regarded as abnormal and anti-social, and that he who turns to the still and quiet life will be despised as a drone, if not hated as an enemy of the serious part of the community (...) for* if property is secure, it may be the means to an end. In contrast, if it is insecure, it will be the end itself.[92]

Summarizing this thread, we can finally identify the addressee of More's rhetoric. He is addressing the wealthy and privileged, likely young heirs rather than owners directly in-

92 Ibid., pp. 146, 148. Emphasis in original.

volved in forging their own success. The aim is, at least partially, to reconstruct an imagination that economic ideals have entirely dominated. The tensions or aporias of the humanitarian religion always create opportunities for this. However, such a procedure's effectiveness is determined not by attempts at establishing a discourse – which would be either trivial and vague, or temporary, short-lived – but by using the sense of existential danger among the rich (that this is the time of Bolshevism and trade unions, that the old rules of the game are a thing of the past). This threat must be properly identified and linked to the "cause" of humanism. So to simplify, we have a peculiar deal: defending property in exchange for defending civilization; because it is worth preserving the privileges flowing from the property, and it is worth supporting the teaching of the classics.[93] The catch lies in the modern understanding of "civilization" – not through the prism of material achievements or gratification through expansion, but a fair political order that would be "gracious" to people focused on the soul, who display genuine spiritual aspirations, drawing on their achievements and shaping, at best, "athletes of the spirit," meaning aristocrats worthy of the name. *We are prone to forget that civilization has always been a* tour de force, *so to speak, a little hard-won area of order and self-subordination amidst a vast wilderness of anarchy and barbarism that are continually threatening to overrun their bounds (...) civilization is like a ship traversing an untamed sea. It is a more complex machine in our day, with command of greater forces, and might seem correspondingly safer than in the era of sails.*[94] More explains the modern illusion of technological power – and the naivete of faith in the beneficial character of man's relationship with nature – with a scene that is highly appealing to the imagination. Namely, he goes back to his memories as a passenger on an ocean-going ship. It was, we read, a cheerful and delightful evening. The rays of the moon reflected on the rippled

93 Cf. ibid., pp. 128–29; and: ibid., pp. 147–48; id., *The Classics* [in:] A. H. Dakin, *A Paul Elmer...*, p. 42.
94 P. E. More, *Academic Leadership...*, pp. 41–42.

Un-Economic Ideals

surface of the water. You could soak up this atmosphere of undisturbed peace for hours, which the author himself did, while his traveling companions took part in a dance party under the open sky. Only one thought succeeded in disrupting the idyllic experiences in the North Atlantic. The *Titanic* sank a year earlier in precisely the same place.

Our modern approach to civilization seems, on the one hand, to express preferences for material expansion (or for the provision of material means to the "machine" of emotional expansion), and on the other hand – to reveal a deep, almost indisputable acceptance of the eighteenth-century – new at the time – vision of dualism. This vision, internalized by the general public through their upbringing (culture, education), can be treated today as an obvious mode of perceiving reality. However, we must remember that political reality is made up of particular opinions that depend on the movement of the imagination; and the imagination seeks support in what is considered knowledge in a given society (or international community). This apparently universal knowledge about man has its roots, according to More, in the views of English deists, who in turn were reacting to the insanities of seventeenth-century Protestants; from them, it moves to the salons of the French Enlightenment, to finally become the material for Rousseau's religious inspiration. The classic dualism of good and evil gives way before the dualism of the individual and the innocent – of what enjoys itself and sympathizes with the fates of other beings, and what is imposed by civilization as it has existed up to this point, things that embarrass the individual and holds his needs in contempt. The new vision turns out to be politically effective and intellectually clever because it is capacious. For, it does not matter that Rousseau did not present himself as a glorifier of scientific progress and did not know the theory of evolution. If we define man by the action of instincts that must be trusted – being natural, they must be good for us – then the seemingly obvious thought arises that these instincts must be liberated and transformed into the appropriate institutions. Thus, we have a reason to develop and invent modern history – with the "end of history." However, what immediately comes to the fore is the tension that constitutes the canvas for the spectacle of modernity.

IV.

On the one hand, the joy of being oneself or self-love, on the other – sympathy with others; and further on – egoism and a lack of divisions. In this way, we recognize, as it were, two types of economic ideals and two goals on either side of the playing field of the imagination. The first type, which Paul Elmer More associated with Nietzscheanism, centers on the image of civilization as a tool in the hands of a weak majority that uses religious authority and state coercion, placing countless obstacles on the path to genuine harmony that can only arise from the fulfillment of the desires of a strong minority. The existing social or political organization is nothing more than a conspiracy hatched long ago against the living will of an individual that knows no limits. The second type encompasses various "theories" of socialism, including the Marxist approach. The working class takes over the role of the individual – insofar as those belonging to it properly understand their interests at the next stage of the history of civilization – hitherto oppressed and disfigured by the privileged class of owners, whose power is identified with the traditional institutional order. The present suffering of workers emerges from economic progress and, as such, is to be overcome when the oppressed people become aware of their plight, take over the means of production, and establish a new ("classless") order, imagined as an emanation of the sympathy that unites all people. *It might seem fanciful –* More states *– to derive systems so contrary in tendency from the same origin, yet both are alike in that they regard the evils of civilisation as caused by that dualism of the individual and society, which was imposed upon the world as a new religion by one who sought in this way to escape the burden of personal responsibility. Both look to relief in the solution of that antinomy through the application of natural science to human affairs and through the resulting free development of man's natural instincts, one in the direction of egotism, the other of* *sympathy. Nor is this difference of direction so real as may appear.*[95] After all, it is not difficult to notice that the rule of irresponsible superhumans can provoke truly superhuman revenge from an equally irresponsible mob. At the same time, the idyllic vision of communism signals an invitation to move from the level of class hatred to the level of a hitherto unknown "anarchy of egoisms." We will come back to this later.

At this point in our discussion, we should become fully aware of the "new" dualism's implications for political thinking; thinking as we know it today, but also as we try to project onto the testimonies and remnants of earlier history. Above all, More writes, *with the idea of an avenging deity and a supernatural test there disappeared also the sense of deep personal responsibility; the very notion of a radical and fundamental difference between good and evil was lost.* Thus, the problem of evil in the world turns into the problem of bad institutions; why they are evil, why we succumb to their evil, and how to replace institutional evil with institutional good – these are our questions. What started as a primarily religious or philosophical question has turned into an economic one. And this is the only issue that occupies our thoughts, since *there is no real distinction between the good and the evil*, and regarding people – beginning with ourselves – we would like to think that *all are naturally good and the superficial variations we see are caused by the greater or less freedom of development.* This may, for example, result in an intense commitment to the modernization of those societies which – from the point of view of the economic ideals assumed – are the least civilized in the dimension of modern civilization (the "good," transformed civilization), i.e., the most entangled in old beliefs and patterns, disoriented, backward, parochial, closed. African tribes, Asian clans, provincial villages and towns, the outskirts of the ecumene, reserves filled with cheap labor, the dwellings of malcontents, various cultural backwaters – such as ours, perhaps – constitute an impressive testing (and combat) ground for followers of the humanitarian religion; an area of

95 Id., *Rousseau...*, p. 240.

intellectual adventures, experiments undertaken in the name of universal liberation. *In place of judgment we are to regard all mankind with sympathy; a sort of emotional solidarity becomes the one great virtue, in which are included, or rather sunk, all the law and the prophets.*[96]

It is worth remembering the phrase about the "drowning" of the old religion. Whenever we are faced with contemporary reinterpretations of classical thought, especially post-Christian versions, where the desire to tame the message or make it more attractive by spiritually disarming it seems to be understood as a way to improve the self-esteem of the defeated or self-affirmation within the discourse of modernity. However, the tension that precedes this discourse raises accusations of decadence; sympathy on the level of all humankind, the totality of the unknown and the small, is, after all, an obvious chimera and an excuse. We know from Babbitt that such "universal" passions in practice favor the emergence of absolute particularisms. In More's view, much of what constitutes the most influential stance against modern decadence, namely Nietzsche's, *was sound and well directed (...) he saw, as few other men of our day have seen, the danger that threatens true progress in any system of education and government which makes the advantage of the ordinary rather than the distinguished man its first object. He saw with terrible clearness that much of our most admired art is not art at all in the higher sense of the word, but an appeal to morbid sentimentality (...) but the cure Nietzsche proposed for these evils was itself a part of the malady. The Superman (...) is a product of the same naturalism which produced the disease it would counteract; it is the last and most violent expression of the egotism, or self-interest,*[97] but also an expression of Nietzsche's illusion that by hitting one of the goals on the pitch of the imagination, inherited from several centuries prior, he can go beyond this pitch. Staying with this

---

96 Id., *The New Morality* [in:] id., *Aristocracy and Justice...*, pp. 201–02.
97 Id., *Nietzsche* [in:] id., *The Drift of Romanticism...*, pp.183–84. Cf. I. Babbitt, *Rousseau and Romanticism...*, p. 198; id., *The Critic and American Life*, "The Forum," vol. 79, no. 2, February 1928, p. 164.

metaphor, the superman is a player who gives absolutely everything in a match that is played to absolute exhaustion either way.[98]

Meanwhile, if we look at the historical dominants in the shaping of the economic ideals' hegemony, the Nietzschean demands for a realistic correction of the political discourse seem to be background noise. The initiative in the game for humanity belongs roughly to the socialist team. Here again, we have to beware of potential misunderstandings. As we have seen, More links radical and revolutionary attitudes to the expansion of feelings awakened by the glaring social inequalities that the free market creates or sustains, rather than to reflection prompted by some new findings on more efficient ways of managing a modern state. In other words, the fight for a new distribution of goods does not extend beyond the horizon of humanitarian thinking. We can say that a socialist's imagination reaches for a tomorrow that is perceived as a better today. "Tomorrow" is something to be won here and now by one means or another. We can treat the antagonism between the socialist and the free-market technocrat as a difference in method, reinforced by appropriate emotional experiences. It is not just anything to take the helm of the ship of modernity! But this bloody or bloodless takeover presupposes complete acceptance of the game's fundamental rules, contrary to appearances. Simplifying somewhat, the point is not to change the way things happen but to make them happen faster. *The tendency of things is to them altogether right; only by persuasion or violence they would hasten its course. Starting with a thorough acceptance of the* grande industrie, *as it now rules society, they aim only to carry this law* (i.e., the law of economic development) *to what they regard as its scientific conclusion. They are not recalcitrant against "the proud magnificence of trade." On the contrary, they are merely a part of the larger tendency, which for a century and more has been gaining visibly in acceleration, to glorify industry, commerce, labour, as things desirable in themselves and inevitable to progress. Their old testament is Adam*

98 Cf. F. Nietzsche, *The Will to Power*, trans. W. Kaufmann, R. J. Hollingdale, New York 1968, fragment 77, p. 49.

Smith's Wealth of Nations, *which from an individualist and collectivist alike take origin; and their Messiah is Karl Marx, with whom they agree in this, if in nothing else, that the domination forces of the world are material, that the changing social order with its creeds and professions is entirely the result of economic forces, that productive labour is the sole economic measure of values, and that the irresistible movement of civilisation is toward the collective control of production.*[99]

Therefore, the rupture that gives rise to – one might say, hard-headed – socialism thus described lies between the eighteenth-century Scottish Enlightenment and nineteenth-century evolution and scientism. Next from this, however, there is a separate but compatible current from which other types of socialist acolytes emerge. In the latter trend, there is not so much a fascination with material progress as a concern about the progressive dehumanization of life under the conditions of ruthless capitalism. From this perspective, socialism is not so much a historical necessity or coming stage of evolution as an object of spiritual aspirations, a state desired by us and achieved in an act of will. This kind of thinking flows from nineteenth-century confusion and delusions about spirituality, reinterpreted by the Romantics and associated with a desperate votum separatum in the interest of loving for the sake of loving,[100] with an inner rebellion against external struggle and rivalry. As More explains, *it is because such religious groping is an emotional and volitional assumption without knowledge, a state of idealism without definite ideal, that the mind, deprived of certain guidance, falls a prey to the dominant party of discontent, and we behold the disconcerting spectacle of idealist and materialist fighting in the same ranks.*[101]

Mixing up the types of "scientist" and "dreamy aesthete" may be the reason why socialism is associated with naivete, obtuse

---

99 P. E. More, *The Socialism of G. Lowes Dickinson* [in:] id., *Shelburne Essays Seventh Series*, Boston–New York 1910, pp. 174–75. The phrase "the proud magnificence of trade" was taken from William Combe's poem *The Tour of Doctor Syntax in Search of the Picturesque* (1812).

100 Cf. I. Babbitt, *Rousseau and Romanticism...*, pp. 224–25.

101 P. E. More, *The Socialism of...*, p. 194.

doctrinairism, or vain daydreaming. However, professed social-ists – Lenin, Stalin, Hitler – were at times terrifyingly effective. Generally speaking, their political achievements tied together not only the countries in which they gained power, but also the rest of the world. Certainly, they were not to be considered sentimen-tal socialists, church orphans, victims of dogma made vague. The ideal of an egalitarian state based on love for humanity or uni-versal brotherhood, renouncing violence in its organization of a new system, departing from brutal divisions between the ruling and the ruled, had to end up being *a dream very quickly extin-guished by the stern lessons of history. Will you find warrant for such a faith in the economic fatalism of Karl Marx? Will you discover it in the theory of the Soviet rulers of Russia, who to the determinism of Marx have added the conscious will to power of the proletariat?* In its con-frontation with the demands of natural necessity, socialism – tak-ing on the form of Bolshevism at a crucial moment – is no less "Nietzschean" than the free-market individualism that refers to the doctrine of the Manchester School. *Lenin understood that the success of revolution depends on capitalizing, so to speak, the individ-ual's will to power as the will of a particular class.* At the same time, the modern *communist as well as the fascist or the monarchist has learnt that an efficient organization cannot be erected on an equalitarian basis. They know that men are divided roughly into three main groups: the mass of those who must be externally controlled by fear or by blind obedience; a ruling body, whether an individual or a committee, which holds the reins and drives, ostensibly at least, for the good of the whole; and an intermediary class who voluntarily submit to direction and upon whose allegiance to the principles embodied in the actual government the stability of the State depends.*[102]

There is a temptation at this point to generalize that the real-ization of economic ideals requires – in every possible arrange-ment – managers, violence, and bureaucracy. The intensity and literalness of terror, the grotesque cult of the individual and the

102 Id., *Church and Politics* [in:] id., *On Being Human...*, pp. 146–47, 152, 154–55.

politburo, the corruption of the clerical and claqueur classes – all these, however poignant, are accidents. The essence of things invariably lies at the heart of the "modern experiment." Thus, a Bolshevik-like real socialist isn't merely a superman's superficial creation or superhumanly desperate in a more profound sense, but, unfortunately, an effective manager in the process of imposing a utopia. But, again, it is worth emphasizing that the humanitarian utopia does not belong to the legacy of one political option or movement. Its sinister effect, so deeply "overworked" in the second half of the last century, does not only inculpate the socialists. A utopia itself does not burn out with, say, the collapse of totalitarian regimes claiming to build socialism (including the "national" variant) or communism – in Russia, Germany, or elsewhere. The threat of absolutely ruthless actions, undertaken in the name of absolute effectiveness in achieving ideals, remains a real threat here and now.

An advantage – of course, only from the point of view of distant observers – of twentieth-century totalitarian regimes was that whatever they did, it could serve to expose evil. Despite all the difficulties, propaganda, and agentry, less than a hundred years ago, a thinking person in the West had the opportunity to observe their actions and find serious premises to understand his fate. Meanwhile, the interwar period's dominant intellectual and political currents might have led to a fascination with Bolshevism more than to its fruitful unmasking.[103] After all, humanitarians living under democratic regimes also dream of a great acceleration – without the dictatorship of the proletariat. More, like Babbitt, saw in Wilson perhaps the worst and most destructive type of democrat. In one of his letters, he stated that *he has certain qualities which appeal to the intelligence of men otherwise clear-sighted and straightforward, and as a consequence he seems to have corrupted the nation at the top, and lowered our whole mental and moral tone.* Responding to one of the president's apologists, he explained that *Wilson's sentimentalism was not a true ideal and was likely to be an important element in*

103 Cf. id., *Religion and Social...*, especially pp. 140–41.

the horrible spread of Bolshevism that threatens the world. For a man in Wilson's position to say, and insist as one of the terms of peace, that all peoples have a right of determining their own government strikes me as nonsense, and perilous nonsense. It is impracticable, the sort of sentimentalism that does not conform with fact or utility yet may be the cause of endless confusion and anarchy. And this sort of thing underlies the whole Wilsonian brand of humanitarianism.[104]

This evaluation doesn't sit well with us. To many Poles, Wilson was considered a hero, or at least a benefactor of the Polish cause, amidst a multitude of disgusting displays of cynicism and disregard on the part of other representatives of Western powers. Regardless of the philosophical motives behind the critique of Wilsonism, its political sense is worth noting. To some extent, More's approach seems improper or devoid of elementary sensitivity, as it is inconsistent with the opinion we accept (for good reasons) about our country, our history, our merits, and the injuries we've suffered. But after all, there is no such thing as the opinion of all humankind. Opinions are, by nature, particular. Moreover, the hegemony of economic ideals can only strengthen this state. If the goals of thinking in terms of expansion aren't balanced by the goals of humanistic and religious experience, then the real – non-false and politically significant – aspiration to rise above particularism disappears. Everyone simply defends his own, what he has earned for himself. He protects it as a last resort, since there is nothing beyond it. From the perspective of our own good – the right to decide for ourselves (however we understand it) obviously belongs to us; from the perspective of the good of the United States, it must be profitable for them for us to get anything. Neither one nor the other falls within the order of philosophical truth, which otherwise loses its universal value. The transformed, adapted "truth," in turn – which by this point is more of a "half-truth" – becomes a tool in the hands of the stronger party, an ideological hammer, a politicized parody of knowledge or spiritual enlightenment.

104 A. H. Dakin, *Paul Elmer More...*, pp. 166–67, note 59.

Let's follow this trail a bit further. America lives and breathes wealth, absorbs wealth, and tempts with wealth. Wealth is, in short, the *raison d'être* of this particular empire, which in itself is a monument to the continual expansion of modern man. For the rest of the world, for at least one century, it was within the American "polis" walls that the tabernacle of modernity was kept, protected by weapons of mass destruction, banks, and the media industry. Of course, one can contemplate the verbal ornaments adorning the imperial political discourse (in relatively repetitive configurations), but it is better to perceive the primacy of economics over politics with all its consequences. More precisely, it was better to have perceived it in advance. In *Wealth and Culture* (1902), an early essay full of vivid irony, More urges his countrymen to stop wandering about in search of a "culture" that has nothing to do with their lives. In the end, we have to ask: *what national ideal has America today on which its culture may be built up? Renunciation, self-development, religion, chivalry, Humanism, pantheistic return to nature, liberty – all these have existed and have born their fair fruits; what have we to offer in their place? (...) wealth and its complement which we call humanitarianism or socialism, and which is, in fact, nothing more than the extension and dilution of this same ideal; wealth aiming at the control of vast material forces, humanitarianism seeking, first of all and above all, material comfort for the multitude while masquerading in the guise of religion, and covering itself with the cloak of brotherly love.*[105] Identifying humanitarianism with socialism is somewhat deceptive, but More's intentions are clear: we must judge economic ideals in their proper order. The meaning of the "sentimental form" – and the practical demand for a just redistribution of wealth – remains secondary to the significance of wealth. The attraction to mammon itself is not a new phenomenon; after all, it results from the natural expansiveness *par excellence* of the human species. What is new is the scale of what we can obtain, as well as the character of the proprietors and their

105 P. E. More, *Wealth and Culture* [in:] *The Essential Paul Elmer More: A Selection of His Writings*, ed. B. C. Lambert, New Rochelle, New York 1972, p. 344.

Un-Economic Ideals

power to influence the imagination of the crowds. Modern wealth triggers a "kind of hypnotic obsession." Its holders are not heirs to those who used to consider themselves – more or less fortunately – to be aristocrats. The civilization they have built seems to exist in a different dimension. They do not belong to the old world. On the contrary, they constitute the avant-garde of the new world, which draws its existence from an expansion that lacks any alternative.

More tells us: *I have traveled a good deal here and there from city to city, but I always come back to this point of land which we call Wall Street as the most genuine expression of our national life.* Wall Street symbolizes the primacy of economics over politics (and thus over every area of life) and determines – literally as well, in architecture – the measures of power born of wealth. *America leads the world in civilization* (the new one!) *because she has most frankly recognized this ideal.* Politically, therefore, under American conditions, humanitarianism will turn out to be nothing more than an action popularizing the sense of comfort guaranteed by money. It is worth emphasizing, bearing in mind the aforementioned "proposal" of the *deal*, that from the humanist's point of view, the tragedy of modernity is not that the layer of great owners appears to be leaky and, in principle, everyone would like to be in their place; it does not consist in errors in recognizing economic ideals or the means of attaining them. Instead, it consists in the undisputed hegemony of one direction of thinking, or to put it another way – in the absence or ignorance of other ideals, other perspectives. Among the humanitarians, or even party socialists (democrats, leftists, whatever), one can surely find people prone to serious intellectual and political confrontation with the diseases of the modern state and society. Such people, unfortunately, end up saturated with nothing but empty words, wandering unhealthily within the vicious cycle of modern thought. *The very bitterness and pathos of it all show that it speaks the revolt of a mind imprisoned within the same material ideal – of a mind that tortures itself to escape, but sees nothing and knows nothing beyond its prison walls.*[106]

106 Ibid., pp. 345, 347–48.

Let us, therefore, create a portrait of America that is most easily criticized by adepts of humanism – this is likely More's perfidious expectation of his artistically-minded fellow citizens. Not records of trauma and resentment, but a joyful profession of faith in economic ideals, bringing to the surface – right before the eyes of those who wish to think for themselves – the long-concealed guts of modernity. Not impressing his audience with caked grime, nor the dark and dramatic "explosion in a cesspool,"[107] but the arch-banality of life in the cell of an empire, which grows thanks to the shrinking of humanity. Finally, the issue of "national" or state culture is part of the recurring issue of imagination and, thus, illusions in political life. More, in Platonic fashion, recognizes the vital importance of myth as a support for established – or rather restored – social order and hierarchy. Visible use of this tool, i.e., opinion management, gives rise to accusations of cynicism and low motives. However, since the majority of people are not philosophers and adhere to some "truths" rather than discover truths, the choice is simple: either order rooted in the illusory belief in the perfection and indispensability of what is already there, or order guaranteed only through a threat of violence in the majesty of the law, through the sight of police batons; in any case, their strength in itself will sooner or later turn out to be equally illusory. At the same time, it is hard not to admit that opinion management can lead to bad, but also to good outcomes, with suitable results on the various levels. *For there is a true illusion, if the phrase will be accepted, whereby the lower nature of man is charmed by the voice of his higher instincts; and there is a false illusion, of the very contrary sort. The one is social and constructive, and is the work, properly speaking, of the imagination; the other is disintegrating and destructive, and is the product of the egotistic desires.*[108]

On the one hand – the illusion of the goods flowing from concentration, on the other – the illusion of the goods flowing from

---

107 Cf. id., *Modern Currents in American Literature* [in:] id., *The Demon of The Absolute...*, p. 63.

108 Id., *Disraeli and Conservatism* [in:] id., *Aristocracy and Justice...*, p. 174.

Un-Economic Ideals

expansion. A "simple" man may not share in the self-fulfillment that is part of a religious or humanistic experience. After all, communing with it, accepting it as an ideal that is binding for everyone, though unattainable for the vast majority, a life conceived vertically, not equal to the (necessarily unequal) sequence of earthly conquests, thus ensuring respect for individual sanctity, and obedience and respect for the aristocratic spirit, which would permeate the institutions of the state... All this, in short, gives a sense of meaning and serves to preserve civilization (in the classical sense). On the other hand, the false illusion concerns the ever-recurring opportunities to be satisfied, here and now, according to the key of our ideas about what we want, what we deserve, what attracts us. The falsehood lies in the fact is that whatever we get, it will literally go to hell anyway. In the end, there must be a disillusionment so intense that it is impossible to imagine anymore. Along the way – a hefty bill for fleeting pleasures, and in the political dimension – a constant threat of the consequences of particular claims and all the effects of decadence.

How can one respond to this situation – a life immersed in illusion and oriented towards falsehood? In *Aristocracy and Justice*, More – and with him, humanism as an intellectual movement – comes closest to adopting a particular way of thinking about politics that historians of political thought used to describe as a conservative doctrine. We are talking about nineteenth-century British conservatism (Toryism), based around the figure of Prime Minister Benjamin Disraeli. Interestingly, despite a certain dose of romantic extravagance in the biography of this politician, for More, he becomes an emblem of leadership that is successful insofar as it combines effective action for the empire with a traditional, non-humanitarian understanding of the real foundations of good politics. We can admire the historic result of this in the practical mechanisms of the substantive United Kingdom constitution. On a side note, we can describe the essence of conservatism very concisely. *The instinctive distrust of uncontrolled human nature and the instinctive reliance on the imagination, – are the very roots of the conservative temper, as their contraries are the roots of the liberal and radical temper, the lack of imagination, if any distinction is to be made, being the chief factor of liberalism and confidence in human nature being the main impulse of radicalism.*[109]

In other words, liberals ask us to simply profess economic ideals, while radicals and socialists ask us to fight for them. A conservative attitude – referring to a specific political framework and a particular era (because you can be a conservative defender of the legacy of the Soviet Union, for instance) – opens itself up to "something more" than the vision of a universal contract or universal emancipation, while maintaining a sober judgment of the changes occurring that we have no choice but to face anyway. Expressing his sympathy for this attitude, More obviously does not join any party. His point – this is how we can put it from our perspective – is to show a place that constitutes a kind of gap in the curtains of modernity. And the political "gaps" lie near the surface, not in the depths of the tormented self. As it is known, the Germans were profound and tormented – and two world wars came out of it. The case is similar with the Russians, or at least the Russian elite. Concerning the Germans, it is worth noting that their "Teutonic" education was second to none in the world. How far removed we are from the final exams in a decent German gymnasium! It was not merely a handful of diligent students who learned Latin and Greek extensively. Intellectual training in the labyrinths of Kantianism and Hegelianism was met with the romantic cult of inspiration, strength, and desperation. Frankly, for the humanists, science and education in *Kaiser* Wilhelm's state create quite a favorable polemical horizon. After all, these are the years of the maturing of modern empires to the "final" confrontation, years of an atmosphere of war. According to Babbitt, the German "philosophy" of the time depicts Rousseau's constantly digested thoughts, to which he adds a staffage – otherwise effective and still not abandoned to this day – of "vague and pedantic phraseology." We cannot deny the Reich's learned elites the ability to penetrate the depths of the human spirit. However, they do

109 Ibid., p. 168.

Un-Economic Ideals

not know the "law of measure" and are therefore enslaved by their own libido sciendi.[110] According to More, what stands out in German thought, which dazzles the Anglo-Saxons with accusations of living a lie and despicable opportunism, is *a fundamental indifference to the truth of first premises, which no logical straightforwardness and superimposed bulk of intellectualism can conceal (...) the hallmark of Teutonic scholarship is an enormous intellectual activity with an initial lack of intellectual integrity.*[111]

Is the humanistic preference for English conservatism and the ostentatious criticism of German thought not merely the result of the natural attachment of our protagonists to their native particularisms? Is it not that they simply choose what is their own? That they write – at least on these matters – with the good of their empire, let's call it the Anglosphere, in mind and without much concern over the universal dimension? Should we trust the "first principles" rhetoric coming from the pen of the American at all? The final decision belongs to each reader individually. However, to better understand this dilemma, let us make a short digression. There is undoubtedly no more touching description in literature of the torment of modern man than the one that emerges from the works of Fyodor Dostoyevsky. *Notes from the Underground* (1864) are a perfect example. In the cold and artificial world of imperial St. Petersburg, thoughts that cannot be brushed off lightly mature; they reveal the future paradise to which we were finally driven. *"Then (...) a new political economy will come into existence, all complete, and also calculated with mathematical accuracy, so that all problems will vanish in the twinkling of an eye, simply because all possible answers to them will have been supplied. Then the Palace of Crystal will arise"* (the figure of the palace may refer both to the literary vision of the triumph of the new civilization, expressed in Nikolai Chernyshevsky's *Fourth Dream of Vera Pavlovna*, and to the actual building – which does not exist today – from the area of the

110 Cf. I. Babbitt, *Literature and the American...*, pp. 136–38.
111 P. E. More, *The Philosophy of the War* [in:] id., *Aristocracy and Justice...*, p. 234.

London World Exhibition, which in the second half of the nineteenth century seemed to confirm the notion that a new civilization was just around the corner). *You believe in the Palace of Crystal, eternally inviolable, that is in something at which one couldn't furtively put out one's tongue or make concealed gestures of derision. But perhaps I fear this edifice just because it is made of crystal and eternally inviolable, and it will not be possible even to put out one's tongue at it in secret.*[112] Does it not remind us of the humanistic diagnosis of the modern world a half-century earlier? And yes, in More's rich legacy, we can easily find chapters that perfectly correspond to Dostoevsky's great prose.[113] However, it is futile to look for any sign of sympathy for the author of Crime and Punishment. Why?

Probably for the same reason that humanists do not call this world the domain of the Antichrist. If the thought overtakes us that we are living on the eve of judgment day, all you can do is smile, turn off the TV and wait for the angels to invade: *nur noch ein Gott kann uns retten*. In such circumstances, one can speak of preserving some form of religious life, while humanism has no reason for existence. After all, it is not time to ask about human measures when the power of God finishes everything. Economic ideals – from pure spoils to welfare systems – belong to the order of *civitas terrena*, of which nothing will be left anyway, so... damn all those drooling sinners!... What if God doesn't exist? If the only thing that awaits us is time-limited duration alone with the "eternal silence of endless spaces," without support, without hope? That's all the more reason to ... damn all of us? For what else is left for us but to move the random mixture of our existence around in vain? And what do we learn at the end of *Notes from the Underground*? *Look harder! After all, we don't even know where*

---

112 F. Dostoevsky, *Notes from the Underground,* trans. Jessie Coulson, Penguin Books, 2010, pp. 27-28, 40.

113 Cf. P. E. More, *Wealth and Culture...,* p. 346; and: id., *The Great Refusal: Being Letters of a Dreamer in Gotham,* Boston–New York 1894, especially pp. 23 ff.; id., *The Paradox of Oxford...,* p. 72; id., Samuel *Butler of Erewhon* [in:] id., *A New England...,* pp. 193–94.

"real life" is lived nowadays, or what it is, what name it goes by. Leave us to ourselves, without our books, and at once we get into a muddle and lose our way – we don't know whose side to be on or where to give our allegiance, what to love and what to hate, what to respect and what to despise. We even find it difficult to be human beings, men with real flesh and blood of our own; *we are ashamed of it, we think it a disgrace, and are always striving to be some unprecedented kind of generalized human being. We are born dead, and moreover we have long ceased to be the sons of living fathers; and we become more and more contented with our condition.*[114]

A king's ransom for whoever can see some way out of the situation in which we recognize ourselves as zombies at the end of history. And while it would not necessarily be the best tagline for all of Dostoevsky's profound work, we are hereby invited to nihilism from a political point of view. For this is what the alternative to modern man seems to look like: either you fit in the pattern of achieving economic ideals, or you fill yourself up with madness and disappear amidst stray atoms. Let's add with a sneer that both options are encompassed within the framework of the "system," so on the whole, it cannot be done. The humanist "project" takes this into account. The political *idée fixe* of Babbitt and More – a *necessary* condition for the preservation and renewal of civilization – provides a way out of this vicious cycle. They must connect the fundamental critique of modern thought with the constant encouragement to be *better* – with the apparent assumption that what is better is not wholly inaccessible. Let us also note that in feeling sorry for ourselves, we cultivate in our own way the praise of human nature, which is the practical antithesis of the humanistic attitude. When we join the side of a desperate rebellion, we inevitably pour out our emotions – however different from the emotions that accompanied Nikola Tesla and other such simple adherents of modernity; in other words – we expand however we can. Humanists, on the other hand, call for concentration and sober judgment. In a reality shaped by the humanitarian

114 F. Dostoevsky, *Notes from the Underground...*, pp. 105–06.

religion, this leads to surprisingly radical consequences for individual thinking and moral well-being, but has nothing to do with the call for a revolutionary crackdown in the here and now. The perspective is much longer, and the responsibilities given to oneself require political prudence. Hence the association of the "first principles" with the British constitution. We have no choice but to tread on the scattered bricks of order. Only by appreciating these remnants in the form of proven institutional solutions and symbols adapted to particular political communities' needs can we influence those who will never be humanists and whose faith in humanity does not have to be the last faith of humanity.

Whatever you think about it, we should not disregard the historical context. World War I brought not only a fundamental reshuffling of military and economic powers, not only human sacrifices and material losses, but also a hitherto unknown global crisis of concepts. This crisis did smolder in places during the previous century, but it was generally obscured by the experience of the development of science, the civilizational supremacy of the West, and the emancipation of subsequent social groups. Among the cacophony of groans and curses, in the face of the disclosure of the defeat of the humanitarian spells of peace and progress, there was also the voice of a humanist, which, unfortunately, went almost unheard: *let us grasp any honourable instrument that works for tranquility without degeneracy.* Politics based on a game of emotions and redefined by sentiments – which therefore cannot go beyond the framework of particularisms – should be opposed to classically understood knowledge and character. According to More, *one thing is sure, we shall not really profit from the frightful discipline of this experience* (a world war) *unless we effect some change in our inner attitude towards life, and so escape from the false dilemma of our philosophy* (...) *we need very much to examine the bases of the absolute humanitarianism* (...) *we need to be less swayed by our sympathies and more guided by the discriminations of reason.* Here is the humanistic "review of concepts" discussed by us in the first essay. More and Babbitt, as we know, did not gain any significant political influence. Still, they left us with a unique formula for the task – a task of the utmost importance, of unfading relevance. If, after a hundred years, we are inclined to share with them our anxiety about the further fate of humanity, this universal anxiety – neither Polish, nor American, not given to anyone proprietarily – it is our duty to examine, at the base, the ideas that influence *great masses of men, both the educated and the uneducated. For if anything is sure in mortal life, it is that if a man thinks the truth, he will in the end find the peace of self-possession; and that if a man thinks untruth, he shall be a prey to the fluctuations of passion. And as it is with a man, so it is with a nation. We are all the servants of philosophy, for good or for evil.*[115]

V.

What has reading the humanists given us? First, we've realized that we live in a world wholly mastered and permeated by economic ideals. Referring to Hulme's prose, today, we don't so much think *about* economic ideals as we think "seeing things through" them, i.e., *in terms of* them. From this perspective, the political differences we've become accustomed to – including those to which our family dispute between the cousin-realist and cousin-idealist referred – are typically inferior, superficial, and limited. It doesn't matter if you're a socialist or a free-market liberal – whether you choose to believe the former or the latter. Second, we've begun to understand that the hegemony of economic ideals is associated with a massive transformation of the religious imagination in the process of transition from classical thought and Christianity to modern faith in humanity. The height of this change seems to fall on the eighteenth century and work of Rousseau. The ideals of modernity, of course, go back even further – look at Bacon's vision of the benefits of scientific progress. Nevertheless, the emergence of a new dualism as a make-shift space for the spirit allowed for the justification of the abandonment, if not murder, of the old civilization in the name of the good of humanity; good reconceptualized in terms of expansion and

115 P. E. More, *The Philosophy of the War...*, pp. 236–37, 241–43.

emancipation. Third, we should view the humanistic response to all this as revolving around the opposite primacy of politics over economics. This model – which could very well be called the priority of preserving civilization over satisfying the needs of the masses – is embodied in the attitude of a gentleman or aristocrat, for whom what matters is rational control over his soul.

This third point, however, turns out to be the most vulnerable. We know that there has never been a humanist political system; at most, some aspects of other regimes – or their philosophical-political interpretations and reinterpretations – could have favored the "cause" of humanism. The historical aristocracy was, in fact, an oligarchy of the "well-born." The title of "gentleman" probably decorated many a vain aesthete, as well as many sly, crafty men. What's more, we learn – especially from More – that political order cannot be a perfect whole, that it requires a compromise with nature, and that nature itself is always deaf to our desires. In natural conditions, we cannot overcome the limitations or indolence of the "broad masses." Although modern democracy – a system that emerged thanks to the achievements of modernity and consistent implementation of economic ideals – does not preclude aristocrats "by nature" from winning over crowds of their fellow citizens, expecting better government within societies brought up on humanitarian thinking strikes us as yet another fantasy. A party of humanism supporters could hardly be created, and even if it could, its platform would not be, in media jargon, appealing to the average voter. Much has changed since the time of Disraeli and Churchill. So, what can we do in *this* world? What can we bet on, really?

Without having freed ourselves from doubt, let's reach for another text by Paul Elmer More (from 1921), titled none other than *Economic Ideals*. This is perhaps one of the best explanations of political reality as we know it and, in a way, constitutes a summary of many of the threads we have touched upon in this essay. The starting point of *Economic Ideas* is a novel by the then-popular left-wing intellectual, Ernest Poole, titled *The Harbor* (1915). Its protagonist is a young man with aspirations, whose story begins with his studies at a prestigious university, where he is disappointed with the academic indifference. After getting out of there, he meets a planning engineer involved in a grand science project to turn New York into a world trade center full of sterile skyscrapers served by a tunnel system. His next interlocutor, a financial tycoon overseeing the entire project, infects him with a vision of the future wealth and power achieved by an alliance of scientists and "strong people at the top" operating under the banner of effectiveness. Later, however, it becomes clear that realizing these plans requires the ruthless exploitation of invisible, cheap labor, which unites and organizes a strike. Their revolt is suppressed, but the protagonist is overtaken with compassion and begins having fundamental doubts, considering these events a prelude to a necessary breakthrough. It is not just about improving someone's living conditions, but rather the "fermentation" *of a new philosophy that is to supplant all the old beliefs – a philosophy of sheer change, involving a perfect trust in the undirected will of the universe, whether manifesting itself in the unreasoned instincts of mankind or in the dumb forces of inanimate nature, to move ever of its own accord on and on to better destinies.* Submission to "pure change" opens up a "philosophical" perspective of inner peace, which does, however, differ from the desired state of a monk insofar as life differs from death. *Thus the idol of Efficiency, whose devotees dreamed of a world manager and made beautiful by the hands of science and money, is shattered before his eyes, while in its place rises the image of the People, as themselves, moving by the blind centripetal force of sympathy and by obedience to their changing instincts, securely onward to happiness and peace.*[116]

According to More, this story about the clash of the two idols – associated with the utilitarian and sentimental versions of humanitarianism, with two types of economic ideals, or, as we called it earlier, with two goals, one on each side of the modern pitch of the imagination – does an excellent job of reflecting the intense intellectual search at that time. The seemingly obvious limitation

116 Id., *Economic Ideals* [in:] id., *A New England...*, pp. 240–41; cf. id., *The New Morality...*, pp. 205–06.

of Poole's horizons pushes one to think all the more. *What* – asks More rhetorically – *if the fluctuation of our minds between the ideals of scientific control and socialistic combination should prove to be a sign that we have lost the clear steady conception of anything really worthwhile to be gained by controlling or combining? Is there no conceivable excellence of the soul itself but efficiency on the one side, with the confidence in progress wrung from the increasing mastery of material forces, or, on the other side, sympathy with the instinctive thrust of masses of men pressing for their close-seen advantage?* This kind of literature (not only fiction), which is supposed to be a response to the real problems of the epoch, is characterized by "naive ignorance" about the most crucial issue: the good life of an individual. A complete misunderstanding of what ancient monks' lives looked like can be viewed in this context as a symptom of a more general ignorance or disorientation. *I suspect that a Saint Bernard, in the seclusion of his convent at Clairvaux after one of his expeditions into the world, won from his absorbed contemplation of a God who knows no shadow of turning, a peace and a strength of which there is no intimation in the fretful literature of change. It was not the love of nature as we understand it which caused him to say to his friends, in his gracious manner of jesting, that his wisdom came less from books than from meditation in the woods and fields; it was rather his conviction that power is gained in the silences of the soul. And he was a powerful man. From his cell he spoke words that shook the governments of the world; there has probably never been a man who exercised more practical authority over his contemporaries than this monk whose life was but a dying.*[117]

Indeed, we have come a long way from universal respect for the contemplative life. Centers for teaching about God have long ago given way to centers for worldly science. And what once bore witness to a scholar's dignity, namely his relative isolation from the affairs of this world, now becomes the seedbed for his becoming a laughingstock. Academic life is to be subordinated to economic life; today, we would say – innovation in the economy;

117 Id., *Economic Ideals...*, pp. 242–.44.

Un-Economic Ideals

university studies are meant as an introduction to a successful professional career. Therefore, the disciplines that provide laboratory knowledge and social sciences that attribute to themselves the ability to create desired behaviors or optimal management come to the fore. Working on something else – once considered more serious, since it is closer to the wisdom of the classics – gives rise to a feeling of uselessness and frustration. Students do not want to listen to lectures that, in their opinion, have no practical value, which are plain-old hassles. According to More, the increasingly visible misery of the academic world, resulting in aversion to vita umbratilis (life in the shadows, devoted to private inquiry), *is in fact only one phase of the general doubt of any positive value in* [an individual's] *life.* Modern man flinches from admitting that *he, who lives in the shadow of intellectual studies is deprived of the narcotic of unreflective action. If the emptiness is clearer to the college man than to his brother in the world, it is because, after all, he still has some opportunity for reflection, and retains a vestige of the habit of self-examination.*[118] This whole process of precipitating non-economic ideals leads to nihilism. This concept, signifying an exchange of the experience of reality for the experience of emptiness – and thus the conviction that nothing matters anymore – was taken from Nietzsche. In *Economic Ideals* More readily agrees with Nietzsche's diagnosis that, first, the "scientific interpretation of the world" renders the world fundamentally senseless; second, that modern morality is rooted in the "tyranny of fear."[119] *As we contemplate the world converted into a huge machine and managed by engineers, we gradually grow aware of its lack of meaning, of its emptiness of human value; the soul is stifled in this glorification of mechanical efficiency. And then we begin to feel the weakness of such a creed* (that is, subordination to efficiency) *when confronted by the real problems of life; we discover its inability to impose any restraint on the passions of*

---

118 Ibid., p. 248.
119 Cf. F. Nietzsche, *The Gay Science,* trans. W. Kaufmann, New York 1974, fragment 373, pp. 334-36; id., *The Dawn of Day,* trans. J. M. Kennedy, London 1911, fragment 174, pp. 177–78.

men, or to supply any government which can appeal to the loyalty of the spirit.[120] This means – no more, no less – that the humanitarian space for the spirit is a space for fear. Or, to be more precise, fear of what others are preparing for us. The fear of man is the great mystery of faith in humanity.

The hegemony of economic ideals introduces a necessary, irremovable division into the somewhat satisfied and somewhat unsatisfied. Excited by the given prospect of expansion, we only see the plane and nothing else, no way up. This plane does not turn out to be – because it cannot be – a plane of "peaceful coexistence," but rather a continuous, hopeless confrontation in which both sides, though differently situated, are equally located at the bottom of humanity. *Fear – there has been, and is, a great fear at the heart of the world. Among the proletariat it is the fear, not wholly unjustified, of being exploited as mere inhuman cogs in a machine; for what, they have asked themselves, has scientific evolution to do with the heart and spirit or with human hopes and joys and regrets? And so the proletariat has banded itself together as a fighting army against its exploiters (...) it may ruin society; it can build up nothing. On the other side, among the intelligent and successful, this fear has taken the form of humanitarian repentance; it has reared a morality of sympathy and sops in place of obligation and command. Humanitarianism (...) is merely an intellectual disguise for the social instinct of fear; the attempt to keep men in subordination by kind words. There is no doubt of the fact. This instinctive fear has been troubling the organizers and masters of society for many years.*[121]

In his argumentation, More refers to the class (and national) conflicts of the first decades of the twentieth century, which may seem distant to us. At least here in Europe, we live in conditions of peace and prosperity, and the rest of the world, in general, envies our problems. The difference between a Pole and a German, say – if viewed from the level of the realization of economic ideals – may seem insignificant in the eyes of most Africans or Asians.

120 P. E. More, *Economic Ideals...*, p. 249.
121 Ibid., pp. 251–52.

Un-Economic Ideals

In their "proletarian" imaginations, we can appear as representatives of a distant caste of administrators, inspiring fear for as long as anyone can remember... and deserving of fear. There is no need to write about the phenomenon of terrorism here, as it is self-explanatory. Let us, however, pay attention to the contexts that were less obvious in More's time. First of all, for over 70 years, our fear has ballooned to the size of an atomic mushroom. Access to weapons of mass destruction shifts particular political creations to the level of gameplay, neatly dubbed "strategic," the possible effects of which are unimaginable. Maintaining a balance between the expanding "players" is therefore imperative for survival. In such a system, the security guarantees *ultimately* count – that there will be *some* tomorrow. Moral judgments fit here like grandma's glasses fit in a slaughterhouse. Critical judgments of political life, based on vertical thinking or questions about the good, encounter a void.

At the same time, what we consider to be the development of civilization, increases particularism and intensifies fear daily. Sure, there were always battles for fields and bays, trade routes and ports. But the more modern the economy, the greater the appetite and determination to access all sorts of resources – fossil fuels, metals, and even water. If you want electricity to flow through your outlets, have no mercy! It was safer, sure, to breed camels than to develop the automotive industry, especially when we're dealing with an insane winding up of the supply and demand for cars (or anything that requires the use of technology). The more needs you find within yourself, and the more ready you are to get into debt to satisfy them, the better – business is running. Shouldn't we still call this insanity? Maybe we should, but we fear the consequences. Fear inevitably reverberates in us whenever we allow ourselves to stand a bit to the side and watch this cycle of changes, successive "revolutions," "generations," and plans for which the background consists in upcoming conflicts and terror. That's why, let's face it, we don't like seeing things as they are. In protecting ourselves from fear, we choose a make-believe life. We live amidst empty words, embedded within the canons of *political correctness* (in one version or another), re-signed to the fact that obtuseness reigns. We move during the course of our thoughtless consumption, focused on scraps – where are we compared to the greats of this world, where are they compared to us? – and wanting only to secure our "rights": to life, to a pension, etc. All this, horror of horrors, fits perfectly within the mental constructs – or, earlier, the trajectories of the imagination – that modern dualism provides. This is because, according to the latter's naturalistic premises, he meets the need to trust one's instincts, and our fear is an instinctive feeling. The "old" dualism, as long as it is not dragged into this framework and not "converted," cannot be treated seriously. How can we go about spiritual ascents when we have to work to pay off our loans? It would be a nightmare to be auctioned off! Truth be told, we have little interest in a good life; we want to live life – simply. Isn't that why we are managed so easily?

What does More think about all this? It seems that the answer he formulated concerning "man's fear of man" should be regarded as an indispensable key to the political interpretation of humanism: *that fear we shall not eliminate by more scientific efficiency; we shall not eliminate it by any means, but we may possibly change its direction and its object.* Obviously, fear as such is not anything unusual; it is a part of human nature. We have good reason to be afraid. *Everywhere about us are unseen forces which, at a moment and without warning, may leap upon us out of the darkness.* It doesn't matter if we imagine another person or a force or a bacterium in this role. The true lesson of pre-modern thought concerns something else: the separation of what is random and what is divine. *Man cannot imagine himself in a world of immoral chance or unmeaning change; if he reflects at all he is driven to translate the devious work of fate into a law of retributive justice.* In other words, the fear of what lurks around the corner disappears in the face of fear of the gods, and finally – of God. It is impossible to escape His judgments – intentional judgments. *The wrath of a celestial Judge we may have reasoned or laughed away, but it does not follow that we have argued ourselves out of the ancient dread; we have merely brought down fear*

Un-Economic Ideals

from heaven to earth, giving to sociology what we have taken from religion.[122]

If the fundamental problem lies in the modern secularization of fear, then the only reasonable response would be to reverse this state of affairs. In a broader sense – which we will try to highlight in the last essay – this entails a re-sacramentalization of life. Contrary to appearances, this position does not force one to seek a relationship with the Church (or any existing religious denomination), so it would be a misunderstanding to put it in the drawer of "political theology." Instead, we should talk about a nemetic (from the word *Nemesis*) theory of politics. The most important part of this approach is its perception of the law, which *speaks to the heart of a man and holds him individually responsible for his acts.* This law does not differentiate people in terms of their effectiveness in achieving and maintaining material status. It does not allow for the depreciation of non-economic ideals. However, it also does not seek to negate what most of society generally lives on. More states: *Even he who, to those absorbed in business, seems to have withdrawn into the contemplation of ideas as into a harbour of refuge, may have found a certain value in life itself which it were good for the world to understand. But at least, whether for the scholar or for the man of affairs, it looks as if, first of all, we needed somehow or other to get the fear of God back into society.*[123]

Just as it is not about one possible confession, it is not about a merely particular good. The attempt to "restore the fear of God in society" does not determine support for any particular form of political system, let alone a specific political party. We are not to create, say, a new version of the hierocracy or establish a party of vengeful priests. Nevertheless, the hint More gives reveals very practical consequences if we read it as marking the level at which it is worthwhile and necessary to make assessments here and now in the field of politics (and in areas related to politics). That default measure by no means grants consent to preserve the remains

---

122 Ibid., pp. 252–54.
123 Ibid., pp. 255–56. Cf. id., *Church and Politics...*, pp. 156–58; id., *Oxford, Women, and God* [in:] id., *A New England...*, especially pp. 284–85, 287.

of a pre-modern civilization, a reference to the old aristocratic ethos, or even an attitude towards the legacy of the churches. The measure of our judgment will be nothing but the ability to manage fear. Whoever has possessed the competence to do so must first have consciously attained the ability to control their fears. What previously served the realization of economic ideals will now be used to regain the horizon of the human spirit that extends beyond the plane of expansion and wealth acquisition and distribution. Otherwise, unfortunately, no spiritual "athletes" capable of taking over and managing a truly post-modern era will appear – and Bacon's "machinery" will remain in the hands of the "cosmic loafers," the children of Rousseau. Like More, Irving Babbitt – seeking an "equivalent of grace" in Buddhist "psychology" rather than in Christian thought – had no illusions about the primacy of economics over politics. *A world of frenzied producers requires as its complement a world of frenzied consumers. The expert in advertising has been gravely praised of late for making two desires grow where only one grew before. The extirpation of desire in the Buddhist sense, or even the limitation of desire in the humanistic sense, would plainly be injurious to trade.*[124] More's attempt at managing fear allows us to face both what in practice makes humanism a position that is politically hopeless and what constitutes a real bastion of the imagination of a man who grew up on a diet of the fruits of faith in humanity. Along with this unpleasant procedure – a descent into the cave of modernity – humanistic realism, in its understanding of human nature, becomes political realism in the most appropriate sense of the term.

VI.

Let's complete the critique of modern thinking about politics outlined above with a few remarks. First, since non-economic ideals should be associated with religious and humanist experiences, the key task must be to describe these experiences from a political

124 I. Babbitt, *Buddha and the Occident (Part II)*..., pp. 84–85.

Un-Economic Ideals

point of view. The issue of religion itself requires a separate discussion. For now, it is enough to emphasize that a religion conceived – or reconstructed – in the spirit of humanism cannot serve to justify moral indifference and the abandonment of work on an individual's character. The non-worldly ideal of contemplation should, in a significant sense, correspond to the ideals of this world: giving them a vertical dimension, refining them, limiting the hegemony of expansion. Unreserved asceticism, with mortification of the body and a refusal to participate in worldly affairs, undoubtedly acts on the imagination, but this action is quite ambivalent because – in More's view – it consists in an attempt to *attain the mystical release by violence rather than by the gradual discipline of philosophy and morality*.[125] This kind of religious experience could prove to be not only useless, but even harmful, leading to a negation of all righteousness (how can I be bound by earthly laws when my heart is devoted to God and Him alone – hands off, gentlemen!). We should also note that the ideal of the "hard" ascetic can be understood as the economic ideal *à rebours*. The total negation of inherent expansiveness directed at material goods betrays the surrender to a desire, no less expansive, to consume – *hic et nunc* – the desire to overcome one's nature. Simply put, according to humanists, the key is not to deny everything material, just not to take it seriously. Better yet, to take all goods seriously as far as they matter to the soul – a soul that, nonetheless, cannot be thought of in isolation from the world.

When we look at philosophers as natural representatives of *vita contemplativa*, putting up, so to speak, signposts of humanistic experience, a paradox of similar measure appears to our eyes. On the one hand, there is a fundamental tension between philosophy and politics; on the other, philosophers' complete isolation from political reality seems to be a sign of decadence. There are stories, some of them hilarious, about people immersed in philosophical discourse, who, wanting to give the world even a bit of the wisdom they have gained, take to practical issues of, say, manage-

125 P. E. More, *Definitions of Dualism...*, p. 293.

HUMANISM AS REALISM

ment, consider their actions exemplary – and fail miserably.[126] Someone may say that such anecdotes describe intellectual clowns and buffoons rather than true philosophers. However, the unfortunate case of none other than Plato comes to the aid of the doubting. Contrary to many school "narratives," he left a very skeptical opinion about serious involvement in politics. His famous "ideal state" (a *polis* ruled by a philosopher-king) is *literally* an ideal state and therefore does not and cannot exist. In the real world, within particular political communities, people who love truth *have also come to understand the madness of the multitude sufficiently and have seen that there is nothing, if I may say so, sound or right in any present politics, and that there is no ally with whose aid the champion of justice could escape destruction, but that he would be as a man who has fallen among wild beasts, unwilling to share their misdeeds and unable to hold out singly against the savagery of all, and that he would thus, before he could in any way benefit his friends or the state come to an untimely end without doing any good to himself or others, — for all these reasons I say the philosopher remains quiet, minds his own affairs, and, as it were, standing aside under shelter of a wall in a storm and blast of dust and sleet and seeing others filled full of lawlessness, is content if in any way he may keep himself free from iniquity and unholy deeds through this life and take his departure with fair hope, serene and well content when the end comes.*[127] The tension between the philosopher and the city inevitably results from the clash between the universality of the good (what is "sound or right"), which is the object of philosophical contemplation, and the particularity of opinions that set the horizon of political life. To put it simply, the philosopher has far more important matters on his mind than those his fellow citizens are concerned with – and it is better for him that these fellow citizens do not fully realize this. There is no such thing as too much realism.

It's easy for interpretations to miss the mark here, though. Socrates could have refrained from making a political career, but

126 Cf. id., *Emerson* [in:] id., *A New England...*, pp. 90–93.
127 Plato, *Republic*, 496 C–E, p. 200. Cf. P. E. More, *Platonism...*, p. 286 ff.

Un-Economic Ideals

he was involved in wars and feasts; he was not a hermit, he fulfilled his civic duties, and – above all – he talked with the city's inhabitants. The latter ultimately took his life, but his death was neither premature nor senseless. We can generalize Socrates' testimony by stating that philosophy – like everything human – emerges in loneliness, detached from the world of opinion. Is one not wise in confrontation with stupidity? What is leaving the cave worth without experiencing that cave? It is certainly no great achievement for a philosopher to *hypnotize himself into empty dreams of his own wisdom.*[128] Perhaps the secret behind this dilemma lies precisely in the fact that it is unsolvable,[129] and philosophers simply like to think most about what concerns themselves.

Secondly, let us look at the practical consequences of the implied advantage of the philosophical life over the political life. Not many thoughts affect our well-being as much as ones placing us into the narrow category of "the enlightened" – or at least of those who have successfully entered onto the path of enlightenment, who look down on the ignorant masses with superiority. In this way, the generally recognized division into the less and more satisfied or, simply, the poor and the rich can be replaced by a less obvious but equally un-humanistic division into those who consider themselves philosophers and those who do not know that it is worth considering themselves philosophers. One of the most significant attempts to revive the Socratic tradition in the twentieth century ends, as Stanley Rosen picturesquely describes it, with the emergence of *infantry troops consisting of those who would believe themselves to be gods merely by their proximity to the revelation of an unrevealed and justifying doctrine.*[130] The intellectual sectarianism of the elites is horrendous for humanists, whose teaching, as we know, is "psychological," not "sociological." We can jokingly point out that the very structure of the word "sociology" contains a difficulty resulting from the creation of a dubious hybrid. This makes

128 P. E. More, *The Paradox of Oxford...*, p. 76.
129 Cf. A. H. Dakin, *Paul Elmer More...*, p. 169.
130 S. Rosen, *Hermeneutics as politics...*, p. 125.

the effects of linking a classical apology of the *vita contemplativa* with modern intellectuals' justification of their life aspirations or position all the more significant. And whatever we have established concerning the issue of "opinion management," it does not mean that we want to "philosophically" segregate humanity. Humanity passionately segregates itself, without the participation of adepts of philosophy, and no "story" about withdrawn elites and frisky commoners should serve to hide this fundamental truth: that the most critical divide runs not outside, but *inside* the soul. My soul.

Thirdly, there is no denying that our reflections also contribute to assessing our native (Polish) political thought. The humanistic critique of modernity makes us aware, above all, of the need to recognize the "first principles" or trajectories of the imagination, preceding discursive and non-discursive complexities in the mutual relations of states and societies. Before we dive into reflections on the history and current functioning of ideas, we should first think seriously about what we expect from the world. If More and Babbitt are right in the main points of their diagnosis, then the problem is not that people are getting richer, but that they believe in wealth; not that they want to expand at the expense of others, but that their expansion seems arbitrary and unpunished, because their ideas about themselves do not reach beyond the plane of economic ideals. Why not cry, then, that it isn't money that rules the world, but the imagination of people who, seeing one good or possibly a type of good, are unable to see anything beyond it? Imagination, stupid! If imagination is limited to the pursuit of wealth – which in our case usually means "catching up with the West" and buying into the grace of the local managerial elite – it's difficult to talk about real political thought. Perhaps we need a long series of discoveries, whose common denominator will be the conclusion that the direction we are heading in is our *choice* rather than the necessary result of some beneficial (mega-)processes; processes that would encompass us more or less in the sense that the vast Milky Way galaxy encompasses the peripheral reference system called the Solar System. Among desirable

Un-Economic Ideals

discoveries, there will be ones that we can simply owe to reading the humanists. At the very least the fact that the plane of economic ideals is an experimental plane based on certain assumptions and predictions, justified or not. We must learn to see and comprehend the gap between the world shaped by classical and – especially – Christian thought and the world we know today. Having understood this, we must overcome this gap and its effects. How nobly naive our tendency to treat the West – the West of our dreams – as a continuum seems: from Socrates and Christ through subsequent eras to a united Europe without borders. No. Recognizing the benefits of the present situation, we must never forget that this is a trade-off. Societies richer than ours, or considered more structured, are not at all better in this respect. On the contrary.

Fourth and finally, the title of this essay is very problematic. The term "ideal" used in reference to religious salvation or philosophical happiness or justice is formally correct. However, More's remark against those who would like to live "as if" Christianity was real is thought-provoking at a deeper level. Their *attempt has taken the form of an Hegelian substitution of ideals for Ideas, of what we should like to be true for what we believe actually to be true.*[131] It is impossible to escape from reflection on how far we have departed from the natural – unmediated by modern thought – experience of reality, from being simultaneously open to being as a whole and responsible for ourselves; to living fully and seriously. Meanwhile, apart from everything else, we're used to being patronized. And this carries with it far-reaching cognitive consequences. Our "realisms" are narrow and imperfect. After all, true political realism must correspond to a proper understanding of human nature. Otherwise, chimerical views, futile intellectual games, and performances calculated to gain the applause of a wide audience are born. The most important findings do not result from the presentation of technical or expert knowledge, but from human efforts to judge the here-and-now from the perspective of what is eternal.

131 P. E. More, *Christ of the New Testament*, Princeton 1924, p. 294.

Reaching this level – to the extent that we are able –we find that economic ideals, which are ideals of expansion, are *solely* particular in nature. For this reason, all faith deposited in institutions created to get rich and gain an advantage over others turns out to be deceptive faith. There is no salvation on the side of expansion, because salvation is not on the side of natural necessity. That kind of offer comes from Someone completely different. *Peace I leave with you, My peace I give to you; not as the world gives do I give to you. Let not your heart be troubled, neither let it be afraid.* (J 14:27). Non-economic ideals – keeping with this term, since it is useful to us for the time being – are universal. Not confusing these two areas is a necessary condition of good politics.

THE ANCIENT MIRROR OF THEOLOGY

I.

Tell me who your God is, and I will tell you who you are. For centuries, humankind has defined its goals by drawing on the fruits of religious experience. This experience, broadly understood, laid the foundations for any significant ideas people could have about themselves. That doesn't mean that all lumberjacks and water carriers contemplated the order of ultimate affairs on a daily basis (although there were sometimes almost overwhelming eruptions of piety). In any case, a horizon of life emerged out of this order – the only true horizon, destined for everyone, which we can gaze at for as long as we wish and at will, facing God's plan or the Law that comes from Him and drawing confidence from the examples given by both saints and non-saints, who nonetheless peacefully fell asleep in the Lord's bosom. A life lived in this way was characterized by a certain spiritual progress or dynamism. Of course, a person could step backward or tread in place; indeed, great communities and entire nations fell into corruption and numbness. However, whatever was done was within the frame of reference provided by religion. The image of possible perfection and its complete contradiction burst into people's minds, definitively expressed in one or another formula of Revelation, superhuman knowledge, prophecy. What gave meaning to moral works – work on oneself, efforts to become better – simultaneously gave reasons to think, generating intellectual works of the highest order, constituting a distant (from our point of view) legacy of Christians, Jews, Muslims, Hindus, and others. Therefore, religious experience was also the experience of philosophers or humanists, who took seriously the needs of a faith that "seeks understanding." The divine was associated with discovering the sources of a rational judgment of experience; religious life – with a philosophical life, a life for the truth; *for as our idea of God is, so do we tend to become.*[1]

All this now smacks of an old fairy tale. Our leaders have long spoken with a different voice. Traditional religion, filled with the vision of a predetermined order and responsibility, gives the impression of having been beaten and discredited by the Enlightenment. The effect of this discrediting, usually referred to as societies' secularization or laicization, can be extended over time and have an unequal impact – like any wave, it can recede and build up. Nevertheless, the general rejection of the old forms of religious life, be it in favor of professed atheism or some version of private "spirituality," appears as an evident and irreversible change in the Western world. It seems impossible to be simultaneously educated, career-oriented, and pious – if the latter is to be anything more than a slightly embarrassing hobby after hours. Sure, the situation differs in different environments, professional groups, and geographic regions. Like the rest of the world, the provinces lag behind the metropolis. But merely, behind! And it's impossible not to move forward – with progress, modernity, development, integration, however. What was good in the past can be discarded, or, if you prefer, adapted, assimilated, distilled, and ultimately safely used to produce new, attractive "goods" for the "marketplace of ideas." The bad things – superstition, the Middle Ages, and claims to eternity – must disappear sooner or later; this disappearance should be assisted here and now in various ways, including by the force of the law. Today, any self-respecting citizen could, if they so chose, shout boldly and with conviction the slogan of nineteenth-century anarchists: *ni dieu ni maître*! An equally strong declaration of adherence to biblical or ecclesiastical tradition would probably cause unpleasant repercussions for them. Well, hardly anyone feels called to be a martyr; we have children and loans. Therefore, the most reasonable attitude seems

1   P. E. More, *Christ the Word*, Princeton 1927, p. 74.

The Ancient Mirror of Theology

to be one that calmly accepts the view that the general direction of this secularization or laicization is good because it frees us from irrational divisions and dependencies, thus increasing the scope of reason so that we will all be wiser in the end.

Unfortunately (or fortunately), we cannot take this opinion too seriously. Its roots lie in certain intellectual claims and the resulting ideas about nature and history, ideas that are not self-evident. As a result of the inherited hegemony of peculiar mental constructs, we become victims of long-term perception distortion. Those who believe that late modern humankind – "our" humanity – having passed the transnational school of enlightenment, are a collection of beings incomparably more rational and therefore less religious than our ancestors, understand nothing of the political and economic reality surrounding them. On the one hand – the Dark Ages, burning piles and the slaughter of infidels; on the other, generally accessible culture and universal education (complaining about the various problems with these and other "problem areas," many will say that they do not intend to go back to the Middle Ages), which are backed by incredible achievements of science and the benefits of technology. But, dear parishioners, a lot has changed since Blake's priest could drag a child off to be burned alive for using reason to judge the "holy mystery"! Much has changed – a doubting person would reply – but do we really comprehend the meaning and consequences of those transformations? Perhaps here in the West, we are dealing not so much with the abandonment of particular denominations and freeing of ourselves from the power of oppressive authorities, but with the negation of the old faith and old authorities in the name of something new, which in itself is by no means guaranteed by reason (and does not avoid the argument of strength). Nature abhors a vacuum. Maybe new believers will come in place of the countless past and present generations of believers. A hundred years ago, a thousand years ago, yesterday and today, very few people could reasonably question beliefs. No, not other people's beliefs, that isn't difficult, but their own! And it is also possible to believe that you are a "liberal ironist" or a non-confessional skeptic. It is possible to believe that you don't believe in anything: *ni dieu ni maître.*

Meanwhile, if we do not differ much from our ancestors when it comes to the needs of faith and submission, if we share the same human nature with them, then we should still view ourselves in the mirror of religion as they did; the challenge is to apply that mirror skillfully. Let us call Saint Augustine to the witness stand. In *De Civitate Dei*, a work conceived as a defense of Christianity against accusations of bringing about the political collapse of Rome, he conducts a critical analysis of the division of theology in the version proposed several centuries earlier by the eminent pagan author Marcus Terentius Varro.[2] Here, the word "theology" does not refer to a specialized field of study at specific types of universities. Instead, it refers to a way of representing the divine, to the presence of religious experience in general, to its impact in a life lived according to one model or another, in the company of other people. First, we have mythical (fabulous) theology entrusted to the work of poets who, with the help of tools offered by the theater of the time (public performances), laid out the winding paths of the masses' imagination. Next, there is natural theology, which can be reduced to philosophers' deliberations on the nature of the world (where various functions are assigned to gods or God), thus more or less corresponding to the ancient mode of practicing "physics" and "metaphysics." Finally, there is state or city theology, that is, a cult organized by the authorities that requires the subordination of citizens based on the veneration of deities important to a given political community. In the pre-Christian approach that Augustine criticizes, the first and third kinds of theology intertwine and ultimately identify with one another. Varro may scold the poets for their idiosyncrasies or for sowing the grotesque, but he realizes that the difference between the gods of the city and the gods on stage is a difference in the degree of seriousness; we need entertainment alongside our

2   See St. Augustine, The City of God, vol. 1, trans. John Healey, J. M. Dent & Sons, Ltd., 1947, Book VI, Chapter X, p. 194 ff.

The Ancient Mirror of Theology

solemn principles. Therefore, theater, run better or worse, is a product of political life. On the other hand, philosophers should remain aloof, with their barely comprehensible debates and ambiguity in their decisions on matters of the utmost importance. From the perspective of the "higher minds," everything that non-philosophers focus on – those content with "experiencing" opinions, seeking only confirmations for their emotional choices, indolent in knowing the truth – exhibits features of both fabulous theology and political theology.

How is it with us? It seems to be the case that all three theologies, though subject to changes in the imagination, accompany us equally (or more) intensely, while simultaneously eliminating clear, useful formulas of the present state of affairs from our consciousness. This is especially true of political theology.[3] For, while the Western perception of the relationship between religion and politics in the Muslim world has sharpened – under the influence of growing concerns about security, the more profound insight into the situation in one's own backyard, to put it mildly, leaves much to be desired.[4] Slowly, we are beginning to realize that all in all, traditional religion has lost its power over souls; it is much harder to explore the supposed void left by Christianity. This is partly because the dynamic processes of secularization or laicization have not just barely begun but have been going on for centuries. It is also because what takes the place of the former religious authority today could, for most of that time, develop and coexist with this authority, get along with it, support and strengthen one another. Either way, our trouble with understanding political theology stems primarily from the modern belief that faith is to be a private, even intimate matter, like the secrets of an alcove. It is worth remembering that the unique experience of

---

3   Cf. P. Armada, *O znaczeniu i problematyczności teologii politycznej,* "Horyzonty Polityki," no. 3(4) / 2012, pp. 21–41.

4   Cf. M. Lilla, *The Stillborn God: Religion, Politics, and the Modern West,* New York 2007, pp. 11, 15, 310; P. Valadier, *Détresse du politique, force du religieux,* Paris 2007, pp. 6, 24 ff.

Christendom itself, consisting, among other things, in the separation of the religious and secular spheres, also distances us from the sober optics of the witnesses of antiquity, whether we like it or not.

Let us try to formulate this issue in the simplest way possible. In the classic medieval model of Christendom, we have two centers of authority between which there is a relative, though uneasy balance: the power over souls (and therefore some practical competencies regarding, for example, getting married) belongs to the Church; to the state (or a secular lord) – the use of a sword, of physical coercion, demonstrations of strength; all for the defense of Christians. When the red line of atrophy of church authority is crossed, the authority of the political ruler takes all. Of course, we cannot associate this level of reflection with ad hoc surveys, such as "what professions citizens value most or least," where the profession of (democratic) politician tends to receive relatively poor results. We should, however, direct our attention to the state as such, with its attribute of sovereignty manifesting itself in the potential for coercion, used to enforce loyalty in a given area and simultaneously to implement any regulations. The modern sovereign, the source of all law, corresponds to the almighty God; this does not make him the *ex nihilo* creator of the world or the steward of miracles in the bosom of nature (unless using technology), but provides unprecedented opportunities – from the point of view of ancient rulers – to shape human fate and opinions about the world.[5] This powerful political creation develops its own interpretation and symbolism, which constitute the material of a state cult of unequal weight and intensity (it is enough to look at the celebrations of national holidays in different countries), which, as a rule, cannot be questioned. Further, most of what we would call political orthodoxy, which in its entirety forms the proper – orthodox – shape of public debate, belongs to the field of political theology. Putting aside the problem of the fluctuation

5   Cf. I. Babbitt, *Democracy and Leadership*, Indianapolis 1979, especially pp. 65–67, 83, 362 ff.

The Ancient Mirror of Theology

of meanings ascribed to key concepts of modernity, at least a few words should be considered highly empowered, such as "democracy," "right" (subjective right, in the sense of "I have the right to something") or "progress" (possibly: "development," "modernization"). Democracy, for example, has been described as "liberal" or "popular." Of course, there are good reasons to choose the former over the latter, but it is worth considering why everyone has long wanted to be considered a "democrat." What is it about this specific form of the political system – democracy? Doesn't its status sometimes reach the theological dimension? Reach representations of what is sacred, inviolable, what should not be doubted? Because why should we liberate this or that – "democratize"? Are we faced with an epiphany of perfect order within which everyone decides about everything? Where there is no God and Lord? Still further, specific movements and personalities in political life can achieve practical sanctification or "theologicalization." It doesn't matter whether we're talking about the communist party, the civil rights movement, Lenin, or Gandhi in this context.

The attributes of the modern nation-state closest to us, the people of the European West, have been redefined based on the tragic experiences of the first half of the last century. Constitutional provisions protect us from being immersed in war and scarcity; there must not be room for more upward mobility for psychopaths. The present-day framework of political orthodoxy includes the established norms of the *welfare state* or the "social market economy," but also a multitude of postulates concerning the sphere of customs and individual morality, which are assessed through the prism of the mysterious vision of an emancipated human being. Persistently going against this vision leads to the "fight against exclusion," the "equalization of opportunities," and the like. Achievements in this area – the effective implementation of appropriate legal acts, sanctioned by coercion – can easily be considered the next stages on the path to all-encompassing development or progress. We could not enter on this path without first giving up the traditional forms of religious life. Hence so many active followers of "political correctness," fighting "hate speech," and wanting, in various ways, to finish off the Christian dragon. On the other hand, we have the new "generations" of human rights ... and the free trade imperative.

So-called secularization can make money – and allow people to indulge themselves emotionally – by proposing new forms of "spiritual" experiences. It is not only about groups commonly recognized as sects, although they also happen to be growing in strength. The ancient concept of mythical theology allows us to look critically – from its foundation – at what seems as obvious to us as the air we breathe: mass culture and entertainment. This topic is too broad for us to attempt to describe. There is no need to discuss the proper functions of the radio, television, or cinema here. We will leave it to the reader's imagination to choose examples of myth-making flair and pressure on reason from the overwhelming selection in pop music, video games, or sports. It is probably enough to suggest the following exercise of the imagination: let us put ourselves for a moment in the central nave of a medieval cathedral, gazing at the rays piercing the stained-glass windows and listening to the dramatic chanting. Then, let's go straight to the dance floor of a modern disco club. Where does the traditional liturgy stand compared to this intensity of experience! Where are the emotions of the past compared to such a concentration of emotions! That we have gotten used to it? Certainly – but what does that mean? That we are less prone to external control of our thoughts – through our sensory impressions and related feelings? Or, on the contrary, more exposed to unreasonable machinations? And isn't it the case, in the end, that from this terrible confusion of images and sounds – for which, by the way, they make us pay! – a modern eschatological horizon is emerging, which, however different from the old way of understanding the ultimate questions, turns out to be equally based on faith or requiring faith?

When considering this, it is worth making an important caveat. Many of us would prefer to relate this type of reflection to the fortunately distant legacy of twentieth-century totalitarian regimes. It was there that, in addition to the enormity of crimes

The Ancient Mirror of Theology

and wickedness, we had to deal with the accumulated transmission of narrowly understood orthodoxy, the deification of leaders, and the celebration of party congresses as if they were monstrous liturgies. Above all, we had visions of a fight for a better future and of a better future itself imposed. We also had a fairly large tribe of intellectuals whose defense of the new faith must have been associated with what had long been branded as pre-Enlightenment Christian fanaticism. Bearing in mind these experiences and not wanting to gloom-monger, should we not agree with the opinion expressed succinctly by American sociologist Peter Berger, that *by contrast with the mythopoetic productivity of socialism, capitalism is and always has been mythically deprived*?[6] In other words, does the free market not invalidate the theological-mythical "narrative," since it successfully functions without the latter? Not necessarily. Perhaps, looking from the present distance, one should distinguish the failed, brutal, grotesque forms of modern theology from its effective forms. Did the West not overcome the socialist camp, perhaps in part thanks to the supply of myths that eventually captured the imaginations of people doomed to a gray life in an inefficient system? Thanks to its movies, television series, music scene? Therefore, did it not display a greater ability to generate and maintain faith in the fulfillment of economic ideals? Finally, isn't the famous "invisible hand of the market" also a myth built on the assumption of a "natural" harmony of human needs and self-interested activities to satisfy them?

It seems that the fundamental relationship between mythical theology and political theology is no different than it was in ancient times. The old "theater" was contained in the "city" (*polis, civitas*) – and it has remained so; various "fairy-tales" serve the "state"; they serve it on many levels, through a multitude of institutional solutions. On the other hand, the problem of natural theology is presented differently. Of course, we could say that today, the speculations of the former philosophical schools correspond to the more well-established and more certain findings

6   P. L. Berger, *The Capitalist Revolution*, Basic Books, Inc., 1986, p. 205.

of modern science. A scientific experiment has created technology thanks to which our repositories of information about the Universe, simply put, beat the possibilities of accumulating knowledge that our ancestors had at their disposal. After all, if we look at it from a slightly broader perspective, it turns out that departing from philosophy as an occupation essentially separate from ordinary human activity, that is, in a way, haughtily independent, comes at a price. Somewhat paradoxically, a science born of philosophy resembles theater; it is politicized, taken over by the city. Enjoying the unprecedented achievements in the conquest of nature, it simultaneously becomes an inexhaustible source of scientific myths (or para-scientific myths along the lines of interstellar travel or bioenergy therapy). Above all, it becomes part of the political offer and an object of consumption. Leo Strauss sums it up perfectly: our *philosophy or science was no longer an end in itself, but in the service of human power, of a power to be used for making human life longer, healthier, and more abundant. The economy of scarcity, which is the tacit presupposition of all earlier social thought, was to be replaced by an economy of plenty. The radical distinction between science and manual labor was to be replaced by the smooth co-operation of the scientist and the engineer (...) in order to become the willing recipients of the new gifts, the people had to be enlightened. This enlightenment is the core of the new education (...) the enlightenment was destined to become universal enlightenment (...) while invention or discovery continued to remain the preserve of the few, the results could be transmitted to all (...) what study did not do, and perhaps could not do, trade did: immensely facilitated and encouraged by the new inventions and discoveries, trade which unites all peoples, took precedence over religion, which divides the peoples.*[7]

Exactly! Where is the room for religion in its "normal" form? One that appeals to God and Revelation? One with real temples and people who really pray? It is hard not to notice that, having picked up an ancient mirror, we see a world full of faith and sub-

7   L. Strauss, "Liberal Education and Responsibility" [in:] *Liberalism Ancient and Modern*, University of Chicago Press, 1995, p. 20.

The Ancient Mirror of Theology

mission, but it is not faith in the Creator and submission to His judgments, but rather faith in humanity (reduced in practice to a small segment of humanity, to particular projects, economic ideals) and the subordination, internally and externally, to emotional expansion. We discussed this modern religion, briefly known as "humanitarianism," quite a bit in the two previous essays. Therefore, our theologies express the reality created for us by the humanitarian use of city resources, theater, and philosophy. But what about the pre-modern tradition, which, although weakened and fought against so much, is not entirely dead? Yes, one should not doubt that here and now, we have a chance to meet people who more than fulfill the old criteria of piety. However, let us not be under any illusions – they are not shaping the face of the earth. Meanwhile, an important feature of modern thinking is the ability to suck in traditional religious and humanistic threads to use them in constructing a "flat" vision of ultimate affairs. Anyone who cares to can describe this process as utilizing existing beliefs, myths, attitudes, or forms of behavior. Defenders of tradition do not necessarily want this, but they sometimes fuel the transformation process literally in good faith. As a rule, ancient records of the Revelation or testimonies of spiritual development are considered difficult to access or even repulsive to younger generations. The whole of the ancient "narrative" supposedly requires refreshing, modernizing, an attempt to make it more appealing. As a result of unsuccessful attempts to (*de facto*) "humanize" Christianity, the faithful lose awareness of the actual direction and meaning of their faith, and generally associated Christian motives begin to function as a capital contribution to the global investment called "modernity." The unsolvable problem lies in the fact that a premise of humanitarianism remains the acceptance of natural man, not oriented towards "vertical" relations with God or Being desired by the mortal soul, but towards the "horizontal" satisfaction of fleshly desires. These are two separate worlds, not to say – the universe of human thought. A humanitarian will gladly take advantage of a Christian, but not marry him or her; in tradition, the humanitarian sees what he

Humanism as Realism

needs for his purposes, nothing more. *But when the Pharisees had heard that he had put the Sadducees to silence, they were gathered together. Then one of them, which was a lawyer, asked him a question, tempting him, and saying, Master, which is the great commandment in the law? Jesus said unto him, Thou shalt love the Lord thy God with all thy heart, and with all thy soul, and with all thy mind. This is the first and great commandment. And the second is like unto it, Thou shalt love thy neighbour as thyself. On these two commandments hang all the law and the prophets.* (Mathew 22:34–40). It is enough to neutralize one's love for God, to suggest the innocence of a man who loves, and things get quite pleasant, don't they?

Christianity's susceptibility to "humanitarianization" must give pause for thought, especially since we are no longer witnessing a crisis, but the outright disappearance of religious practices. This is sometimes the result of direct efforts to "atheize" (de-Christianize) the state and violence by the state apparatus, which of course took place in countries ruled by communist parties (the French Revolution was a much older, and perhaps less contemplated precedent). At the same time, the tragedy of the Christian faith is that, in the absence of identification of the religious and political spheres, it can function as an "asymptomatic" religion. In other words, you can ask yourself if you want to be a Christian all your life, weigh it in your conscience, wait for signs, try to force your mind, and it still won't matter, since Jesus will take you to Himself anyway, because He loves you, as well as all people, and he knows that your heart desires the salvation of your soul, that you have enough disgust with evil and contempt for sin, even if they were invisible. This kind of not-overly-serious, but legitimate from the point of view of an individual, interpretation of religious experience fits perfectly into the general attitude of a modern consumer, a representative of, as sociologists wisely define it, "selective religiosity." For him, what he grasps from the experience of piety has mainly an emotional and temporary, sometimes merely relaxing value. It is on this ground, that of mythical theology, that perverse, extreme attempts to "utilize" Christianity arise from within. It is easy to see how successful

The Ancient Mirror of Theology

Pentecostalism is today and how similarly inspired movements of nominal Catholicism are. There appears – not necessarily out of ill will – the expectation that a religious service will resemble a rock concert or a smoky disco rather than a humanly sublime celebration, requiring at least a certain amount of self-control and focus on what is beyond us and irreducible to the noisy spectacle of emotional self-expression of those gathered. We thus receive "organized praise of our human nature"[8] – and nothing more. The new religion of humankind devours the religion of the revealed God. The priest becomes a jester.

Comparing this post-Christian solution with what appears against this backdrop as a crystal of faith of Muhammad's followers also requires reflection. While you can be a Muslim in various ways, you cannot be "asymptomatic." Religion oriented towards rigor in observing God's law, as is Islam, does not know, in principle, the aporia of faith that discourages us from living in this world and is thus doomed to dangerous conditions of coexistence with the authorities of this world.[9] For Christians, religious experience is almost on the verge of political experience: *Then saith he unto them, Render therefore unto Caesar the things which are Caesar's; and unto God the things that are God's* (Matthew 22:21). The most important thing is happening within the depths of the soul. Behavioral regulation is secondary. Therefore, the theological and political dimension of Christianity seems a negative necessity often leading to disastrous compromises (the greatest of them, in the form of fratricidal religious wars in the sixteenth and seventeenth centuries, turned out to be a prelude to the new era) and somewhat underestimated at its starting point: *For here have we no continuing city, but we seek one to come* (Hebrews 13:14). In turn, Muslims think in terms of a "city" that exists here on earth, not one foretold to exist in the afterlife – and this is their theology.

---

8   Cf. P. E. More, *The New Morality* [in:] id., *Shelburne Essays Ninth Series: Aristocracy and Justice*, Boston–New York 1915, p. 208.

9   Cf. E. Gilson, *Christianity and Philosophy*, trans. R. MacDonald, New York 1939, p. 92.

Moreover, looking from the perspective of the history of civilization, we see that the situation in Islam is the norm, while the experience of a double life within Christianity is a surprising novelty. As French scholar Rémi Brague puts it in a highly apt and suggestive metaphor: *in some animals, the hard parts of the body are on the outside and the soft parts are on the inside. This is referring to crustaceans: their shell protects the soft tissue. But there are also animals where what is hard is inside and what is soft is outside; these are vertebrates whose muscles cover a rigid skeleton. It is dangerous to be a vertebrate because the body is not protected. Most civilizations chose a solution based on crustaceans, hammering themselves into a corset of extremely rigid traditions, rules, codes (...) From the very beginning, Europe has opted for a certain type of man with a backbone, fast, adaptable, but weak. Not only Islamic women wear veils, we also wear them. Our veil is inside, it is our skeleton: morality, honor, kindness, a sense of dignity – according to our will. The problem is that for some time, our civilization has insisted on shedding its own backbone, which it wrongly considers a shell. And that is why it risks resembling a third type of animal: a jellyfish that floats on the waves by submitting to the sea's currents, absorbing everything that passes by and being entirely at the mercy of predators. We understand why the idea of "shelling up" seems attractive to so many people, not just Muslims.*[10]

After all, it would be a complete misunderstanding to view today's Muslims (and other "crustaceans") as non-modern people. The phenomenon of Islamic fundamentalism, which is particularly disturbing in its strength and vitality, should be considered within the context of a reaction to modernity.[11] Confronted with a refusal to accept *his* "secular" values and disloyal attitude to the *modus vivendi* in the West, a post-Christian person

10 R. Brague, *Wtórność Europy (rozmowa z Rémi Brague'm)* [The "Secondariness" of Europe (a conversation with Rémi Brague], trans. Institut Français de Pologne à Varsovie, "Teologia Polityczna," no. 2/2004–2005, pp. 68–69. Translation from the Polish: L. Fretschel.

11 Cf. P. Kłodkowski, *Polityczna misja islamu*, "Teologia Polityczna," no. 2/2004–2005, especially pp. 40–42.

is at first surprised that someone is taking the old religion seriously. However, amazed at this, he will probably be inclined to explain the onslaught of fundamentalists by recalling the medieval disputes between Christianity and Islam as two civilizations. Regardless of how wisely and honestly this distant history is presented, one must remember the limitations – and futility – of an anachronistic approach to theological and political issues. Today, there are no monk-knights or Saracens. Humanitarianism – belief in humanity – reaches the bowels; what is outside is secondary; the same garments may lie similarly on people of dissimilar souls. A devout Muslim always reveals the "symptoms" of his religion; he must obey God immediately, tangibly and visibly, by obeying his law. On the other hand, if the form of human behavior matters rather than the content of conscience, and the uniqueness of God is a function of the singularity of the law, we are faced with a paradox. For, while the very provisions of divine law should be considered non-negotiable, the framework and techniques of its application can be defined, as a consequence of the goal set, in terms of political expansion (as long as this goal does not signify the denunciation of obedience). Perhaps then, the (unintended) contribution of Islam to the "modern experiment" will end up being the otherwise effectively implemented template of a universal legal system, global casuistry? Who knows. Such considerations certainly make sense after we become aware of the political and philosophical distance between us and our ancestors' religions.

II.

It is unfortunate that today, the term "humanists" is used to describe those who unreasonably and unwisely *believe* in the birth of a "rational" society, likely seeing themselves as the avant-garde of a new experience or formula of existence. We do not need to analyze their views. The interested reader will easily be able to find the low-hanging fruits of "secular humanism." They do not arise from the classical approach to human affairs, but from the very center of the mythological turmoil into which the humanitarian religion of modernity drives us. A true humanist, as we know from Paul Elmer More and Irving Babbitt, is one who becomes proficient in the art of mediation. One of the poles of this mediation is pre-human necessity, contained in the nature of everything and revealed through the course of events, circumstances, and situations. The other extreme should not be identified with any goal or system of values; brutally speaking, officers of the SS were also striving for something and encountered resistance, which they had to face. We begin to comprehend the proper sense of humanistic mediation only when we turn to vertical ways of thinking, having rejected our prejudices and corrected our dull senses. To fully realize our humanity, we should look as high as possible; having enumerated the contours of earthly dreams, we then reach the superhuman horizon of religious experience.

The art of humanism is a universal art, not confined to the heritage of Western countries. Nevertheless, there is no doubt that the aforementioned "experiment" of Christendom requires special consideration on the part of those who would like not so much to escape from the world, but to regain the space of humanistic experience – in the conditions of material transformations that this world undergoes and the "sham spirituality" reigning in it. It is also worth thinking about because the tangled paths of humanitarianism seem to emerge from the assumptions of the Middle Ages; that – in many respects – modern faith in humanity is nothing but a parody of the Christian faith. First, however, it is necessary to establish what is at the root, what separates us from the conversion of imaginations carried out in previous centuries. What is *true* faith? Faith that in no way serves the needs of "horizontal" expansion that is so obvious to us? According to More, *it is that faculty of the will, mysterious in its source and inexplicable in its operation, which turns the desire of a man away from contemplating the fitful changes of the world toward an ideal, an empty dream it may be, or a shadow, or a mere name, of peace in absolute changelessness. Reason and logic may have no words to express the ob-*

ject of this desire, but experience is rich with the influence of such an aspiration on human character. To the saints it was that peace of God which passeth all understanding; to the mystics it was figured as the raptures of a celestial love (...) to the ignorant it was the unquestioning trust in those who seemed to them endowed with a grace beyond their untutored comprehension.[12] Already based on the above quote, we can conclude that the humanistic approach to the object of "inverted" desires (by definition, faith would mean – focusing the individual's will on the realization of *precisely these* desires) implies the memory of the effective influence of a handful of the few who, while living in spite of worldly matters, nevertheless constituted living witnesses to the reconciliation of man's limited and imperfect nature with eternity; a relationship with God, which gives measure and meaning to the actions of unholy people as well, living here and now; a *memento vitae* and *memento mori* in one. Therefore, the starting point of the religious experience that emerges from this judgment is not a commitment to defend dogma or even an aesthetic taste (after all, many people are quietly enamored by chorales), but the adoption of a mediation perspective.

Contrary to More (who near the end of his life decided to don the robes of a Christian apologist), Babbitt was considered a thinker fundamentally at odds with the traditional approach to faith, with the transmission of knowledge about God and with the ultimate questions, referring directly to Revelation. As we know, he draws a strong opposition between the "total positivism" at the foot of truly "modern" humanism and the dogmatic – thus also somewhat *quasi*-theological[13] –attitude of its supposedly scientific, naturalistic opponents. He does not speak in the name of authority – neither the one that reigns today, nor the one that has effectively been overthrown and replaced – but

---

12 P. E. More, *The Quest of a Century* [in:] id., *Shelburne Essays Third Series*, New York–London 1907, pp. 249–50. Cf. Phil. 4:7.

13 Cf. I. Babbitt, *The New Laokoon: An Essay on the Confusion of the Arts*, Boston–New York 1910, pp. 209–10.

from a position of rebellion against authority.[14] Such rebellion seems immune to ridicule insofar as we have good reason to regard authoritative teaching as harmful or insufficient, inebriating and deceptive. Viewed through the prism of individual ambitions (or individual dignity), Babbitt's humanism is a search for full humanity in the conditions in which we live. However, a necessary condition for this search must be some idea of what we are looking for. Since we are not to rely on theological doctrine, which is firmly established by a given denomination, as that would mirror our reaction to the limitations of humanitarian thinking, what is supposed to cause our thoughts? How are we to know that we are not going astray? That the models of humanistic mediation we have anticipated are not a chimera in the same sense as visions of universal well-being and the emancipation of humanity, or of crossing the horizons of faith and submission? At the same time – and this is a crucial issue – Babbitt consistently emphasizes the independent status and intrinsic value of the "humanist experience,"[15] clearly warning against getting involved in disputes over issues traditionally debated by theologians. It is not the calling of a "modern" humanist to protect himself under a canopy of dogmatic statements and vicariously teach the truths of faith. At the same time, it is not right to give up the field of one's own inquiry and avoid responsibility in this regard.

Nevertheless, whether successfully or not, the discovery of the humanistic experience is constantly accompanied by reflection on the religious experience and concern for the proper grounding of humanism (as a movement) vis-à-vis Western religious tradition. In one of Babbitt's later texts, we read that *between the humanist and the humanitarian (...) there is a clash of first principles. Between the humanist and the authentic Christian, on the other hand, there is room for co-operation (...) for my own part, I range myself unhesitatingly on the side of the supernaturalists* (believers in the

14 Cf. id., *On Being Creative and Other Essays*, New York 1968, pp. xii-xiv.
15 Cf. ibid., p. xvii.

The Ancient Mirror of Theology

supernatural). *Though I see no evidence that humanism is necessarily ineffective apart from dogmatic and revealed religion, there is, as it seems to me, evidence that it gains immensely in effectiveness when it has a background of* religious insight. *One is conscious of such a background, for example, in Sophocles, who ranks high among occidental humanists, as well as in Confucius, the chief exponent of the humanistic idea in the Orient.* Babbitt, however, does not enter into analytical deliberations on ancient Greek and Chinese religiosity. Instead, he is interested in the power of a supra-historical dimension provided by the primal religious experience in confrontation with a sloppy and purposeless life, in the work of self-mastery, verification of desires, and distortion of feelings. Looking at the root of the word, this force may simply be described as "enthusiasm." *Humanism is not primarily enthusiastic, whereas religion is.*[16]

Indeed, both kinds of experience are characterized by a fundamental lack of permission for the individual to submit to natural expansion consciously; for a life that is unreasonable, instinctive, dominated by impulses – "sinful." However, in the case of religious experience, an alternative (and redeeming) solution is the decision to submit to a different (implicitly disproportionate) category of impulses or instincts that lead a person to negate or renounce what is changeable and tangible or filled with sin. Therefore, the most urgent task of a true *homo religiosus* will be to tear through the walls of a dying world in response to a voice coming from eternity. Humanistic experience, on the other hand, indicates an alternative solution in the volitional act of concentration itself, opposed to all expansion. This act reveals itself on the grounds of the supreme ability to suspend judgment (*inner check*); "suspension" which can – and according to humanists should be practiced purposefully, deliberately, not to say with premeditation. Overall, we come to the seemingly unambiguous conclusion that religious experience in its pure form does well

16 Id., *Humanism: An Essay at Definition* [in:] *Humanism and America: Essays on the Outlook of Modern Civilization*, ed. N. Foerster, New York 1930, pp. 37, 39, 41.

without humanistic experience ("mediation"), while this is not the case the other way around. Is it really so? Firstly, the trouble is that the vast majority of traditional adherents of religion, including undeniably pious people, do not spend time transcending sensual reality daily but instead spend it trying to live a decent life in this temporal sphere. In Babbitt's view, *the man who sets out to live religiously in the secular order without having recourse to the wisdom of the humanist is likely to fall into vicious confusions – notably, into a confusion between the things of God and the things of Caesar.* Religious enthusiasm, simply put, fails when confronted with the realities of political or economic life. The city – in every age – requires sober judgment and prudent action. It is easy to be "sinfully" optimistic here; it is also easy to fall into paralyzing pessimism in reaction to sin. Secondly, this enthusiasm can be false, rooted in one or another imitation of religious experience, bewildering and destructive. Thus, "humanist wisdom" is not "merely" about methods of achieving a useful balance between a life directed towards the afterlife and life in this world. The humanist may not be concerned with defining God, but whether he likes it or not, he faces *the difficulty of determining what is genuine religion. Religion, not merely to-day but always, has been subject to extraordinary perversions. It has ever been the chosen domain of self-deception and "wishful" thinking.*[17]

However, while the problem of the influence of religious experiences on the experience of political and economic life is universal and eternal, we must not lose sight of the peculiarities of our situation. For, if the humanistic diagnosis of the modern state and society is fundamentally correct, that is, in line with the intuition we demonstrated earlier in picking up the ancient mirror of the three theologies, that means that we are living amidst the gusts of enthusiasm and dead calm of decadence present *within* the general experience of humanitarianism. Real, as opposed to "sham," religious experience appears to us to be somewhat incomprehensible and uninviting. We "invest" our faith in the

17   Ibid., pp. 44, 46–47.

The Ancient Mirror of Theology

ideals of expansion – gaining what is outside and extracting what is inside of us (both of earthly provenance, at least in the eyes of an "enlightened" man). Hence why, generally speaking, only some forms of the old religion remain, from temple celebrations, through everyday habits to literary clues. We can answer any doubts that – despite the condition of the group of parishioners – we still see monks who devoted themselves entirely and seriously to the service of God in numerous monasteries, thus – agreed; pure, individual religious experience is beyond question. However, these people did not come to the monastery out of nowhere. They are, like everyone else, imbued with the religion of this world that reigns supreme among the masses. Therefore, we can assume – assuming the monks' best intentions (that they do not think of their abbeys as, say, profitable companies on the herb or alcohol market) – that they will encounter overwhelming difficulties not only in working on "tuning" their soul in contact with the Creator, but even more so when they want to return to the city where their loved ones live to bear witness to their faith. Will their service to God not then turn into service to humankind? To humankind, who craves the fruits of past enthusiasm to chew them up for the purposes of horizontal expansion? Concerning American society (one hundred and twenty years ago), Babbitt states: *we are still living on the capital of moral Energy inherited from Puritanism.*[18]

Behind such observations, however, there is a suggestion that is much subtler and more disturbing. *Though the traditional habits survive the traditional beliefs, they do not survive them indefinitely. With the progressive weakening, not merely of the Puritan ethos, but of the Christian ethos of the Occident in general, it may become harder and harder to justify humanitarianism experimentally.*[19] What does this mean? It seems that here, we are dealing with a very ambivalent

18   Id., *A Century of Indian Epigrams* [in:] id., *Spanish Character and Other Essays*, eds. F. Manchester, F. Giese, W. F. Giese, Boston – New York 1940, p. 145.
19   Id., *Democracy and Leadership...*, p. 317.

perception of the issue of preserving traditional forms of religious life. On the one hand, there was talk of an "important space of co-operation" between humanism and traditionalism; on the other, however, the duration of the old forms contributes significantly to masking the true character of modernity. Thus, if we assume there is a chance that the Humanist Movement will be successful, then – according to Babbitt – it is worth connecting that chance with the direct, "experimental" confrontation between the findings of the humanists and the dogmatic *modus operandi* of the followers of humanitarianism. It is better, in short, that the king should be naked, that his practical weaknesses and the harm he causes may be attributed to what he truly believes in, rather than to what he retains by the power of inertia or in the fashion of consumption. *The various naturalistic philosophies that have been built up on the ruins of tradition should, at all events, whatever their merits or demerits, be made to stand on their own feet.*[20] Yet another gloomy observation corresponds with this. Under the modern hegemony of economic ideals, the inertia of formalized religious beliefs guarantees tensions leading to madness and bloodshed. In one of his earliest texts (from 1898), *Lights and Shades of Spanish Character*, Babbitt considers the perspective of a country whose pride and identity stem from a sense of the continuation of Christendom, in which the desire to jump into reality born out of promises of humanitarianism swells at the same time. *It is curious* – we read – *this spectacle of a nation hesitating between contradictory ideals. Spain looks doubtfully on our scientific and industrial civilization, and in the very act of accepting it feels that she is perhaps entering the path of perdition. She does not share our exuberant optimism, and has misgivings about our idea of progress. She cannot, like other Western nations, throw herself with fierce energy upon the task of winning dominion over matter (...) she is haunted at times by the Eastern sense of the unreality of life (...) we may be sure that Spain will not modify immediately the mental habits of centuries of spiritual and political absolutism. In attempting to escape from the past, she will no doubt shift from the fanatical belief*

20 Id., *Humanism: An Essay...*, p. 48.

in a religious creed to the fanatical belief in revolutionary formulae, and perhaps pass through all the other lamentable phases of Latin-country radicalism.[21] Anyone who knows the further history of Spain (and Spanish-speaking countries) needs no convincing that this was quite an accurate forecast. From the perspective of a humanistic diagnosis of this sequence of events, a similar relationship exists between the two sides of the Spanish Civil War, the rule of conservative oligarchs and the legend of Che Guevara, the lofty ethos of the church hierarchy and popular piety, such as so-called liberation theology or the current eruption of Protestant sectarianism among Hispanics. Humanitarianism absorbs, but does not tolerate serious competition.

A simple but essential caveat is needed at this point. Namely, the key feature of a society dominated by modern theologies is not the sheer propensity to sin (reinterpreted by us as losing oneself in the satisfaction of natural urges). People have always sinned, and they have always looked for opportunities to do so – and be forgiven for what they have done. Humanitarianism, impregnated in this regard by Rousseau, fulfills itself by offering one mode or another of self-absolution. We are thus used to loving ourselves, liking ourselves, or at least accepting and "tolerating" ourselves. Different orchestras can play this melody in different keys (because sometimes everything is great and happy, at other times – barely bearable, and in the end – inevitable), but its basic notation remains relatively unchanged. *In a period like the present every man is his own Jesuit.*[22] The figure – caricatured by Pascal – of the seventeenth-century priest as a clever master of moral casuistry was certainly not closest to Babbitt's heart. However, he sees the justification for the Jesuit reaction to the outbreaks of Christian asceticism and the demands that we examine our dirty consciences with all severity, a reaction which, having revealed itself within the framework of the old religion, became the canvas

21 Id., *Lights and Shades of Spanish Character* [in:] id., *Spanish Character*..., pp. 13, 19.
22 Id., *Democracy and Leadership*..., p. 304.

for the new religion. *We cannot blame the world for having risen in revolt against so horrible an obsession* (the wrath of God, the fires of hell, the depths of damnation), *for refusing to be frightened into heaven. But the reaction against the theological terror has resulted in turn in an almost equally violent and dangerous extreme.*[23] Babbitt's approach corresponds, perhaps, to the rhetorical expectations of the circle of his readers, who strongly hesitate at the mention of their Puritan grandparents' fear of the devil. Nevertheless, it seems clear that he did not sign up to participate in the hopeless defense of the fortress of the Church of God besieged by human-itarians on all sides. Suppressed desperation – at the level of ideas – is not conducive to efficiency. And since the key to the spiritual dimension of modern society turns out to be its susceptibility to offers of self-renunciation, since modern theologies – our city, the-ater, and philosophy – find their raison d'être in the supply of such offers, the proper task of a humanist – who in the old days would aim to make real the claims resulting from a belief in the supremacy of religious experience – should be the effective ques-tioning or exposing of the falsity of "sham spirituality." *When one considers (...) the multitude of those who have hoped to combine peace and brotherhood with a return to nature* (i.e., that through the liber-ation – absolution, redemption – of the natural instincts, a state of beneficent harmony will be created), *one is forced to conclude that an outstanding human trait is a prodigious and pathetic gullibility. The chief corrective of gullibility is, in an age of individualistic emancipation, a full and free play of the critical spirit. The more critical one becomes at such a time, the more likely one is to achieve standards and avoid empty conceits.*[24] It is not difficult to understand that the criticism postu-lated by Babbitt seemed to him incompatible with references to dogma or with the call to rebuild Christendom. His humanistic realism prevented him from believing that people would believe as they once did. To "reach the standards" again, one has to go beyond the measure of tradition.

23   Id., *Pascal* [in:] id., *Spanish Character...*, p. 78.
24   Id.m, *Democracy and Leadership...*, p. 304.

The Ancient Mirror of Theology

Christianity is not, however, the only great ancient religion. Of those appealing to the authority of Revelation, Babbitt barely mentions Islam – only to stigmatize the concept of God's will *that has been revealed once for all in words of literal and plenary inspiration (...) the effect is to force human life into a rigid and definitive mould (...) when will is conceived as absolute and irresponsible and at the same time as transcendent, the individual is made humble, indeed, but he is so far from being made self-reliant that he is prone to fall into the Oriental form of fatalism.*[25] Ab oriente lux! What if we turn our attention further, into the center of the Asian melting pot? Regarding the religious experiences of Chinese civilization, which constitute the eschatological horizon of the Confucian order that Babbitt admires – and perhaps somewhat idealizes – Babbitt also has little to say (though his criticism of partial anticipation of contemporary visions of a return to nature in Taoism is interesting[26]). The situation changes dramatically when we ask about India. The spiritual heritage of this subcontinent is undoubtedly one of the pillars of humanistic reflection. From a very impressive essay, which More dedicates to a deceased (in 1933) friend, we learn that *literature and the problems of education were much in his thought; but the staple of his more serious talk (...) was ethical and religious (...) from the beginning, Babbitt was drawn to the Buddhistic side of Hinduism rather than to the Brahmanic, and to the Pâli language, in which the most authentic record of Buddha's teaching is preserved, rather than to the Sanskrit.* Therefore, there is a verifiable agreement, or a practical synergy of conclusions, between the findings that come from reading the Western classics and those from the Pâli texts. Meanwhile, according to More, *the dogma of Grace, the notion of help and strength poured into the soul from a superhuman source, was in itself repugnant to him, and the Church as an institution he held personally in deep distaste, however he may have seemed to make an exception of the disciplinary authority of Romanism (...) on the other hand, he was*

25 Ibid., p. 201.
26 Cf. id., Rousseau and Romanticism, Boston – New York 1919, pp. 395–98.

much closer to Buddhism than would appear from his public utterances (…) in private as well as in public he refused to be denominated a Buddhist, and with perfect sincerity. But in the denial by Buddha (the real Buddha as seen in the authentic texts) of anything corresponding to Grace, in his insistence on the complete moral responsibility of the individual, in the majesty of his dying command (…) Babbitt perceived the quintessential virtue of religion, purged of ephemeral associations, of outworn superstition, of impossible dogma, or obscurantist faith, and based on a positive law which can be verified by experiment, pragmatically, step by step. It was in this way he sought to bring together a positivism in the religious plane with a positivism in what he distinguished as the purely humanistic plane of life and letters.[27]

Let us try to briefly analyze Babbitt's position, sticking to More's guidelines (who at the same time makes us pay attention to the rhetorical sense of statements serving, in a way, to prepare for the war against humanitarianism). The problem is twofold: first, the assumed advantage – in the eyes of a humanist – of Buddhism over Christianity; second, the synergy suggested earlier between Buddhist religious experience and humanistic experience, or perhaps more precisely, between the effects of describing both experiences. Above all, we must avoid associating what we call a "religious experience" with the popular image of exotic, readily available after-hours therapy that does not require significant sacrifice, a romanticized image that has been included in the offer of "spiritual" palliative measures. We are not interested in hippie games or para-scientific methods of treating shattered nerves. Babbitt's Buddhism has nothing to do with practicing relaxation techniques. Nor does it reveal any unhealthy fascination with immersing oneself in the colorful waters of Far Eastern myths and superstitions. It is, in short, a testimony to the recognition of the importance of the spiritual experiment and the civilizational importance of the teachings of Gautama (the historical Buddha). Moreover, these ancient teachings should not only be

27 P. E. More, *Irving Babbitt* [in:] id., *On Being Human* (*New Shelburne Essays III*), Princeton–London 1936, pp. 31–32, 37–38.

The Ancient Mirror of Theology

freed from the burden of later reinterpretations and applications contrary to the spirit of the original – the modern "utilization" of Buddhism has been going on for some two centuries – but also carefully separated from the rich resources of the Hindu tradition, as well as dubious internal tendencies towards development or enrichment of doctrine, mainly in the Mahayana schools.

One of Babbitt's best short essays is revealingly titled *Interpreting India to the West. If Buddha –* we read there *– was like other ancient Hindu teachers in stressing the inner check* (a concept, as we remember, explaining the act of concentration and thus the humanistic experience in general), *he was unlike them in combining this astringency with an extremely positive temper. In the face of the sixty-two systems of philosophy current in his time he declared the inanity of metaphysics. He looked with disfavor on those who had "views" (...) one is not to trust anything that is not immediate and experimental.* Babbitt's "experimentality" does not mean reducing all knowledge to the results of laboratory work carried out according to the method of the natural sciences. It is about a tedious and self-conscious examination of the individual experiences of each (potentially) human being. A similar imperative, that of knowing oneself, constitutes the basis for Socratic philosophy. What is the difference between a philosophizing Greek and a Hindu liberating himself from the fetters of this world? *The essentially Buddhistic act is the rigorous tracing of moral cause and effect. It was by an act of analysis, namely, by following the chain of evil, link by link, back to its beginning in ignorance, that Buddha attained supreme enlightenment. In tracing evil to ignorance Buddha is at one with Socrates and Plato, but in refusing therefore to identify the opposite of ignorance, knowledge, with virtue, he agrees with Aristotle. One may know the right, but fail to do it. What stands in the way, says Buddha, is the most subtle and deadly of all the sins – moral indolence, the tendency to drift passively with temperament and desire. Man's laziness cannot, from the positive point of view, be considered merely an aspect of his ignorance: man is ignorant and lazy.* Therefore, if we define evil as moral laziness (that we "ordinarily" do not want to "know what is right"), then as a consequence, we get the concept of virtue as strenuousness (appamāda) and not being subject to the power of impulses or self-determination. In Babbitt's view, *Buddha seems to have the facts on his side: nothing is so vital and immediate as the act of self-control by which one rises above the temperamental level.* At the same time, this means that the creation of illusory mental constructs – the culmination of which are metaphysical systems with their claims to be fully and ultimately reflected in the word of the nature of all things – is not a manifestation of the real effort of thinking humans, but, on the contrary, the fruit of indolence. The "beings" "known" by metaphysicians are like verbal palliatives, meaning that they provide "false security" to the individual in relation to the world. Nothing else matters but dealing with yourself. *If Buddha will not hear of a soul or self in the sense of a metaphysical entity, he takes as his starting point (...) the psychological fact (...) the presence, namely, in man not merely of one but of two selves and the conflict between them (...) the opposition as one may say between an element of change known experimentally to the individual as vital impulse (élan vital), and a permanent element known to him experimentally as vital control (frein vital). The escape from sorrow (i.e.,* suffering in the face of the necessary loss of all that we are given to have and to experience; the "liberation" that is, let us emphasize, the goal of all religious experience in Buddhism) *can come only as a result of the strenuous exercise of the principle of control. No man and no god can be strenuous for another.*[28]

This last statement indicates the moment when Buddhism was superior to Christianity. The salvation of Christians happens individually, but not independently; it does not presuppose the possibility, let alone righteousness, of an attitude of the kind that would treat the totality of creation as something with which we, as it were, deal with "on the side," preoccupied only with our toil. In its original form, the Buddhist experience is thus situated at the antipodes of humanitarianism much more obviously than it is for genuine followers of Christ. For these, through Him, turn

28 I. Babbitt, *Interpreting India to the West* [in:] id., *Spanish Character...*, pp. 152–54, 155, 157. Emphasis in original.

outward to their neighbors and all creation; they trust in Him who manifests Himself from Without. There is no path to holiness here without faith in the common Lord and joint participation in His plan. Babbitt, however, tries to soften this difference by saying that every *saint, whether Buddhist or Christian, who knows his business as a saint is rightly meditative and in direct proportion to the depth of his meditation is the depth of his peace.*[29] Meditation, the equivalent of humanistic mediation in religious life, requires the highest level of concentration... on oneself. For, what – from our human perspective – would the competency of a religious man be if not the ability first to perceive, then by the strength of his will to overcome the conflict in his soul? To *truly* understand, on account of yourself, that *none is good, save one, that is, God* (Luke 18:19)? The crux of the matter is that for the humanist, holiness is by no means compatible with a "spiritual" departure or a disregard for natural necessity. In other words, a holy man should appear responsible for himself most of all.

Perhaps the fullest account of Babbitt's reflections on religion can be found in the posthumous essay *Buddha and the Occident* (1936). It was initially intended as an elaborate introduction to his translation of the Buddhist *Dhammapada*, and as such focuses on showing the obstacles that separate us, readers, attempting to get out from under the burden of modern authorities, from a correct and fruitful reading of the classical description of religious experience. The instruction of the Buddha, says Babbitt, expresses a fundamental opposition to the affirmation – inherent in humanitarianism – of what is changeable, fluid, and transient (progressive, emotional, etc.). But *in his rejection of the transitory for the eternal he is (...) neither metaphysical nor theological, but psychological. One needs only to take a glance at the four noble truths of Buddha to perceive that his doctrine is in its genuine spirit a psychology of desire.* In traditional Christianity, the human will meets the will of the eternal divine Being. *The Buddhist sets up a similar opposition between a higher and lower will, not, however, on dogmatic but on*

29 Ibid., p. 164.

psychological grounds.[30] However important this distinction seems – one can ask whether the concept of a revealed God, indeed contained in dogma, is only a theological thought construct without which *homo religiosus* (let us emphasize – not "natural man"!) is able to cope – it is not on him, from a humanist point of view, that the fate of civilization depends. *In its essence Buddhism is (...) a psychology of desire, so that all that is needed for a reply to the question what Buddha would think of us is to compare positively and critically our attitude towards the expansive desires with that of Buddha. The movement that became predominant in the Occident with the emergence of the middle class in the eighteenth century and which still continues, may be defined in its two main aspects as utilitarian and sentimental. The outstanding characteristic of the movement in both of these aspects has been its enormous expansiveness (...) to both types of expansionist (...) Buddha's psychology of desire seems intolerably astringent. To Buddha, on the other hand, a view of life that combines the extreme of outer activity with the extreme of spiritual indolence would have seemed one-sided to the point of madness.*[31] How the Buddha explains his religious experience also indicates the appropriate mode of humanitarian criticism.

The shift towards the "positive" language of the "psychology of desires" is especially evident in Babbitt's later statements. In his opinion, such are the requirements of modern man's situation. We need operative simplicity, so to speak. *It is desirable (...) under existing circumstances, to get at humanistic or religious truth with the minimum of metaphysical or theological.*[32] Traditional churches defend – at least at the level of a confession of faith – the memory of someone whose eschatological horizon was not that of emotional expansion (at least not exclusively); of someone who worshiped a "will" or "being" infinitely better than any emanation of his own desires or natural

---

30   Id., *Buddha and the Occident (Part I)*, "The American Review," vol. 6, no. 5, March 1936, pp. 534, 537.
31   Id., *Buddha and the Occident (Part II)*, "The American Review," vol. 7, no. 1, April 1936, pp. 84–85.
32   Id., *Democracy and Leadership*..., p. 251.

The Ancient Mirror of Theology

urges. This defense against humanitarianism – based, it is worth emphasizing again, not on the realistic recognition of the expansive side of human nature, but on the belief in the necessary self-fulfillment of man on this side – turns out to be fundamentally ineffective. *But why – Babbitt asks – abandon the affirmation of such an "essence" or higher will, to the mere traditionalist? Why not affirm it first of all as a psychological fact, one of the immediate data of consciousness, a perception so primordial that, compared with it, the deterministic denials of man's moral freedom are only a metaphysical dream?*[33]

While the natural sciences absorb modern psychology (hence the intellectual phenomenon of twentieth-century behaviorism), we can *conceive of a humanistic or even a religious psychology,* the science of which we are "directly" aware. *This awareness, to be sure, exists in very different degrees in different individuals, so that one encounters in purely psychological form the equivalent of the mystery of grace* (which in such an approach would mean the action of the will to transcend oneself, i.e., our "mood level," the plane of élan vital). "Psychology" in the service of humanism is associated with a critical recognition of the poles of mediation. Mediation itself is possible as long as we can – consciously – suspend the affirmative judgment regarding the impulses or instincts that influence us. *If anyone sets himself the humanistic task of achieving the intermediary term between extremes, he will find that it is not enough to exercise an inner check on temperament, he will need to exercise this check intelligently; and to exercise it intelligently he will need to look up to some norm.* The origin of this "some" norm is not as clearly laid out as one might expect. It is undoubtedly related to the action, not so much of the will, as of the imagination, which gives a vivid quality to the very human experience of an inner rupture or conflict of two "selves" – the perception of the "element of change" against the unchanging, an imagination fulfilling itself primarily in the description of a religious experience. However, here enters the *analytical reason that discriminates and tests this unifying activity of the imagination, not with reference to any theory, but to the actual*

33   Id., *Humanism: An Essay...*, p. 39.

data of experience.[34] The initial analysis of "consciousness data," associated parallel to the Buddhist inquiry into the origins of evil and the path of freeing oneself from evil, ultimately leads to an "experiential" critique of the two forms of the absolute – "pure" change and "pure" following of the unchanging. Finding an "equivalent to grace" is "merely" an introduction here.

A further detailed description of the terms of humanistic "psychology" would be quite tedious. However, it is worth considering the reason for Babbitt's (at a particular stage also More's) usage of the language of scientific description. Undoubtedly, this action's most essential practical premise is the intention to be effective. *His mind was eminently practical in that he aimed at getting results and thought much of strategy in attack.*[35] Simply put, Babbitt wanted to be "scientific." As an academic teacher at Harvard and wishing to attract the flower of his students, he must have deliberately used the splendor and attractiveness of the natural sciences. After all, whatever the feeling of the crisis of Western civilization or the need to deal with nineteenth-century optimism meant in those years – especially just after World War I – the fantastic achievements of scientists and engineers remained something evident and tangible, even on the battlefield. Of course, studying at a renowned university was the starting point for a successful career in politics or business. Hence, ambitious individuals from around the world, including the Asians who inspired hope in the humanists, were drawn to Harvard as if to the very tabernacle of modernity. Under such special conditions, it was possible to dream up – deceptively hilarious – plans for a "Humanist International" that would ally itself with a future neo-Confucian movement in China to fight the humanitarians "in the field of education."[36] However, it is necessary to be credible and

---

34 Id., *On Being Creative...*, pp. xviii-xix, xxii, xxx. Cf. id., *Democracy and Leadership...*, p. 332.
35 P. E. More, *Irving Babbitt...*, p. 36
36 Cf. I. Babbitt, *Humanistic Education in China and the West*, "The Chinese Students' Monthly," vol. 17, no. 2, December 1921, p. 91.

The Ancient Mirror of Theology

persuasive when creating such incentives. Why, watching the successes of adepts of physics and other fields of natural science, not announce – in the heart of the academic world – the birth of a new science, equally necessary, studying consciousness? Is it not possible that some of those who have come to learn about wealth creation will become interested in "making" a real human? And this "humanistic" (or "religious") psychology could draw from the fascinating fabric of Buddhism, viewing itself in the highly useful terms of "moral laziness" and "mindful toil." After all, the traditional Christian view of Adamic sin and Redemption is a much worse fit here, or would at least cause unnecessary opposition and controversy. Moreover, the characteristic comparison of Buddha and Aristotle as masters of "positive" thinking – of which only the former gives a clear analysis of experiences at the religious level – can also be assessed through the prism of efforts to attract readers (listeners). The respectable teaching of the *Nicomachean Ethics* as a propaedeutic to help demonstrate the meaning of the Buddhist "middle way" – why not? Buddhism, which is the heritage of the peoples of Asia and a pillar of their traditions, could not *take the place of our Western wisdom*.[37] The trick is to associate the best of what is determinable with the best of what we know and value. Finally, the language of humanistic "psychology" meets the American ethos of work and action. The "experimental" opposition of two wills in man can be read – up to a certain point – as a proposal for a scientific improvement in the implementation of leadership. Let us remember that this leadership already showed signs of global aspirations in those years. Maintaining the universal vision of breaking humanitarianism's spiritual hegemony and educating a new type of leaders, people responsible for the fate of the world, we must also notice the *signs* (...) *that if America ever achieves a philosophy of its own, it will be rather a philosophy of will*.[38]

When discussing the intention to attack the dogmatic vaults

37   Id., *Interpreting India...*, p. 168.
38   Id., *Democracy and Leadership...*, p. 320.

HUMANISM AS REALISM

of modern religion effectively, are we giving the final word on Babbitt's attitude to religion in general? It seems not. Not forgetting his declared aversion to the metaphysical and theological discourses he is familiar with, it is worth considering the thesis that Babbitt – as a scholar and thinker – is concerned with nothing but the practice of natural theology. At the same time – however risky this association might look – the humanist critique of humanitarianism, at its base, turns out to have a lot in common with Augustine's critique of pagan religions. Of course, the very concept of humanism as the art of mediation, by which *only the humanistic virtues* are achieved, contains the indispensable postulate *to restore the teleological element to life*. The need for a goal beyond ordinary goals (beyond what we desire from day to day, fitting into the continuum of natural phenomena, expanding); hence the standard mentioned above. There must be a supernatural pole or point of reference traditionally defined by religion in this system. The question remains as to the method of determining the shape of the supernatural – and here, Babbitt's answer is clear: it is wrong *to start with dogmatic assertions about God and the soul rather than with psychological observation.*[39] Therefore, he is looking for a version of (natural) theology that would be digestible for modern man and simultaneously capable of blowing up modern myths – without burning cities at the same time. Okay, but what does Saint Augustine have to do with this? We know that, in defending Christianity, the author of *De Civitate Dei* critically analyzes the earlier view of tripartite theology, according to which a pagan philosopher and citizen of Rome who hears a call to reflect and study nature makes concessions to the city and its political theology. By acting in this way, the Roman in practice transmits the *imprimatur* of the learned authority to those who, being farthest from philosophical inclinations, cultivate mythological delusions, increasing general ignorance and depravity. After all, there is no significant difference between indecency in the theater and indecency in the temple – with the caveat that *if we mark the truth, the*

39   Id., *On Being Creative...*, p. xxxii.

The Ancient Mirror of Theology

temples where these things are done are worse than the theatres where they are but feigned.[40] The real effect of the philosopher's insurmountable isolation – or simply hypocrisy – is that natural theology is imbued with myth. In this way, every possible representation of the divine contains the flaws of mythological disorder, a deficit of seriousness, and moral simplicity. Christendom is the answer to this. With the progressive collapse of the Christian model, the taking over of the competencies of eroded church authority by the political authority, and the instrumentalization of teachings, the ancient problem takes on more and more radical forms. The humanitarian transformation of the imagination – replacing classical dualism with its successful parody – ultimately completes the process. We lose the chance to participate in a purpose-oriented arrangement beyond "ordinary" nature.

Modern natural theology – the object of fundamental criticism on the part of humanists – is based on the forcible reconciliation of "the Law for Man" with "the Law for Thing." We discussed this in the first essay. What we call "the Law for Man" is now associated with the inhuman dictates of religious fanatics and the unlawful hypocrisy of the churches. *Tantum religio potuit suadere malorum!* Isn't it better to educate people to live according to the voice of nature – the voice they usually hear? Without claims to the divine (the perfect, the holy)? But the natural man still demands divinity, only brought down to earth and appropriate to his state, which is not that of a philosopher, but of someone who enjoys going clubbing. So, in the end, we get theater; theater founded by philosophy and belonging to a city that believes in the theater. The effect is not good for philosophy, just as it is not good for the city. Babbitt contrasts this with his interpretation of classical natural theology, which may – perversely – do without God, but will not do without an extraordinary, definitive, allowing itself to be expressed only in an apophatic way – will of the soul. Saint Augustine writes: *I desire to know God and the soul* – and adds, soon after: *I love only God and the*

---

40   St. Augustine, The City of God, vol. 1, trans. John Healey, J. M. Dent & Sons, Ltd., 1947, Book VI, Chapter X, p. 194; cf. ibid., pp. 379 ff.

soul, and know neither the one nor the other.[41] The humanist remains out of love for the soul, at least initially. More tells us that we need to distinguish between the supernatural and the superhuman to understand Babbitt. The Christian God is something "superhuman," above the human soul. Though created in His image and still able to follow Him, man is defined by a vertical space, an ineffable distance from above to below, which cannot be breached without grace. Meanwhile, humanistic "psychology," using Buddha's vision, rejects – or omits – the "superhuman" moment, fully preserving the "supernatural" – and precisely very human – moment of volitional concentration within the human soul. This way, the continuity between the humanistic experience and the religious experience is maintained. Although they have different practical effects because they refer to different types of vocations and different needs, the foundation of their *modus operandi* remains the same: the "higher will" is measured against the "lower will." No external element is added to this. There is no space between us mortals "below" and the eternal absolute "above." Like a political leader, a monk must count on himself – to be able to defeat himself and overcome his "ordinary self."[42] Later we will see that this approach signifies, beyond all else, an attempt to break the impasse that emerges from the pages of Aristotle's *Nicomachean Ethics*. For now, let us note that the will – in its double dimension – unites philosophers and non-philosophers. Seen from this angle, Saint Augustine's revealed God plays a similar role in similarly trying times. Incidentally, it is hard to resist the impression of a further analogy when we think of the art of humanism through the prism of an individual examination of the soul, knowing what a master in this field the author of *Confessions* was.

We said earlier that the characteristic feature of a modern man would be – from a theological perspective – not so much the

---

41 Id., *The Soliloquies of St. Augustine*, trans. Rose Elizabeth Cleveland, Boston: Little, Brown, and Co., 1910, Book I, Chapter II, Section 7, pp. 10-11.
42 Cf. P. E. More, *Irving Babbitt...*, pp. 38–39.

intensity of sin, but the naive covering up of the need for an interior confrontation with his own propensity to sin. To recall one of Babbitt's favorite quotes, such a man refuses to participate in a "civil war in the cave." This phrase, taken from Diderot, boils down to the supposition that everything that stands in the way of the fulfillment of natural (instinctive) human desires should be rejected as an artificial interference and the cause of futile anxiety ("war"). Modernity would then mean less and less internal torment and more opportunities to act on the external front. Though he likes to be optimistic about human nature, the humanitarian would not so much be obliged to believe in anyone's natural goodness as to accept the most basic imperative of surrendering the higher to the lower in the name of peace through natural expansion.[43] Is this not what our state or "municipal" theology is based on? Is this not what our fairy tales and myths serve to do? And does this command not return, as if it were a necessary requirement of all reasonable findings, to people who think and study reality and are capable of being philosophers?

Regardless of the rhetorical tools used and all his prudence, Babbitt speaks in the mode of a prophet who has read the books of nature. Citing Buddha and Aristotle, he explains patiently that *the true drama of war and peace (...) is enacted in the breast of the little "fathom-long" creature; whatever prevails there extends in widening circles into society. All other forms of war are reflections, near or remote, of "the civil war in the cave."*[44] It is impossible to understand the political or economic reality by looking only at the "extreme periphery" occupied by external conflicts, conflicts between states, etc. Therefore, the reflection proper to humanism, which assumes "bringing the teleological element back to life," turns out to be in practice theological-political reflection. From the point of view of the classical approach, both Christian and Buddhist, as reconstructed by Babbitt – *any conquest that the individual may win over*

43 Cf. I. Babbitt, *The Bicentenary of Diderot* [in:] id., *Spanish Character...*, especially pp. 107–08; id., *Rousseau and Romanticism...*, pp. 130, 187.
44 Id., *Interpreting India...*, p. 161.

his own inordinate desires will be reflected at once in his contact with other men. If the individual happens to be one in high station, such a conquest may have almost immediate consequences in the field of political action.[45] This is the noble dimension of politics. It is somewhat unfamiliar to us.

Let's summarize. Babbitt is not lying when he says that humanism is not a religion and is not intended to replace religion. However, this does not mean that the problem posed by religious experience can remain ill-thought-out. On the contrary, Babbitt's struggle with this problem – with his realization of the contemporary hegemony of the humanitarian attitude – leads to findings that inform all of his thought, both in terms of its form and its content. We are dealing entirely with thought permeated by a vision of ultimate matters, which is not dogmatic thinking. *Wherefore by their fruits ye shall know them* (Matthew 7:20). *A great religion is above all a great example; the example tends to grow faint in time or even to suffer alteration into something very different.*[46] According to Babbitt, Hinayana Buddhism turns out to be a model that is the least transformed and thus the most hostile to that rhizome of theology from which the modern religion of humankind grew.

III.

Comparing what we consider Babbitt's version of natural theology with the wealth of theological reflections by Paul Elmer More forces us to consider the significant differences between these two friends and thinkers. However, do not be too quick to place them on the axis of faith and unbelief. More was undoubtedly a more openly religious writer; in any case, he wrote much more than Babbitt. At the same time, strong, even unbearable tensions are visible in his legacy. From a letter to Thomas Stearns Eliot (from 1930), we learn that *theology is the only really interesting subject* and that, in connection with this, *I do want to tell you that I hate your*

45 Id., *Buddha and the Occident (Part II)...*, p. 85.
46 Ibid., pp. 92–93.

theology, and love you as a theologian.[47] A dozen years earlier, the same More spoke about theology in the spirit of Babbitt's formulations, but with greater severity and consistency: *theology is an attempt to superimpose the abstracting activity of metaphysics upon the personal dualism of spontaneous mythology (...) theology thus involves a self-destructive process, and either kills mythology or abdicates in a superstition which has lost connection with our better inner life (...) for most men the consequence of theology is a state of fluctuation between rationalism and superstition.* Between a living religious experience (that is, a special experience of the effects of "personal dualism") and any attempt by reason at explaining it, there is not only a contradiction, but a literal threat. Such an interpretation does fit with the humanist view of *immediacy* – "unmediated data of consciousness." So far, however, we have not yet come across the notion of "mythology" in this context. *Spontaneous mythology,* More explains, *is the unreasoned work of the imagination projecting our imperfect self-knowledge into the void in the form of daemonic personalities (...) belief is the acceptance of the creations of mythology as real; it is not to be identified with faith, any more than mythology is to be identified with religion.*[48]

The passage we cite comes from the text *Definitions of Dualism* (1913), which as a whole could provide an excellent illustration of what could be called More's "psychological" phase. At this stage, the humanist imitates contemporary users of the scientific language in his writing, using the concepts he needs (such as "will" and "imagination," but also "theology" and "mythology"), which together make up a description of human experiences (humanistic, religious) parallel to the description that is being created

---

47 Quoted in: A. H. Dakin, *Paul Elmer More*, Princeton, New Jersey 1960, p. 292.

48 P. E. More, *Definitions of Dualism* [in:] id., *Shelburne Essays Eighth Series: The Drift of Romanticism*, New York–Boston 1913, pp. 298, 295–96. Cf. id., *The Forest Philosophy of India* [in:] id., *Shelburne Essays Sixth Series: Studies of Religious Dualism*, New York–London 1909, pp. 2–4, 20–22.

on the part of the natural sciences. However, while Babbitt – a "moral positivist" – remains faithful to this method, More, during the last two decades of his life, transforms his writing to the point that one could speak of an apologetic-theological phase. Its beginning (seen from the perspective of his public addresses) can probably be marked by the call to "restore the fear of God in society," presented in the previous essay. In his subsequent books from the 1920s onward (composing the collection *The Greek Tradition*), our author increasingly appears to be more a curator than a critiquer of Christian thought. The old "psychological" criterion of *immediacy* seems to give way to the new. However, the "new" generally does not mean a refutation of the previous position, but its specific recapitulation based on Catholic doctrine viewed in the mirror of Greek philosophy. So, we now have a double criterion: inner experience (awareness of the *inner check* of action) and the *logos* tradition. Late More appears as a supporter – though not a nominal follower – of the Church of England. And perhaps it should not come as a surprise that his Anglicanism – or, more precisely, Anglo-Catholicism – fits easily into the rhetoric of "New Humanism" with its persistent emphasis on the benefits of moderation and prudence.

Christianity in its Anglican version emerges from a massive breakthrough in world history – the turmoil known as the "Reformation." Albion's sixteenth-century elite simultaneously feared the dictatorship of the implacable papists and radical Protestant ideas. *Between these opposite intrusions from the Continent the Church of England was thus directed, primarily by reasons of State, to the via media ("the middle way") which has been her watchword from that day to this (...) it may have begun as a protest against the political claims of Rome on the one side and the Genevan (i.e., Calvinist) theories of State (...) but behind it all the while lay a profounder impulse, pointing in a positive direction, and aiming to introduce into religion, and to base upon the "light of reason," that love of balance, restraint, moderation, measure, which from sources beyond our reckoning appears to be innate in the English temper.* Interestingly, this formula, which is pleasant for the English, refers to a genuinely Catholic attitude.

The Ancient Mirror of Theology

Avoiding extremes (in the form of heresy), focusing enormous intellectual efforts on discovering a common path, but one that is not reducible to an ad hoc consensus – is this not what the Church Fathers' greatness is founded on? Especially those who prepared and edited the documents closing the most critical dispute in the heart of early Christianity on the divinity and humanity of Christ? In More's view, *the Church, by the Definition of Chalcedon, simply thrust its way through the middle by making the personality of the Incarnate so large as to carry with it* both *natures* (divine and human). *Evidently in this case at least the principle of measure does not produce a diminished or half-truth, but acts as a law of restraint preventing either one of two aspects of a paradoxical truth from excluding the other. Nor is the middle way here a mean of compromise, but a mean of comprehension.* Unfortunately, this rational – because it considered the limitations of reason – approach that theologians had at the dawn of the Catholic faith was no longer the norm at the threshold of modern times. *The course of the Anglicans was peculiar in this, that deliberately and courageously they clung to the principle of mediation in regions of doctrine and discipline, where, as they contended, the Romanist and the radical Protestant did in fact stray aside into vicious extremes.* By contrast, the spiritual leaders of the Church of England tried to read the letter of the Scriptures and the messages of church tradition in a pragmatic manner, assuming the need to separate the fundamental from the incidental and the secondary, but also rejecting any claim to an infallible judgment in matters of religion. More adds that if, therefore there is *any outstanding note of the English temper it is a humility of awe before the divine mysteries of faith and a recognition of the incompetence of language to define the ultimate paradox of experience.*[49] It's worth remembering these words, even if they cause dissonance in the ear of anyone who comes across a more modern dimension of English spirituality.

49 Id., *The Spirit of Anglicanism* [in:] *Anglicanism: The Thought and Practice of the Church of England, Illustrated from the Religious Literature of the Seventeenth Century,* eds. P. E. More, F. L. Cross, Cambridge 2008, pp. xxviii-xxxi, xl. Emphasis in original.

HUMANISM AS REALISM

The problem for us, who want to read humanistic reflections on the ultimate questions seriously and with benefit, does not concern how the sheep baptized in the Church of England really behave today (it's simple – they were brought up to adhere to the religion of humanity and know nothing else); the problem lies in reconciling what could be considered the acceptance of the faith based on revelation (apparently at its best) with the overall philosophical diagnosis proposed by More. In one of his earliest texts, written as a commentary on his translation of Plato's *Apology* (1898), he states that *we cannot hold confidently to the belief in a personal God as anything more than a projection of man's own soul into the void (...) a prudent man will not prophesy. He may, however, feel safe in predicting that humanitarianism will accomplish its measure of benefit and injury, and then pass away – rapidly (...) by reason of its flagrant falsehood and inadequacy; but what will take its place? Some new expression, no doubt, of that inherent sense of self-division which man can satisfy only by the delusion of ever-changing myths and philosophies; but what its form shall be, the years alone can reveal.*[50] Moreover, from our point of view, Christianity turns out to be "a historical error." Faith in humanity has blossomed through the discreditation of ancient forms of religious life. *It is possible that Zeus and Apollo, the nymphs and dryads, may retain their appeal as symbols of the religious imagination, when Jehovah and Jesus, Allah and Mahomet, have been dethroned as false gods and denounced as priestly impositions.*[51] This last, somewhat dubious, suggestion is, after all, "only" a humanistic encouragement to an unbiased reading of the Greek classics. Either way, More seems to share the opinion that the Christian religion, with all its theology, is a thing of the past. From where and for what did this later apologetic-theological stage arise? Someone may say: the man was converted. It might have been good for his soul, but his thought lost its continuity and coherence as a result of this personal transformation. Is this really the case?

50 Id., *Socrates* [in:] id., *Studies of Religious...*, pp. 243–44; cf. id., *The New Morality...*, pp. 213–14.
51 Id., *Plato* [in:] id., *Studies of Religious...*, pp. 323–24.

The Ancient Mirror of Theology

Above all, it is not for us to judge what only God knows, what filled the recesses of Paul Elmer More's soul. We can, however – it would probably still be worthwhile – try to understand his work. Having some understanding of this vast legacy, we would be inclined to point out a particular, significant undertone that appears in various ways in perhaps all of More's writings. So, what do we hear? The reality perceived by the senses, ladies and gentlemen, is *invariably* paradoxical, illusory, and incoherent. Human judgments have been, are, and will forever remain disturbed and uncertain, as they have been eaten through at their foundation by our desires and emotions. Despite this, or perhaps because of it, there is no intellectual justification for the negation of reality as such. There is no justification for irresponsibly situating oneself outside the sphere of human nature, outside the sphere of participation in what is real, for what in practice could be called a carefree departure, floating freely, self-forgetfulness. The point is not that this tangible reality does not exist, but that it exists *despite* its *ultimate* incompatibility with us, despite the offense of human hearts. Insofar as we can transcend it, it appears relative or insufficient, as if it loses itself "in existence" along with our individual spiritual progress. However, what makes sense at the end of the road is not given at the beginning. It is a dynamic, not a static take; dynamic from the perspective of the individual, who does not emerge from a vacuum at that moment, but reaches out to the available memory of how the fact of being human was dealt with in the past.

In short, there are many different consequences of truly agreeing to disagree. The expected tension between More and Babbitt – the deeper dimension of which we will try to reveal in further considerations – most often comes down to a different distribution of accents. The paradoxicality or illusory nature of the things of this world is a thread present in both of their thought. According to a neat formula of Babbitt's, *life is at best a series of illusions; the whole office of philosophy is to keep it from degenerating into a series of delusions.*[52] However, More emphasizes the constancy of human

52 I. Babbitt, *Rousseau and Romanticism...*, p. 259.

nature, the continuity of the experiences given, the irremovability of the irrational element contained in them. Thus, it betrays a greater distance to the effects of the historical enlightenment ("modern experiment"), and therefore also to the need to meet the demands of the "era of individualistic emancipation." A very telling testimony of the resulting difference is found in More's letter to Maurice Baum (1924), written after the beginning of the apologetic-theological "phase" and referring directly to the apparent rupture in the bosom of the "New Humanism." For Babbitt, *the only way by which the world can be brought to sanity is the Aristotelian positivism, though with this he harbours a sympathy with a thoroughgoing mysticism (...) I cannot see things as he does. To me the only possible release from the present trend towards materialism and dissipation seems to lie through the awakening of the sense of what I call otherworldliness. I do not believe the mass of people ever was or ever can be rational or positive; I do not believe the positive scientific view of life will ever have the power to restrain the passions – and there we are.*[53] Philosophy (natural theology) is not and will not be given the power over souls. And no reasoned science about the soul will capture the imaginations of societies.

His studies of Sanskrit had an undoubted influence on More's general position. Nevertheless, what turns out to be the backbone of his reflection is – just like in the case of many other authors – the frequent reading of Plato's dialogues. More admitted having an affinity with Plato (as a dualistic skeptic). He had what, in his opinion, was the most important quote from the *Laws* carved in large letters above his mantel. Therefore, on a daily basis, he could contemplate the first sentence of this chapter, which has a specific context: *human affairs are unworthy of earnest effort, necessity counsels us to be in earnest; and that is our misfortune. Yet, since we are where we are, it is no doubt becoming that we should show this earnestness in a suitable direction (...) what I assert is this, – that a man ought to be in serious earnest about serious things, and not about trifles; and that the object really worthy of all serious and blessed effort is God, while man*

53 Quoted in: A. H. Dakin, *Paul Elmer More...*, pp. 221–22.

The Ancient Mirror of Theology

is contrived, as we said above, to be a plaything of God, and the best part of him is really just that (...) they are puppets for the most part, yet share occasionally in truth.[54] According to More, on the other hand, *philosophy and religion agree then in this, that they both leave man in a combined state of ignorance and knowledge, scepticism and faith; they agree in telling us that we are morally responsible and intellectually impotent.*[55]

The combination of moral responsibility and intellectual helplessness – that is, the realization of the lack of access to absolute knowledge, a unified view of everything, the ultimate satisfaction of reason (to say nothing of philosophers' political effectiveness) – is the shortest expression of the fullness of human experience; the experiences revealed to us by the "inexorable law" of being in this world. It is a law that we cannot say is a good (desirable) law; rather, it is a fatal compromise that we cannot get out of. The formula of helplessness accompanying responsibility also seems to indicate the most concise possible approach to the content being the subject of cognition in the way of *common sense*. As we tried to present in the first essay, the concept of *common sense* can be regarded as extremely useful and even central to humanism, if only we associate it with some kind of inner sense of humanity, a "shared sense." This "sense" encompasses, on the one hand, the basic awareness of our human limitations (our entanglement in *real* illusions or paradoxes), and, on the other hand, the first fruits of any conjecture about human greatness or perfection; a perfection that is not related to external gains, but to the mastery of one's inner self. We feel that each of us should be responsible for ourselves to the extent we are able. The perspective of *common*

---

54 Plato, *Laws* [in:] *Plato in Twelve Volumes*, vols. 10 & 11, trans. R. G. Bury, Cambridge – London 1967 &1968, 803 B-C, 804 B Cf. P. E. More, *The Religion of Plato*, Princeton–London 1921, p. 332; A. H. Dakin, *Paul Elmer More...*, p. 168.
55 P. E. More, *Hellenistic Philosophies*, Princeton–London 1923, p. 257; cf. ibid., pp. 384–85; id., *The Sceptical Approach to Religion*, Princeton 1934, pp. 89–90, 106, 173, 191.

sense outlined this way goes beyond the important distinction we used to associate with the birth of classical political philosophy, namely between *physis* (nature) and *nomos* (convention). This "sense" is generally revealed through conventions (laws, traditions, etc.). Still, it does not result from a secondary perception of these *nomoi*, but rather from the prior (pre-philosophical) self-perception of human nature. This leads to the finding, based on *common sense* thus understood, the relationship between the natural good of an individual and the good of the political community. Socrates' tradition of teaching politics (i.e., living in a "city" and managing a "city") seems to be conceived as a response to the challenge of sophists – ancient paid intellectuals who equated what was good with what was natural and what is political with what is contractual, imposed, and relative. In More's view, *it was the battle of one man for the deeper common sense of mankind against the sophistries of a people that had lost its Anchorage and was drifting it knew not whither.*[56] Babbitt shares a similar approach. According to him, while Socrates was *working out the new basis for conduct he continues to observe the existing laws and customs; or if he gets away from the traditional discipline it is towards a stricter discipline; if he repudiates in aught the common sense of his day, it is in favor of a commoner sense,*[57] while the "commoner" sense should be understood as meeting the universal needs of the imagination to a greater and greater degree. In More, the historical Socrates himself is the epitome of a paradox – the simultaneous presence of skepticism, "spiritual affirmation" (the belief that it is worth being just), and rationalism (identifying virtue with the benefit of knowledge). On these grounds, there appears the philosophical and political justification of living in obedience to laws or conventions (being a good citizen of one's *polis*), but also the prospect of the farthest path – fulfillment in a philosophical life; a vision of a life that is truly free (from the omnipotence of impulses or passions), expe-

56 Id., *Platonism*, Princeton–London 1917, p. 21; cf. ibid., pp. 49–53.
57 I. Babbitt, *Rousseau and Romanticism...*, p. 245; cf. ibid., p. 175 and id., *On Being Creative...*, p. xii.

The Ancient Mirror of Theology

riencing genuine reassurance (as to the sense of individual existence), and heading towards true autarky, the self-sufficiency of an individual.[58]

The timeless importance of the Socratic tradition stems precisely from the fact that its cornerstone is a proclamation of the principles of *common sense*, in isolation from which the philosopher's mind fails. Plato creates myths in the name of the success of this proclamation. Thus, we can say that he harnessed fabulous theology to the service of natural theology. However, he does not pay the price that Christianity later paid. Let us give the floor to More: *when I see the perplexity into which even St. Paul could be thrown by the fear of losing his belief in a particular miraculous event* (i.e., Jesus' Resurrection), *I appreciate the force of Plato's boast that he alone, with his master, had the courage to rest his faith on the simple common sense of mankind. This is philosophy. Having expounded the meaning of the commonplace that it is better to be just than to be unjust, and having thus given authority to the affirmation of the spirit, philosophy does not seek for extraneous proofs of this truth, but proceeds to use it as a principle for investigating the manifold life and activities of the soul.*[59] And it is precisely at this point that the correction takes place, which brings More to the apologetic-theological "phase" of his writing. Why? Because no poetic spells of a philosopher can match the power of the revealed Word, which grants hope of salvation to all humanity. A man tortured with fire cares little for the beauty of discourse. Simply put, *common(er) sense*, discovered by the Greeks, demands Revelation.[60]

We are not, as of yet, resolving More's relation to faith treated – according to the Christian, Pauline tradition – as accepting the deposit of Truth into our hearts. Suffice it to say that the way of thinking we have reconstructed – most likely better than the approach dominant in Babbitt's works – fits what we call the ancient mirror of theology. As long as we remain people of flesh and

58 Cf. P. E. More, *Hellenistic Philosophies...*, especially pp. 9–10.
59 Id., *Platonism...*, p. 76.
60 Cf. id., *Christ the Word...*, especially pp. 251–61.

blood, the most profound dilemma of Revelation and philosophy remains our dilemma, a riddle *par excellence* and, as it were, the first entry on the hefty bill of humanity we've been handed; regardless of whether or not we look at the majority of those whose horizon of life is within the walls of the *polis*, who need, above all, reassurance from an external authority; or – at adepts of the philosophical life who are able to approach spiritual autarky. Against this backdrop, the "late" More unequivocally states that humanism without (revealed) religion as a source of "purpose and value" is "incomplete." So, he is approaching Eliot's position. The latter, having undergone an official conversion to Anglicanism (Anglo-Catholicism), speaks openly from the perspective of someone who has received the Revelation. This point of view also allows him to indicate, with almost daring clarity, the proper place of the Humanist Movement. Eliot thus asserts: *I believe that the sceptic, even the pyrrhonist, but particularly the humanist-sceptic, is a very useful ingredient in a world which is no better than it is (...) the ideal world would be the ideal Church. But very little knowledge of human nature is needed to convince us that hierarchy is liable to corruption, and certainly to stupidity; that religious belief, when unquestioned and uncriticised, is liable to degeneration into superstition; that the human mind is much lazier than the human body; and that the communion of saints in Tibet is of a very low order (...) criticism, infidelity and agnosticism must, to be of value, be* original *and not inherited. Orthodoxy must be traditional, heterodoxy must be original (...) and precisely I fear lest humanism should make a tradition of dissent and agnosticism, and so cut itself off from the sphere of influence in which it is most needed.* For, bearing in mind the good of religion, we must remember *that religion without humanism produces the opposite and conflicting types of religious bigotry (liberalism in religion is a form of bigotry).*[61] Eliot's statement leads to the conclusion that humanism, as a "heterodox" attitude in the eyes of God's people, cannot afford the ambition to "delve" into natural theology and replace

61 T. S. Eliot, *Religion Without Humanism* [in:] *Humanism and America...*, pp. 105– 06, 108. Emphasis in original.

The Ancient Mirror of Theology

tradition. What comes to mind here is a – somewhat inelegant – comparison to the symbiosis of two organisms, the smaller of which is a parasite, but a necessary one. Therefore, "true humanism" should be seen as an elite activity within a faith-based system. It has nothing to do with humanistic "zeal," that is, the alleged desire of the "New Humanists" to offer secular *ersatz* spiritual experiences. *Humanism* – Eliot writes – *makes for breadth, tolerance, equilibrium and sanity. It operates against fanaticism (...) it operates by taste, by sensibility trained by culture. It is critical rather than constructive. It is necessary for the criticism of social life and social theories, political life and political theories (...) humanism can have no positive theories about philosophy or theology. All that it can ask, in the most tolerant spirit, is: Is this particular philosophy or religion civilized or is it not?*[62]

The above approach, referring to the supreme authority of Revelation, seems close to what More arrives at. Here, we would be dealing with the opposite view: "orthodoxy" serves "heterodoxy," and no, the latter cannot pretend to be the former. *Can humanism, of itself, unaided, provide the purpose and values it needs for its fulfillment and without which it cannot pass from the purely critical to the productive state? Must it not for its driving force depend on religion? The question is primarily pragmatic, but at the last it involves a whole philosophy of faith.* Thus, what emerges is the somewhat disturbing prospect of the judgment of religion – through and through – according to the criterion of "fueling" attitudes that favor the idea of humanism (or the preservation of civilization). *It must be a militant force that will intermeddle with the whole of life, exacting obedience and arousing enmities. Nor, on the other hand, can it, for the humanist at least, be such a sublimation of the ethical will as would deprive this transient world of significance and demand the total renunciation of mortal ambitions and desires. On the contrary it must come into the heart of man, not without austerity of command, yet with salutary hope, assuring us that our practical sense of right and wrong,*

---

62 Id., *Second Thoughts about Humanism* [in:] id., *Selected Essays*, London 1999, pp. 488–89.

of beauty and ugliness, is justified by the eternal canons of truth, and that the consequences of our deeds in this little segment of space may follow the soul in its flight into regions beyond our utmost guessing. It must fortify the purpose of the individual by inspiring him with a conviction that the world in which he plays his part is not a product of chance or determinism, but the work of a foreseeing intelligence, and is itself fulfilled with purpose. It must lend new meaning and larger values to visible phenomena by seeing in them shadows and symbols of invisible realities, and by exhibiting them as servants to a spiritual end.[63]

Revelation – a pragmatic matter? How should this be understood? Are we not faced with the – vulgar – temptation to instrumentalize the effects of religious experience? Is it even possible to speak of a serious attitude toward traditionally-understood faith's (intellectual) claims? Will religion, framed on the basis of the theological image of Divine Providence or the mythological description of the relationship between a man and his Lord, prove to be only a useful "superstructure" of the interpretation of human nature provided by philosophy?[64] That, therefore, we are not so much returning to the classical understanding of natural theology as an extra-political activity of "higher minds," but rather that we wish to engage these minds in constructing political theology and mythical theology, which constitute the most effective possible translation of practical aspects of philosophical life into the realities of "urban" life? Undoubtedly, as a fully mature thinker, More undertakes a reinterpretation of the fundamental truths of Christianity. He tirelessly discusses their roots, which lie in what he calls "the Greek tradition." Its axis is marked by "true Platonism"; "true" because it differs not only from the philosophical schools of antiquity that bear separate names, but also – especially – from the ecstatic-metaphysical formula of Neoplatonism. Therefore, it tries to bridge the gap between the era of humanitarianism, from the center of which it speaks to modern

63 P. E. More, *A Revival of Humanism* [in:] id., *On Being Human...*, pp. 15, 22.
64 Cf. id., *The Religion of Plato...*, p. 109.

adherents of the religion of humanity, and the era of the Church Fathers, more or less distancing itself from the achievements of the long-standing Christian interlude, that is, the historical formation of Christendom. In his view, *it remains true that in some important respects the Occident, in so far as it has been dominated by Roman legalism and medieval scholasticism, has added elements unfortunate in themselves and alien to the original spirit of the faith. From these religion, if it is to hold the modern mind, must be freed, and can most easily be freed by returning, for the moment at least, to the more Hellenic type of theology. We need to reintegrate for ourselves the Gospels and the philosophy of Plato, as this was once done in the dogma of Christ the Word.*[65] But what is this connection supposed to consist in? How can we judge the Bible's message? Based on what findings? One might suspect that we are moving towards a view of religion in which it does not necessarily have to be true according to its own claims. What matters is its place in our civilization's log of profits and losses.

Let's put it another way. Is it not the role of Christianity (and other belief systems or cults directed at the afterlife) to provide effective tools for exercising power over the masses? Isn't the point simply to raise a faithful, obedient people, ensnared by the fear of punishment for their sins? Among More's numerous publications, there is a lecture titled *Religion and Social Discontent* (1921), where our author evokes the classical understanding of religion in the spirit of political theology as an *instrumentum regni* with ambiguous approval. Plato, Polybius, Tacitus, John Chrysostom – all of them linked the presentation of divine matters with the need to ensure a stable social order and a general sense of well-being. Interestingly, More sees a continuation of this approach in modern times: *passing on to the eighteenth century, one finds the politico-religious thought of England and France dominated by the Polybian notion that religion was imposed more or less deliberately on the people by their masters as an instrument of government, only with this important difference, that in England the*

65 Id., *Christ the Word...*, p. vi.

HUMANISM AS REALISM

imposition was commonly regarded even by the more radical deists and freethinkers as a salutary and necessary fraud, whereas across the channel a more logical and less prudential habit of speech led the bolder spirits at least to spurn the whole fabric of traditional religion as an impediment to liberty and progress. The British elites of the time were still able to hitch Christianity to the "miraculous fiction" of their system. This was possible because their education allowed them to see in advance the damage of propagating, say, Eliot's, heterodox attitudes. However, the teaching of the classics itself is not a monolith in terms of judging the truths of faith. According to More, *classic philosophy, the philosophy of idealism properly so called, which underlies all religion, whether Platonic or Christian,* treats religion *as a conservative, or at least as a regulative, force in society. But thinking men have differed profoundly in their valuation of such a force.* The political result of godliness appeared to those who followed the notion of a soul related to God (or ideas) as the apparent correlate of true knowledge. In turn, *those sceptically and materialistically inclined, to whom the spiritual world of Plato and St. Augustine is merely an insubstantial fabric wrought out of the discontent of mankind with the actualities of life, have been divided in their attitude. By some, this dream of the unseen (…) has been accepted* with the awareness of its falsehood and its *de facto* irremovability in the name of order and well-being. In such a system, *the enlightened few might indulge their superiority of doubt, but without the restraining content born of superstition the turbulent desires of the masses would throw the world into anarchy and barbarism and universal misery. That was the prevalent attitude of ancient rationalism; and it is still common enough today* (i.e., about one hundred years ago), that the association of the social functions of the Church with the maintenance of public order, appropriate for this tradition, makes itself felt. However, this is not the only, nor the main, variant of heterodoxy. *To others, a rapidly growing number, it seems that the spirit of content engendered by religion, if based on a falsehood, must be detrimental to the progress of mankind. Or perhaps their position might be expressed more accurately by reversing the terms. They would not say that religious content is false and therefore must be detrimental; but rather, religious content is inimical to progress and therefore must be false.*[66]

What can we conclude from this? First, we should certainly note the theological and political mode of defining the "modern movement." Classical thought – as defined by More – is divided into the "philosophy of idealism" and naturalistic rationalism. In both cases, there is a sense of illusion: either of the things of the world or how we deal with the things of the world. Either one considers faith ("the dream of the unseen") to be adequate because it is philosophically justified, the reaction of a thinking man to reality, or it is assessed through the prism of natural necessity (people in their mass are not philosophers), as a practice not resulting from knowing the truth, but politically adequate. On the other hand, the humanitarian attitude should be understood not as the result of a skeptical perception of religion in a broad sense, but, as we have tried to show, of internalizing a competing vision of revealed truth. The new faith revolves around the promise of beneficent expansion and emancipation of humanity. The fact that traditional religion is doomed to extinction is not a consequence of a philosophical rejection of Revelation. Whether we look at the eighteenth-century French revolutionaries or the later advocates of progress associated with the theory of evolution, they all cannot come to terms with practical "contentment" on the path of faith. This is precisely where the battle for power over souls unfolds. From the point of view of classical political theology, mature humanitarianism remains a form of heterodoxy, but a special and, in fact, illusory one. There is, inevitably, a continuous reproduction of predictable "mental shortcuts" or fruits of the imagination drawn from a long tradition – or anti-tradition – of overthrowing (ridiculing) Christianity. Here and there, from generation to generation, the family ethos of being a "liberator" is passed on. If only there were something to be liberated from!

Let's try to summarize some of our reflections. As More in-

66 Id., *Religion and Social Discontent* [in:] id., *On Being Human...*, pp. 120–21, 123–24.

structs us, what *really* touches people's hearts is not laborious introspection (or discourse that would encourage it), but hope in pursuing a goal (which may be a spiritual goal). This is the lesson of the Fathers of the Church, who, being heirs of philosophers, were ready to condemn *philosophy with its inability to convert the stubborn hearts of men and to save the masses. And the Fathers were right (...) it is simply true that, in setting the emphasis so strongly upon knowledge and intelligence and in leaving so little room for the will and the instinctive emotions, classical philosophy, even the philosophy of Plato, had left the great heart of mankind untouched. Christianity, by transferring the source of good and evil to the will and by appealing more directly to the emotions and imagination, had in a measure succeeded where philosophy had failed – yet, even so, how small has been that measure of success! Looking back over all that Christianity has done and has not done, we may ask ourselves whether God meant to save His people by the emotions alone any more than by the understanding alone; we may broach the question whether the tragedy of Christianity was not just there, in its failure to achieve, or at least to impose on the world, a sound combination of dialectic and emotionalism (...) in the West also theology received a strong Neoplatonic (i.e., not "truly" Platonic) bent from St. Augustine; and then (...) there flowed over East and West alike the desiccating winds of Aristotelian scholasticism. As a consequence our Latin Christianity has been largely a mixture of unbridled emotion, running up into pure mysticism, with scholastic metaphysics – a mechanical, unstable mixture and no true marriage of the intellect and the will.*[67] It is not difficult to notice that historical Christianity – according to this interpretation – for most of its existence is situated on an inclined plane, descending downward in a zigzag of tensions between equally destructive attitudes: optimism about the possibilities of reason on the one hand, and optimism about the effects of engaging one's feelings – on the other. We will come back to this later. Meanwhile, the outline of More's intellectual search and the main reason why it was undertaken become

67 Id., *Hellenistic Philosophies*..., pp. 299–301; cf. id., *Platonism*..., pp. 89–90 and id., *Irving Babbitt*..., p. 41.

The Ancient Mirror of Theology

clearer. They are not conditioned by abandoning a critical assessment of theology's centuries-old struggles or strengthening approval for Christianity's civilizational achievements. We may even be offended by this cold distance to Christendom's legacy. After all, this is about "only" one key element that distinguishes the Christian faith from the other great ascents of the spirit, especially Buddhism. *Christianity may seem to have failed in so many ways; it has done so little for the morals and intelligence of civilization, so little to mitigate the evils of social and international injustice, so little to impose the restraint on the insurgent passions of mankind; but this one thing it has effected, the offering of hope, the long hope, to the souls of individual men.*[68]

The presentation in the foreground of the hope that stimulates individual spiritual development, which is like a natural promise of supernatural happiness, does not preclude the recognition of the ordering aspect of religious life. Of course, we cannot suppose that More pays tribute to rulers or "gentlemen" for whom theological-political manipulation would be a means of realizing their own ideals of expansion. This type of cynicism of the distinguished, socially privileged, and rapacious deserves condemnation, at least in principle, because we face unwanted compromises in practice. And what situation should be considered desirable? Likely one in which mass piety could feed on the image of natural aristocrats' religious life (and humanism). These, in turn, would be taught to draw – wisely – from the experience of people guided by religious instincts. This unique instinct, acting in opposition to wants or desires on a biological basis – that is, despite (horizontal) expansion – determines the presence of enthusiasm. We remember Babbitt's remark that enthusiasm is a feature of a religious experience, not a humanistic one; from More we learn – to simplify a bit – that there is no better (more effective) version of enthusiasm than that produced by Christianity. To understand

68 Id., *Marginalia* [in:] *The Essential Paul Elmer More: A Selection of His Writings*, ed. B. C. Lambert, New Rochelle, New York 1972, p. 41; cf. P. E. More, *The Sceptical Approach...*, p. 185.

this, one must first grasp the very concept of the religious instinct, which in its action *is based on the two contrary tendencies in the soul of man, by one of which he is dragged down to the desires and painful satisfactions of this world, which by the other he is lifted out of changing impressions into the serene contemplative possession of himself. Faith is the faculty whereby the world becomes unreal beneath the light of the greater inner reality.*[69] In other words, the essence of the experience induced by following the religious instinct would be a fundamental shift of desires (and not their extinction at their source, which would be improbable and inhuman): from what the visible world offers to what appears to be an otherworldly, inviolable horizon of the soul's existence; from what must turn out to be impermanent, to what cannot be questioned.

At the same time, however – and this is the point of contact with humanism and political thinking – traditional *religion has always recognized the legitimacy of another standard of life besides the one peculiarly its own. It has seen clearly that the ideal of poverty and chastity and obedience, which would uproot altogether the natural instincts, is possible for very few men, and that the attempt to enforce such a standard absolutely on society at large would result in a world of hypocrisies, if it did not actually run counter to the command of the Creator.* In this respect, says More, Buddhism and Christianity behave similarly. Severe asceticism, or following the religious instinct, never becomes the universal norm. Next to monks live the fathers (and mothers) of families; next to the saints – ordinary people. The law given to them cannot be religious in the strict sense – directing one, here and now, to the afterlife. But by no means can they – those loving and arguing, sweating, and trading with one other – be left to their own devices. The world we live in every day – the world of "horizontal" desires and goals, the world of things – is nothing but an arena for the hopeless struggle for existence and meaningless passings, and *both Christianity and Buddhism held that the natural instincts were ruinous if left to themselves, and that they became salutary instruments of welfare only when limited*

69   Id., *The Bhagavad Gîtâ* [in:] id., *Studies of Religious...*, p. 43.

and softened and illuminated by a law not of themselves.[70] So we return to the basic formula of the humanistic judgment of religion: that is good (politically), which serves the preservation of civilization. What is good, then, is order that is sanctified *from above* and, possibly, once and for all.

However, the difficulty in recounting More's position and showing its advantages results from the intrinsic intricacy of linking the political aspect (effects) of religious experience with experience – the divine – *par excellence*, individual and spiritual. Many of the proclamations and observations of our thinker seem to concern a personal experience of faith or the desire to live in faith. The most important chapters in this regard can be found in a peculiar little work entitled *Pages from an Oxford Diary*, stylized as the notes of an old Oxford lecturer, written in the mid-1920s and published, at More's request, in the year of his death (supplemented at that time with a very concise preface in which he describes the text as "a transcription of a very real experience on my side"). The author mentions *a passionate search to discover the eternal verities behind the veil* (the illusion of the material world) – *the realm of Ideas which Plato taught, and in which my soul could move, some day if not now, in liberated joy. I can say simply and without reservation that to this goal I attained, and that I shall end my days a conscious, as I was born, an unconscious, Platonist. The visible world of things has contracted into comparative insignificance save as a symbol of that which is unseen; the Ideal world has become the vivid reality upon which all my deeper emotions are centered (...) but here I could not rest. Is that realm of Ideas a cold vacuum of inanimate images? (...) I knew that what I still needed was God.*[71] This poignant confession must be confronted with a critical opinion on the fate of Plato's teachings in the past. For, *in a manner not given to any other writer Plato must be regarded as the liberator of the spirit, who has set wings to the human soul and sent it voyaging through the empyrean* (divine heaven). *But*

70 Id., *Religion and Social...*, p. 136.
71 Id., *Pages from an Oxford Diary*, Princeton–London 1937, chapter VI (no page numbers present).

Humanism as Realism

in that flight how many have mounted too near the sun, and fallen to earth in ruinous combustion! How many others have forever lost their way in those thin heights! Alas, for the weakness of mankind, and their "blind hopes"! It is a fact, sad and indisputable, that no one is more likely to call himself, or to be called by his admirers, a Platonist than the reformer with a futile scheme for the regeneration of the world, or the dreamer who has spurned the realities of human nature for some illusion of effortless perfection, or the romantic visionary who has set the spontaneity of fancy above the rational imagination, or the "fair soul" who has withdrawn from the conflict of life into the indulgence of a morbid introspection, or the votary of faith as a law abrogating the sterner law of works and retribution. Half the enthusiasts and inspired maniacs of society have shielded themselves under the aegis of the great Athenian. Not to mention the detected mountebanks, the list is replete with the names of accepted sages whose wisdom, if brought to the test, would prove to be only a finer form of spiritual flattery.[72] But where can we look for a criterion that would separate the false application of Plato's teachings from their true continuation?

It is the direction of thinking about God that indicates it. Ironically twisting around the words of Mephistopheles from *Faust* – about "the Spirit that denies"[73] – More makes one of his most important statements: *it is God that denies, not Satan.* How does this relate to the evaluation of Platonism? A man who enters on the path to a philosophical life is faced with a promise to get out of the "house of slavery," which is how the world of opinions professed by his loved ones or fellow citizens appears to him; opinions as if pinned to a given place and time. Rightly then, his eyes look to the horizon, beyond the farthest limits of the city (culture, epoch); they go to what is eternal, unblemished, divine. Here, the adepts of philosophy begin to divide into two groups. *To the true Platonist the divine spirit, though it may be called, and is, the hidden source of beauty and order and joy, yet always, when it speaks directly in the human breast, makes itself heard as an inhibition; like the guide*

---

72   Id., *Platonism...*, pp. 270–71.
73   See J. W. Goethe, *Faust*, trans. G. M. Priest, Chicago 1952, p. 33.

of Socrates (i.e., a daimonion), it never in its own proper voice com-
mands to do, but only to refrain. Whereas to the pseudo-Platonist it ap-
pears as a positive inspiration, saying yes to his desires and emotions
(…) what is reverenced as the spirit becomes a snare instead of a monitor:
liberty is turned into license, a glamour of sanctity is thrown over the
desires of the heart, the humility of doubt goes out of the mind, the will
to follow this or that impulsion is invested with divine authority, there
is an utter confusion of the higher and the lower elements of our nature.[74]
What follows from this? We can again, for the sake of clarity, indicate two dimensions. In the political dimension, such an approach opposes – taking Plato as a witness – the affirmation of
satisfaction that permeates modern thinking about the state and
society. There is no universal (supra-political) warranty for universal comfort or satisfaction. In particular, one should not believe
in the divine provenance of what we desire instinctively, mas-
sively. On the other hand, in the spiritual (philosophical) dimension, More's Platonic *dictum* exposes the errors of individual
self-assertion, failure to think about natural limitations, and over-
estimation of the strength of one's intellect. The beginnings of the
knowledge of God (divinity) come not so much through speculation, which is potentially deceptive, but through the practice of
suspension of judgment, an *inner check*, which is itself subject to
critical reflection.

But haven't we hit a dead end? What does this *ex post* corrective concept of practicing philosophy in the Socratic spirit have
to do with the Spirit understood as the personal Creator of "all
things visible and invisible," as Judge and Savior? The "late"
More is shifting towards the theistic formula (God is a person
who is not indifferent to us). However, he still holds onto his interpretation of Platonism, directly referring to the *inner check* criterion introduced earlier. *The danger of fanaticism or sentimentalism*
from assuming we have positive knowledge where we have none must
not be minimized (...) but I think that admission of the visible effect of

---

74 P. E. More, *Platonism...*, pp. 272–73. Cf. I. Babbitt, *Rousseau and Ro-*
manticism..., pp. 147–48, 179–81, 255–56, 360–61.

HUMANISM AS REALISM

inhibitions in beauty and order and joy should be understood more lib-erally in accordance with the Timaean allegory (i.e., the hypothetical image of the creation of the world by Demiurge as presented by Plato in the dialogue *Timaeus*). *If God works with His eye upon an Ideal pattern, then at least His knowledge has a very positive content, and His will is fixed upon a very positive goal, though their operation in this composite sphere of existence may appear to our understanding as a bare checking of excess.*[75] Thus, we come to an analogy between the deliberate action of man, the proper field of which is his own soul, and the action of the Creator based on His plan of forming wayward matter. A man correctly, that is, in his own measure, im-itating God – a man of true faith – affirms creation in the cosmic dimension when he chooses the matter within himself as the raw material he wishes to sculpt and overcomes the resistance of the body, thus contributing to the overall work of salvation.

All these twists and turns of More's thoughts become much more understandable when we consider the fundamental impor-tance he gives to a sense of illusion. The word "illusion" does not mean "false" here. Instead, it is intended to express both how re-ality appears to us and how we react to what becomes manifest. The key, then, will be to distinguish a "true illusion" from a "false" illusion and, respectively, "false disappointment" or "dis-illusion" from a "true awakening." What's behind this? Well, it is undoubtedly easier for us, modern humans, to grasp the meaning of a "false illusion" – and to describe our participation in experi-encing its effects (although we are faced with the age-old reluc-tance to tell the truth about ourselves). Indeed, an illustration immediately comes to mind: a man manipulated by advertise-ments; a dull consumer who thinks that the more he enriches himself in life, the more he will have in the end; meanwhile, it is known from the start that he will not take nondescript gadgets and discounts with him to the grave; the prospect of the painful falsehood of such an existence is all too apparent. Let us look at another example. Here in the "spiritualized" version of moder-

75 P. E. More, *The Sceptical Approach...*, pp. 200–01.

The Ancient Mirror of Theology

nity, and certainly closer to the main thread of our considerations, a sad old hippie looks at us. This gentleman has been through a lot; drank from many decanters; been carried time and time again to the ends of the galaxy among fragrant vapors; free in love like a migratory bird; chasing after his heart's desire without hesitation; a geyser of "positive emotions"; a master of "being himself." Now, he would be a guru for young, hungry people, but why so... sad? Well, because young hungry people do not need a decaying old guru. Which grandson is taking grandpa to the party? Don't get your hopes up, you morbid old man! Your reckoning is poor ... But let us be fair. If not he himself, then the people of his generation have made a lot of great music. Do we deny that their sounds call us with their beauty? That we want to imitate this beauty, to bask in it? That we want to be like them ... but young and hungry (still or again), not – corrupt old men...? We won't deny it. This is what the "false illusion" is all about.

You have to be very careful which poets (prophets, gurus) you put your faith in. Where they promise us the fulfillment of our desires and the liberation of our hearts, where the pinnacle of thought may be an exalted phrase about our "right" to this or that, where there is no room for "something more," which is not a further affirmation of satisfaction, but the acceptance of the presence of the One, who says "no" – *there shall be wailing and gnashing of teeth* (Matthew 13:42). More writes: *at first this false illusion is sweet, but soon it is troubled with the bitterness of satiety; and the awakening from it leaves only the emptiness of endless regret and self-tormenting. The false disillusion is a discovery that the looker-on who masqueraded as the spirit is merely a phantom of the body; it is a perception of the hollowness of the old illusion without the power of escaping therefrom (...) the disillusion of the flesh is perhaps the saddest chapter in human experience.* What, then, would a "true" illusion be? First of all, it doesn't lead anywhere because it doesn't combine *the things of the spirit with the things of the world.* It does contain the knowledge that *the way of the spirit must lie through this meadowland of calamity*; a man who understands its course can – thanks to "deliberate efforts of the will" – *throw the glamour of light and joy and freedom on the objects by the roadside, so that the spirit may journey swiftly and pleasantly to its own upland home.*[76] In other words, the concept of a "true illusion" refers to conditions conducive to the true fulfillment of our humanity; true – that is, not confined to the horizontal order. A man striving for holiness, a man of faith – in More's understanding – does not want to be the master on the lower level; with the sure step of a self-aware pilgrim, he travels through the ungrateful meadow-land to find peace of mind at the end of his pilgrimage – in an "upland home." The "true illusion" allows us to think – for ourselves – in a vertical fashion, to live "upwardly," to climb spiritually. It is a gift of meaning (hope, enthusiasm). It makes what surrounds us, which in itself ultimately has no value, become a herald of or encouragement to a "true awakening." It gives the world higher laws and measures that are not of this world.

It is difficult to say about someone that s/he could be a fully intellectual steward of "true illusion." Plato certainly came close to this role. As More writes: *the ideal world, created or, it may be, obscurely grasped by the imagination, is thus at once an illusion and a reality, with this difference, that when we deal with philosophy as a mere dead corpus of speculation these Ideas fade away into an illusory make-believe, whereas such is the constitution of our spiritual nature that the more we take philosophy as a principle of life the more vivid and real do they become. That is a truth which can be demonstrated only by living, not by argument. But of the facts of ethical experience underlying the Ideas there is no such halting tale, no question at all of make-believe.*[77] Further, however, since the relationship between the world of ideas and the world known by the senses appears to be unbearably paradoxical, so that it is impossible to propose a credible and

---

76 Id., *Arthur Symons: The Two Illusions* [in:] id., *Shelburne Essays First Series*, New York – London 1904, p. 128, 127–28; cf. id., *The Forest Philosophy...*, pp. 14–15.
77 Id., *Platonism...*, p. 195; cf. id., *The Religion of Plato...*, especially pp. 309 ff., 328–32; id., *The Sceptical Approach...*, pp. 11 ff.; id., *The Catholic Faith*, Princeton 1931, p. 218.

The Ancient Mirror of Theology

meaningful transition from one to the other, then the work of the best minds, weaving the garments of true illusion, does not stop there. There is a need for a Creator, a Judge, a Savior; a need for the Word. Someone may say: It comes to them by Itself, as long as they keep their minds open to It; and to them – as ones of many, because Revelation is not the property of philosophy. Maybe. In any case, this is the task of the true philosophers: to create a theater of moral imagination. After all, true philosophers are responsible philosophers.

It is this problem of philosophical responsibility that casts a shadow on the history of Christianity. In More's view, *Augustine opened the door to a perilous intensification of the religious emotions with his famous reduction of all reality to God* and his own soul. For while Ideas are retained *as independent realities the purpose of creation and deliverance is directed by the external canons of beauty and order; without them right and wrong cease to have any final validity and the universe is left with no ultimate law of responsibility. The will of God becomes purely self-centered, while on the part of man there is the ever present danger of arbitrary fanaticism.*[78] What is the modern faith in humanity if not the result of this state of affairs? A false version of the Good News, a crazy tale of self-renunciation and the conquest of nature by natural instincts; a story that otherwise adopts a naturalistic view of the things of this world? For all his greatness, and perhaps unintentionally, St. Augustine began the great spoiling of the Christian myth and thus the disarming of the "true illusion" that could arise and develop on the foundation of the revealed Word.

IV.

In the age of humanitarianism, it's hard to talk about evil. Terms such as "diseases," "pathologies," "problems" are encountered much more readily. They correspond, roughly speaking, to the postulates of "treating," "isolating," and "eliminating." So, we

78   Id., *The Catholic Faith...*, pp. 309, 308. Emphasis in original.

have advice for all kinds of evil – therapies, services, projects, etc. That all of this is temporary and apparent? As a last resort you can always say to yourself: don't think about it, don't ask, forget it. It is, in turn, a sign of the truthfulness and completeness of the record of human experiences to face the topic of evil openly and seriously. The traditional message of faith retains its value – at least for some – insofar as it reveals, at bottom, a genuine "sense of evil" in its true magnitude. *How otherwise* – asks Paul Elmer More – could *religion meet those harder questions of experience when its aid is most needed? And in like manner* will they *say that the power of philosophy as the* dux vitae *depends on its acquaintance with the scope and difficulties of skepticism? Both religion and philosophy would seem (…) to rest not only on a statement of the dualism of good and evil, knowledge and ignorance, but on a realization of the full meaning and gravity, practical and intellectual, of this dualism.*[79] How are we to understand this?

From our point of view, a useful procedure may be to discuss moral evil and natural evil, as a starting point. The former is usually associated with meanness and brutality; at least some people reflecting on evil would add licentiousness and insolence (others might prefer to discuss liberty and equality in this context). A bit of reflection then leads us to link the various manifestations of evil in human behavior with a character deficit: man indulges; he loses control of himself; he succumbs to evil desires and emotions. More's position – as well as that of Irving Babbitt's – fits in well with the "common sense" mode of judgment. Regardless of our views on specific issues, each of us *somehow* knows that in the end, we are responsible for what we do. On this level, the cause of evil is submission to the power of impulses, to moral indolence. Therefore, the blade of humanist opposition will be directed

---

79 Id., *Emerson* [in:] id., *Shelburne Essays Eleventh Series: A New England Group and Others*, Boston–New York 1921, p. 89. Cf. L. Kołakowski, *Can the Devil be Saved?* [in:] id., *Modernity on Endless Trial*, Chicago – London 1997, pp. 149–67 and C. Schmitt, *The Concept of the Political*, Chicago 2007, especially pp. 229 ff.

The Ancient Mirror of Theology

against the clear tendency to make the victim out to be guilty of, say, the prevailing social relations; to make misdeeds – the fruits of a non-culpable affliction. What is needed here, of course, is an agreement as to what behavior is to be considered vicious; it is easy to condemn the disgusting rapist, but the limits of the accepted freedom may expand significantly (especially after the "sexual revolution") or, at other times, narrow. Either way, the general rule seems clear (and politically hopeless). But what about natural evil? When it is not moral indolence, but blind luck, misfortune, and inevitable human fate that we – equally "commonsensically" – disagree with? Deformed fetuses, children dying of cancer, a "broken" life, a sudden end to life. How many people brought up in the traditional faith lose it when they cannot explain to themselves why He is doing this to us! And how many not brought up in this way look with pity on the tormented child of the cruel Father in heaven! After all, there is a difference between evil in the hand of a sinner who brings hellish torments on himself, and evil as if from the devil that for us constitutes suffering for nothing! Let us add that not only people suffer. We can at least – according to the formula of Revelation known to us – count on reconciliation with God. What about the senseless suffering of animals? What was the fault of the antelope being torn apart by lions?

More undertakes this topic – of evil in all its dimensions. Certainly, especially in his late works, he goes further beyond the humanistic rhetoric of character and moral discipline than does Babbitt. Therefore, it may be argued that his arguments fall all the more within the classical realm of natural theology; that is, they serve to present a unified view of the nature of reality, of human and divine affairs. However, this is not entirely true. More's position is based on a consistent negation of reason's claim to explaining categories such as "good" and "evil." He is interested in the mythological "management" of experiences, the final perception of which cannot be translated into the language of metaphysics or optimistic theology, confidently using the tools of discourse. There is no recognition whatsoever of attempts to outline a theodicy; peculiarly, he does not accept the image of divine omnipotence as the source of evil (namely, everything that we cannot come to terms with here and now is some expression of a perfect plan realized in the afterlife). *In some sense* – More writes – *the imperfection of the creature is the weakness of the creator; no amount of sophistical theology can avoid the shuddering conclusion that tracks the causes of evil back to the first Cause of all.* The Augustinian concept of *felix culpa* betrays a false attempt to cover with a beautiful word what must be a rock of offense to a thinking man. The ancient Gnostics, on the other hand, *despite the grotesque puerilities of their mythology, saw deeper into the possible truth when they raised the tragedy of human life into a cosmic drama wherein the celestial Aeons were involved. Only, the Gnostics were bitten by the same metaphysics as the Christians, and so insisted on positing a God above the Aeons – the Abyss, or the Silence, as they named Him, a pure Abstraction of reason, unconcerned with the troubled facts of existence. Plato, from whom in part they took their ideas, had dealt more wisely with the matter when he attributed the imperfections of the world to the dark unfathomable Necessity, clinging to the very act of creation and obstructing its execution.*[80]

So, briefly – what is evil according to More? It is the result of the overall resistance of matter to a subject's intentions – a subject which, in the cosmic dimension, is best described in Platonic terms as the Demiurge. At the same time, perhaps contrary to the vision outlined in the pages of *Timaeus*, there is no place here for lesser deities, weaker and more tainted. All responsibility rests with one Creator; responsibility – not for evil as such, but for the efficiency in overcoming the resistance of matter. Evil in itself remains something irreducible to any parts of the description of reality, inexplicable and unacceptable at its root. If it is possible to speak – conditionally, "mythologically" – about its source, it would be a natural necessity (*Ananke*), inseparable from the divine intention (which expresses a willingness to share the good

80 P. E. More, *Pages from an Oxford...*, chapter XXII (no page numbers present).

The Ancient Mirror of Theology

or implement "at the bottom" the ideas that it has at its disposal "at the top") and the act of creation (giving forms, liberating matter from its original formlessness). In the most far-reaching, though still on the proper scale of human comprehension, understanding of the causes of evil, we reach a point where it feels as if there was a lack of energy to complete the work of creation. At the same time, we see an obvious analogy between what resists in us, what is therefore revealed in the experience of moral indolence, and what does not submit – from our point of view, within time – to the divine work of transforming chaos into cosmos. In both dimensions – the moral and the cosmic – the idea or goal (*telos*) turns out to be the key concept, always achieved at a certain cost and never fully. More's position appears, indeed, as a certain version of a teleological vision of the world (teleological – from this *telos*; everything, except the original formlessness, exists "for something," and this "something" comes "from above," from God's mind). However, at the heart of this conception turns out to be the most fundamental discrepancy between the world which is slowly "becoming" and the absolute good, which cannot be spoken of in a "rational" or "positive" fashion, and which we recognize only by the traces of the action of the One who sees it. We are given – perhaps indispensable – participation in the general process of becoming and perfecting things, that is, deliberately overcoming the resistance of matter, and not – perfect order, complete satisfaction, or reconciliation of everything with everything else. The reality of the natural world may seem cruel, but since there are laws imposed on it, such that an antelope does not eat a lion alternately with a lion eating an antelope – this is already a success.[81]

The problem of evil – its philosophical foundation – is related to the understanding of "dualism." More uses this word in various contexts. The dualistic mode of reflection on oneself and the world seems to support, or even enable, a correct evaluation of

81 Cf. id.., *The Sceptical Approach*…, especially pp. 74–78; id., *The Religion of Plato*…, especially pp. 216 ff., 232–61.

HUMANISM AS REALISM

moral (and political) issues. It is not a specific theory, however, but the way in which we relay our pre-philosophical experience of being a conscious subject. In the aforementioned *Definitions of Dualism*, this central formula is as follows: *consciousness, the more deeply we look into ourselves, tells us that we are ceaselessly changing, yet tells us also that we are ever the same. This dualism of consciousness, it seems, is the last irrational fact, the report behind which we cannot go, the decision against which there is no appeal, the reality which only stands out the more clearly it is questioned. If a man denies this dualism of consciousness there is no argument with him, but a fundamental difference of intuition which will follow into every view of philosophy and criticism.*[82] Of course, More could not have had many people to debate in his day. He would also not have them today, since we are used to treating the completely dissimilar theses of naturalistic monism as the essence of thought and the educational canon. Meanwhile, a slightly different approach to "dualism" can be found in one of his last statements (addressed, interestingly, to two European students asking about the "thread binding" the works of the American thinker): *in every field of experience, if I push my analysis to the end of my resources, I find myself brought up against a pair of irreconcilable, yet interrelated and interacting, contraries, such as "good" and "bad," "mind" and "body," the "One" and the "Many," "rest" and "motion." The dualist is one who modestly submits to this bifurcation as the ultimate point where clarity of definition obtains. Beyond this he refuses to follow reason in its frantic endeavor to reconcile these opposites by any logical legerdemain which one of the controlling factors of consciousness is brought out as an Absolute while the other disappears in the conjuror's hat.* If, then, the classic vertical (higher – lower) opposition between reason and the passions should be regarded as permanently binding, we must avoid believing in, let us call it, impractical reason. There is always a verdict of experience that stands over the strength of the mind, however unbear-

---

82 Id., *Definitions of Dualism...*, pp. 248–49; cf. id., *Platonism...*, pp. 216–17; id., *The Religion of Plato...*, pp. 53–56; id., *The Forest Philosophy...*, pp. 16–18.

The Ancient Mirror of Theology

able or provocative for our intellect it is. However, this anti-rationalist message becomes muddied, when we read that *this (...) is only the superficial aspect of dualism; for the root of the matter, it should seem that we must look not to the logical faculty at all, but must penetrate to some deep substratum of the temperament or the emotions, to some obscure region of the soul itself, out of which spring the conflicting impulses to the religious and the worldly life.*[83] Thus, that from a certain perspective appears to be a decision concerning human nature, a natural and theological concept, turns out to be – from a different point of view – a thinking man's strategy in the face of the apparent weakness of reason and strength of the "substratum." *A dualist* – More will state – *might be defined as a philosopher with a sense of humour.*[84] *Sit anima mea cum philosophis,* he adds elsewhere (following Averroes).[85]

This dualist is the skeptic's "half-brother." We might consider him a representative of the practical "party" in the skeptic school, as a truly mature lover of truth who, as effectively as possible, protects his thoughts against the philosophical illnesses of rationalist pride and delusions. The "model" monist, on the contrary, is a fully "metaphysical dogmatist" who thinks that his "theory" or "worldview" ultimately explains everything, and so in practice, that view serves humanity most perfectly. For him, evil is something intellectually excluded (or possibly in the process of being excluded). *All monistic theorizing on the ultimate origin of evil turns inevitably to an apology for evil.* But monism has two faces: naturalistic and spiritual. In the first case, the world "makes sense" if we reduce *all* reality to a description of physical phenomena (or our attitude to these phenomena). It is worth noting that metaphysical pluralism is also one of the versions of naturalistic monism; according to the schema binding there, the "hard" image of the insurmountable multiplicity and relativity becomes

83 Id., *Marginalia...*, pp. 37–38.
84 Id., *Christ of the New Testament,* Princeton 1924, p. 9, note 5.
85 Id., *The Drift of Romanticism...*, p. xiv; cf. id., *The Catholic Faith...*, p. 98.

that wholeness-devouring "absolute." In general, the "absolute" truth of naturalism is well suited to "give up" from the beginning, without self-reflection, to the aspirations of the spirit, to what we previously called "self-remission." The downward indolence commands *men to rest lazily in a materialistic philosophy, explaining their actions by those mechanical causes which are first visible to the eye, and forgoing the search after the ethical motives which are the true springs of our life. It is against the innate indolence of the will that the whole scheme of Platonic education* of the king-philosopher *is directed.*[86] It's just that today, it is futile to summon philosopher-kings ... but we have plenty of lazy materialists. What about evil? It disappears with the madness of the cultural backwaters. It is treated, isolated, and condemned to elimination.

More's reluctance towards attitudes resulting from the adoption and use of doctrines founded on a naturalistic-monistic basis seems perfectly understandable. But what about spiritual monism? Should we not expect a much milder judgment of those who are simply devoid of the urge to face the miserable monotony of physical phenomena? Of people determined "vertically" by the action of the religious instinct, for whom the only meaning and the only law is in achieving an eternal union with the Absolute? Of those who, then, rushing to the top, seem to brush away all evil, like dust from the sleeves of a jacket? There is no reduced fare for them. If the "earlier" More sounds ambiguous in this respect, the "late" More presents a very strong, even devastating critique of the mystical tradition. Its beginning can be traced back to considerations on the Hellenistic schools, among which a daring analysis of Plotinus' thought shows the moment of transition from philosophy ("true" Platonism) to metaphysics, from rational insight into a reality full of illusions or paradoxes, to a uniform way of explaining everything based on the thinker's ecstatic experiences. *One may suspect that a terrible confusion of emotional values has played into a like intellectual confusion to create a strange and fascinating philosophy (...) but the record is too clear and*

86 Id., *The Religion of Plato...*, pp. 241, 257.

too disastrous; mysticism of the Plotinian type is almost certain evidence of a physical or mental or moral taint somewhere in the devotee.[87] Transferring this "error of the spirit" from the crisis-stricken pagan world to Christian grounds does not make things any better. Although the theistic confession of faith – the personal God of Scripture and the Church cannot be a pure abstraction – soothes the language of mystics, they still allegedly experience their supernatural "leaps," bringing reports of their own "self" dissolving into the immensity of the benevolent Absolute. In the notion of the faithful "babes," it makes them holy heroes, who sit through the night with God. At the same time, the incomprehensible Absolute becomes the obligatory conceptual coin in the field of ever more refined metaphysics. So, in our (pre-modern) civilization we deal with *this junction of religious enthusiasm and metaphysical abstraction*. We can boldly classify More's lecture on the historical role of Christian mysticism as one of his most outstanding texts. According to humanist rhetoric, mystics' spiritual monism appears as a mirror image of naturalistic monism here. Yes, this sender of *imprimaturs* for the sluggish, light-hearted, and sybaritic, as well as ardent advocates of self-fulfillment by way of the senses. No more, no less, our author judges, but *mysticism is a disease of religion, and not its perfection, and the impulse to hypostatize the unifying energy of the soul into an absolved Unity must be regarded as a temptation of the reason just as surely as the impulse in the opposite direction must be so regarded; and the effort to lose our sense of conscious responsible being* (in the world) *in the gaping abyss of the unconscious is a temptation of the spirit just as surely as the surrender in the opposite direction is a temptation of the flesh. Mysticism, in a word, is the handiwork of the Demon of the Absolute* (i.e., a living metaphysical temptation), *showing itself in the field of religion exactly as it does in the fields of philosophy and art and science. And as in the secular fields so in the religious, the temptation comes most strongly to the higher natures* (...) *their virtues are maintained at the cost of a certain tension between theory and practice. However he may act, the*

---

87   Id., *Hellenistic Philosophies...*, pp. 252–53.

mystic is one to whom, theoretically, the existent world has been denuded of all meaning and purpose, and whose will is set ultimately not upon taking his part in God's task of evoking order and beauty and design out of things as they are, but upon such an absolute withdrawal as in the eyes of the mystically-minded (recognizing illusions and paradoxes) *Platonist is a plain defalcation from duty.*[88]

It is undoubtedly worth examining this harsh assessment of the effects of the autocracy of the spirit, taking into account the theological and political context. Mysticism weakens religion, if only because it ultimately leads to a complete separation of the standards of religious life – wrongly validated – from the binding moral standards or, more broadly, the requirements of *common sense.*[89] Why should "simple" people look to those who, looking upwards, melt in a sense of complete liberation, at the cost of losing their real subjectivity? Where is the lesson in fighting evil, dealing with the "ordinary," everyday malice of the devil? Where is the incentive to be better – in the world? What consolation could there be in seeing this "absolute withdrawal" amidst emotional spasms and intellectual cabalism? What hope is there for those who do not share the fate of a mystic, and, in truth, when they take a close look at it, it is neither attractive to them, nor able to be translated into their "ordinary" desires? Further, the morbid experience of mystics breeds melancholy, a feeling that is in a way constitutive of "later" states of the spirit. It corresponds to the "false disillusion" of a man who does not know higher laws and belief in the afterlife. Since everything *worth* living for is "downstairs" in the natural order, we only have "horizontal" expansion and the emancipation of humanity. The fear of other human beings shown in the essay on ideals becomes the highest form of fear, and inevitable death – the only imaginable form of "entering" the Absolute. The historical role of mysticism – which is married to Western metaphysics, let us remember – boils down to the

88 Id., *The Catholic Faith...*, pp. 259, 297.
89 Cf. Ibid., p. 265 and: id., *Platonism*, p. 273; L. Kołakowski, *Diabeł* [in:] idem, *Czy diabeł może być...*, p. 181.

The Ancient Mirror of Theology

violation or destruction of the mythological credibility of Christianity. This is the vestibule of the real faith of the last few centuries: not so much the emergence of new aspirations as a transformation of the imagination based on fundamental doubt. Before it leads to great edifices and revolutions, the gust of religious enthusiasm collides with the naked wall of absolute negation and, if not completely absorbed by its desire for self-annihilation, turns back, thus creating the vortex from which modernity emerges.

The image of the vortex is good in that it also shows the specific shape of the surface over which our thoughts move roaringly – while seeming to fly. Their limited course and extent results from what would best be described as a "metaphysical hole." Whether we like it or not, we must limit ourselves at this point to merely suggesting that the reader follow the trail of a certain anomaly. Anyone who has flipped through Aristotle's *Nicomachean Ethics* is given the impression of an almost bizarre inconsistency in arguments that are otherwise a model testimony to the record of ancient thought. For, while the subsequent books of the treatise teach us to live based on civic virtues, to live "in the city," in the end, we learn that "perfect happiness" belongs only to "theoretical contemplation," to the "divine" life. *Nor ought we to obey those who enjoin that a man should have man's thoughts and a mortal the thoughts of mortality, but we ought so far as possible to achieve immortality, and do all that man may to live in accordance with the highest things in him* (i.e., in accordance with reason as an "element" that betrays divine provenance); *for though this be small in bulk, in power and value it far surpasses all the rest.*[90] We are therefore left with, so to speak, a mechanical juxtaposition of the two currents of existence; moreover, Aristotle's vision of divinity – absolutely pure, unblemished, fully devoted to its calling – does not allow a solid bridge of belief and enthusiasm to be built between them.

According to More, *in place of the living concrete dualism of Plato's*

---

90 Aristotle, *Nicomachean Ethics* [in:] *Aristotle in 23 Volumes*, vol. 19, trans. H. Rackham. Cambridge – London 1934, 1177 b – 1178 a.

divine energy working upon the slowly yielding potentiality of the world (the formation of matter), *we have in his successor a metaphysical dualism which partitions the universe into two incommunicable realms: on the one side a congeries of individual things and persons, each with its own energy and potentiality and its own end, and on the other side, set in remote isolation, God conceived as a goal of absolute goodness utterly unattainable by any individual of this world (...) Aristotle's Absolute (...) is pure energy and no potentiality of becoming anything, and pure causality which yet of itself causes nothing, a* telos *at which nothing arrives. Now it is just this final disjunction of the abstract and the concrete against which Plotinus revolts. His ultimate reality will be as metaphysical as Aristotle's, but at the same time he will find some way to connect it with the sphere of phenomenal existence.*[91] This method is embodied in the image of the successive levels of emanation of the Absolute, forming a sort of staircase for the spirit, on which the mystic climbs "from below" in ecstatic jumps. It seems that we can translate this process into the categories of modern naturalism – we change the vertical dimension of thinking into a horizontal one – by evaluating the eschatology of gradual, benevolent expansion (economic, technological, moral, etc., especially in the historiosophical version) emerging on their basis, through the lens of the extant discovery of the metaphysical hole. Let us note that Aristotle's conception itself is not naturalistic-monistic in its intent, but it does replace properly understood – and meeting the requirements of *common sense* – dualism, generating at the same time a vacuum of experience which is then buried (or covered) by the monists, with all the consequences of their desires, visions or interpretations of the world. These consequences concern, in particular, the problem of evil. As a result of the marriage of mysticism and metaphysics so strongly emphasized by More, natural ("dark") necessity is no longer associated with the resistance of matter that causes evil, but, on the contrary, with an emanation of the Good. Where would

91 P. E. More, *The Catholic Faith...*, pp. 226–27; cf. id., *Christ of the New...*, p. 137; id., *The Religion of Plato...*, p. 283, note 3; id., *Christ the Word...*, pp. 38 ff.

The Ancient Mirror of Theology

this world come from, with all of us, if our calling to life – a life that returns to the Absolute – was not somehow necessary? In the order of ultimate affairs, what is evil (imperfect, unhappy) loses its raison d'être; the Creator does not face it, since He faces nothing but himself; burdened with our fate, facing our weaknesses – we lose our best chance at imitation. It turns out that a myth that would link the purposefulness of human aspirations with the eternal goal and the realm of ideas cannot endure.

Finally, let us try – very succinctly – to reconstruct the general outline of the history of religious thought in the West that emerges from the findings of More (and, in part, Babbitt). At the starting point, we have the "Greek tradition," which culminates in Plato's "philosophy of the soul." Christianity is – in this sense – a healthy continuation (reinforced by the reception of Revelation) insofar as it *maintained what may be called a secret dualism as Plato maintained it openly (...) the serious rift is not between Christianity and Platonism, but between the common Greek sense of religion as it developed unchanged at the core through all the changes of the eight hundred years from the death of Socrates to the death of St. Chrysostom, and as it persisted, though with graver alterations, in the western world until a comparatively recent date – the great chasm is between that religious spirit and the prevailing modern ethics.*[92] After all, already in antiquity was philosophical dualism confronted with metaphysical monism, tried by the Stoics, as well as with the position of Aristotle, which More calls "transcendentalism." The mystical current grows on the frontiers of theoretical discourse. We do not have to view his relationship with metaphysics that distorts real experience as necessary. Mysticism in its Buddhist version – the best version of Far Eastern religion according to the humanists – becomes understandable based on "absolved dualism." A vital sense of the illusion and paradox objectively existing in the "lowest layer of human consciousness" is retained here, at the cost of a complete detachment of spiritual aspirations from the ordinary mode of existence, from thoughts and feelings that do not correspond in any way with the attainment

92   Id., *The Religion of Plato...*, pp. 241, 299–300.

of nirvana. Simply put, a Buddhist mystic turns his back to us (and apparently also to himself) and runs away. *The Absolute of monism is the next step metaphysically after an "absolved dualism."*[93] However, note that the characteristic phrase about "deliverance from guilt" (or "absolution") also expresses the critical distance between More and Babbitt. The latter, from the philosophical (Platonic) point of view, falls into the trap of a metaphysical hole, proclaiming his "positive," nontheistic "psychology" (in place of classical natural theology) and on those grounds merging humanistic and religious experiences. Of course, when we look at their fruits, Buddhism has an advantage over Christianity. There is no personal God in this tradition who would guarantee the reconciliation of everything with everything else – and which could as such be secularized. Dark fanaticism can only weakly be rooted in it. The world as it is, is being abandoned rather than brutally transformed or blown up. In short, there is no food for modern enthusiasm.

Let's move on. The Middle Ages, seen through the eyes of our humanists, were far too optimistic about affairs of the spirit. They culminate in the "Age of Reason,"[94] scholasticism, and religious life; in constructing metaphysical systems and simultaneously being open to mysticism – both tendencies, as we know, turned out to be disastrous for religion. We can look at Thomas Aquinas as a brilliant thinker, but also as a beneficiary of his times. About another figure (from the first half of the fourteenth century), Richard Rolle, More writes: *in his glorification of the emotions and of the contemplative love of God there was always a lurking element of self-exaltation, and his praises of the secluded life were filled with outbursts of indignation against society which was only too willing to take him at his word and leave him to his seclusion (...) he is consumed with ennui and the feeling of futility; he cries out to heaven to remove him from a community of fools and worldlings among whom he languished in unregarded uselessness.*[95] Here, we can see an anticipation of the moods cher-

---

93 Id., *The Catholic Faith...*, p. 69, note 13.
94 Cf. id., *The Quest of A Century...*, p. 250.
95 Id., *Cardinal Newman* [in:] id., *The Drift of Romanticism...*, p. 40.

The Ancient Mirror of Theology

ished by romanticism. However, the road to true celebration of the instinctive "truth" of feelings, to primitivism, impressionism, etc., is still a long way off. To be facetious, we can say that the Middle Ages end up sizzling on Savonarola's stake; Machiavelli, who followed him, was a preacher of an entirely different type. Now is the time to ask who we "really" are – according to our tendons and bones, not according to monastic phantasmagoria; that is when naturalistic monism enters the scene. However, while it is difficult to overestimate the impression of scientific progress on the dawn of modernity, the great transformation or conversion of the imagination – which we tried to illustrate in the previous essay – would not have been possible without the success of the new doctrine of dualism, which was, in fact, a successful parody; a doctrine in which the old religion is "drowned." It is worth emphasizing that the distinction – in fact only apparent – between modern monism and modern dualism has nothing to do with the ideological divisions that are usually used to organize various technical-structural political propositions or "narratives." It would be a complete misunderstanding to speak of, for instance, liberal monism and socialist dualism. In any such arrangement, the fundamental body of thought turns out to be the same: based on naturalistic assumptions, drawing on the "spirituality" of humanitarianism, and eschatologically oriented towards the benevolence – or necessity – of expansion. Modern dualism means, so to speak, "energy support" for modern monism; there is – *ultimately* – no difference in philosophical or spiritual experience.

Still bearing in mind the question of evil, one should consider the genesis of modern dualism. This is too broad a topic to be elaborated on here. Suffice it to point out that the Reformation became the grounds for influential religious thought. It gave rise, especially in the Calvinist current, to an absurd theology, boldly rationalist and at the same time corresponding to the disastrous experience of mysticism.[96] The complete incapacitation of a

---

96 Cf. id., *The Catholic Faith...*, pp. 303–04; *The Sceptical Approach...*, pp. 17–18.

depraved humanity cannot, in the long run, be a good premise for life in society. Thus, with the inevitable burnout of reformers' religious enthusiasm, the cynicism of "it does not concern me" took root very easily. As a consequence, at the level of reflection, there is a kind of "sociologization" of the fight between good and evil; evil, as we know, is eventually identified with a defective institutional order. If we apply the measure of ancient Christian heresies, it is quite possible to conclude that *we are all Pelagians today;* Pelagianism, on the other hand – as More writes – *pretends to save for man his freedom, but essentially is a denial of free will, in so far as free will implies a radical separation from a transcendent God.*[97] Art, as we can see, consists in being "radically separated" from the Creator, not in being so far away from Him that there is nothing left for us to do but to *necessarily* relieve Him in His grace.

V.

In an anecdote cited by Paul Elmer More, he is referred to as a "philosopher" while his friend Irving Babbitt is called "a saint."[98] Meanwhile, referring the ancient mirror of theology to the legacy of both thinkers and not wanting to be merely superficial recipients of their texts, we would be inclined to associate the first-class findings of the latter with the field of natural theology, and those of the former – with the field of mythical theology; the common center of their reflections would, in turn, be situated in the area of political theology, where, from the perspective of the classics, the humanistic art of mediation and the experience of self-mastery easily fit. As for More, it is worth noting that he reflects on the key issues of the creation of the world and the presence of evil – in a way determining the direction of his later statements – in a part of a book (*The Religion of Plato*) marked by the brace of "mythology"; he also consistently, at every stage, gives Christianity the status of a myth or a religion based on a mythical event. The devil lies in the explanation

97   Id., *Saint Augustine* [in:] id., *Studies of Religious...*, pp. 98, 96.
98   Cf. id., *Irving Babbitt...*, p. 42.

of the word "myth" itself. It is certainly not limited to the approach to theater as a place of frivolous and entertaining art, which ultimately serves to channel common emotions and pacify moods, i.e., opinion management. It does contain a certain ambivalence, but it is not intended to depict a predetermined falsehood or flight of fancy, but only a "superstructure" of experience understood by philosophers, an experience that by no means excludes the inherent role of Revelation – it even demands it. Of course, recognizing – for one reason or another – the objective need for divine intervention is not the same as confirming that God has revealed Himself to us. The life and resurrection of Jesus is not a truth proven by reason, but a myth that clashes with reason. Nevertheless – according to More – *by the use of the word "myth" nothing is implied prejudicial to the truth of the event so designated. It simply means that any commingling of the two spheres of the divine and the human, any revelation of God to man, must assume an anthropomorphic character,*[99] that is, it must be understandable for people, corresponding to the horizons of common experience or the requirements of *common sense*, that is to say – it must be generally attractive. Therefore, the concept of "myth" is equal to a concrete form of "true illusion," which is both a gift for all and a signpost for those called.

On this basis, Christianity is distinguished as a religion that most profoundly and effectively binds the teleological image of the world (whose ultimate nature must remain a mystery to us) and an individual sense of purpose (that we are responsible for ourselves). In the doctrine of the *Logos made man, in the intrinsic meaning of the Logos apart from Incarnation, Christianity has mythically (a true myth – we will say) brought together the objectivity of the ethical law and the subjectivity of personal morality.*[100] The *factum brutum* of the revealed Word is evaluated here through the prism of the surprising harmony of the traditional record of God's presence on the one hand, and the universal needs of human nature,

---

99 Id., *Christ the Word...*, p. 5, note 3; cf. id., *The Religion of Plato...*, especially pp. 14–15; id., *The Sceptical Approach...*, p. 17.
100 Quoted in: A. H. Dakin, *Paul Elmer More...*, p. 364.

HUMANISM AS REALISM

on the other. It can be argued that, on the contrary, the original shape of the biblical tradition resulted from particular needs; Yahweh, some will say, was for the chosen people nothing but a figure of a super-ruler capable of defeating the pharaoh (and ultimately all hostile monarchs) completely and irreversibly, extrapolated to the heavens. However, this Jewish political theology, reconstructed by us for better or worse, was able to "establish" a unique message, potentially important to every human individual in any place and time; although this message, as a myth, as the substance of imagination – is prone to corruption. *Few things are more interesting to the student of this period* (the era of the birth of Christianity) *than the gradual assimilation of the Biblical kingdom of heaven and the Platonic world of Ideas, whereby the former sheds its temporal and national limitations and assumes the aspect of universal philosophy, while the latter acquires a dynamic hold on the imagination and will which as pure philosophy it could not possess.*[101]

Indeed, it is hard to escape the assertion that – with all its anti-rationalist rhetoric, profound reluctance to create all-explanatory systems, sensitization to vain intellectualism, and bending facts into theory – More places religion before a tribunal of reason. After all, he does not do so from the position of triumphant enlightenment. All the great humanist's arguments are based on skeptical reflection on man's "intellectual powerlessness" and "moral responsibility." In practice, this leads him to provide philosophical support to the Christian faith; support – despite the well-known problems, roughly speaking, of a theological-political nature ("a healthy connection between dialectics and an emotional approach") that have haunted it from the beginning, not to mention more modern distortions or even the sucking up of its internal resources by humanitarianism. In one of his letters (from 1928), More writes about himself: *as you probably know, I am not even a communicant, and it is not likely that I ever shall be (...) I am fixed now, and my habit towards matters of that kind is, and will remain, primarily intellectual – though my nature is*

101 P. E. More, *Christ the Word...*, p. 264.

268

emotional enough (...) I do honestly believe that the best service I can render the (Anglican) *Church is by arguing for her fundamental truths as an unconcerned advocate. I think my position gives me a certain claim on educated readers, which I might not have if I were a recognized member of the organization – I think that, while admitting that the claim has not been widely heard.*[102] He creates his "apologies" of Christianity with the critical reader in mind, meeting the expectations arising from the popularization of texts that fit into the current of Protestant biblical criticism (e.g., Adolf von Harnack). In short, he tries to replace the explainers of "fundamental truths" in this role – authors who profess a "purely humanitarian view" of religion. Hence, many of his judgments, such as those concerning the interpretation of the Holy Spirit, may be considered too distant from the canon of Christian (Catholic) orthodoxy; whatever value we assign to them, we should take into account various external premises, More's sometimes – in the eyes of a late grandson – overly ostentatious nonconformity; that – it was expected of him. Wouldn't he have done better by cutting himself off to a greater degree from the rules of the game set by liberal Protestantism and devoting more attention to the universal content of Christendom? Who knows. Perhaps he did not have time to fully consider and say many things (he died ailing in 1937). However, the essence of his thought, as he himself stated, was "established." In the middle of his "apology," we find praise for the work of the Council of Chalcedon (AD 451), which, after long, deep, and violent disputes, adopted the definition of the person of Christ as uniting two natures. These two natures, the divine and the human, are unmixed, inseparable, and complete. However, what from the point of view of a modern church historian would probably mean stifling further intellectual searches, is, for the humanist, an edifying example of a skillful cutting of hopeless speculations and thus a successful turn in the spiritual history of the West,

102 Quoted in: A. H. Dakin, *Paul Elmer More...*, pp. 259–60; cf. ibid., p. 316.

which could henceforth focus on "consuming" the ripe fruits of "the Greek tradition."[103]

As a critic of traditional religion, More strikes in two directions simultaneously. First, at mysticism, emotionalism, unbalanced asceticism. Second, at the rationalist (and Roman-legalistic) mode of practicing theology, in metaphysical discourses. The common denominator here is detachment from real experiences and linking piety with abstraction. Therefore, critical judgment falls upon the concepts used to describe the divine Absolute, qualities of God like "eternal" and "almighty." They convey the spirit of reverence towards What (Whom) is beyond our understanding, what is beyond our perception of everyday matters, towards things perceived by the senses; in this sense, they confirm the mind's natural limitations – and that's all. *But when a thinker goes beyond these bounds to direct our worship and our moral sense to pure abstractions, then I hold that religion has been betrayed by reason and faith has been attenuated to nihilism.*[104] The very concept of the "Absolute" seems to be a philosophical chimera corresponding to both Aristotle's divine vision and the Stoics' deceptive hope that one can experience being a sage and not merely one seeking wisdom. In one of his last works, More advocates the abandonment of the word "Absolute" (in the sense of "that, which is unconditioned") in favor of "the Ultimate." In such a system, the description of God is derived from attempts to define the (vertical) boundaries of human experience and not from the negation of that experience. So when, for example, we declare Him to be "eternal," we are not concerned with some essentially unimaginable existence beyond time, but with a subject who is untroubled by the passage of time, so to speak; from whom nothing is hidden, and who loses nothing of what has happened; the attribute of "eternity" is therefore associated with perfect knowledge. Similarly, when reflecting on His Passion, we should not deny Him –

103 Cf. P. E. More, *Christ of the New...*, p. viii, 50; id., *Christ the Word...*, pp. 69, 243 ff.
104 Id., *Pages from an Oxford...*, chapter XI (no page numbers present).

The Ancient Mirror of Theology

as God – real participation in suffering (as if it was an offense to God's consistency or the Lord's omnipotence), but to perceive what we are not capable of, namely the perfect steadfastness of our will and the immutability of our intention. In More's view, *to stop with the Ultimate does not mean that we are presuming to draw an artificial line about the power of Perfect Goodness, or to define the essential nature of Death in terms of finite understanding; rather it is an honest recognition of the limits of the human mind. Our knowledge of God ends with what ultimately He is to us and for us; what, if anything, stretches beyond that the humanist leaves reverently in the vast unknown.*[105]

This *ultimately* mysterious nature of the world from which we derive our sense of illusion or paradox – and secondly, our religious enthusiasm (in the proper sense)[106] – cannot be explained through discourse. The interpretation of reality that is binding for us results from pre-philosophical assumptions, which are neither arbitrary nor – in essence – numerous. First of all, we can think about the world (and ourselves) solely based on the perception of natural necessity, sooner or later reaching a monistic image of *perpetuum mobile*, encompassing all phenomena and processes, i.e., a kind of sovereign omni-mechanism through which everything happens and without which nothing happens, but which has no regard for our needs and no connection with my or your self-awareness. Second, we can go beyond the level of determinism (or whatever you would call the intellectual derivatives of faith in what is necessary) and then create discourses according to our spirit (thinking about ourselves and for ourselves seems to prompt this going beyond). As More writes: *there are only two conclusions in which the philosophic mind can abide. Either, as the Hindu in his more courageous moods taught, the whole thing, this globe and this life, are utterly without design, a phantasmagoria in which we can*

105 Id., *A Scholar-Saint* [in:] id., *On Being Human...*, p. 182; cf. A. H. Dakin, *Paul Elmer More...*, p. 360.
106 Cf. P. E. More, *The Religion of Plato...*, pp. 17–18; id., *The Catholic Faith...*, pp. 215–19.

detect no meaning and to which we have no right to apply any interpretation, not even that of chance, a huge illusion of ignorance which simply vanishes into nothing at the touch of knowledge; or else, if we see design in the world, then there is no holding back from the inference of the theist. The agnostic will say that this is to fall into anthropomorphism. It is.[107] In other words, the philosopher – not only the rationalist-dogmatist or some other lost soul – reveals to us (at first equally probable): nothingness or the cosmos.

Reflection on the cosmic order or the purpose of creation occupies, as we have already indicated, a special place in the works of the "late" More. We can assume that this is the point of arrival of all his reflection. This final message of More's is contained in the peculiar notion of "sacramentalization." What is needed, what must be confronted with the raped and stunted imagination of modern man, is *a sounder conception and a broader expansion of the Catholic doctrine of the sacramental nature of life.*[108] It refers to *the purposeful adaptation of material resources to spiritual ends, whether it be seen in the cosmic work of Providence or in some specific act of human design.*[109] God's work on the world and man's work on himself are connected, on the one hand, by creative, ordering thought, and on the other – by the presence of inertia on all sides, which has arisen in a necessary and unwanted way as the result of the resistance of matter. And this world – "mythologically" being a patch of matter saved from nothingness – should seem mysterious to us again, while simultaneously containing clear reasons for us to become better than we are. Only by rational imitation of the Creator, through his Son, will we perhaps be able to get out from under the tentacles of humanitarianism, from the embrace of false faith.

The necessary condition must, of course, be to treat seriously – the independent experience of – the thought that guides tradi-

---

107 Id., *Christ the Word...*, pp. 286–87; cf. id., *Pages from an Oxford...*, chapters XV, XXVIII (no page numbers present).
108 Id., *Church and Politics* [in:] id., *On Being Human...*, p. 159.
109 Id., *The Catholic Faith...*, pp. 154–55.

The Ancient Mirror of Theology

tional religion and philosophy: that not everything is "all right" with us, that our nature demands "something more"; that *something is wrong with existence and that somehow the wrong can be, and ought to be, escaped. He who does not feel that wrong is no longer a human being, but a mere automaton, a dull-witted animal with no part among men; he who has lost the accompanying sense of possible allevi-ation has sunk to the most terrible of all shapes of madness, which is called melancholia.*[110] The leaven of philosophy turns out to be the study of the causes of what is "wrong" in us and of how to get rid of the "error." In turn, religion becomes something important, since it offers our imagination a dualistic vision in which what is natural (and "wrong") is opposed to what is supernatural, oth-erworldly, divine. If the letter of the teaching of the great reli-gions takes on such different patterns, if we then come to humble ourselves before the mystery of God's presence – that He seems to be present... so unevenly – it only confirms that *tragic rift some-where in the dark backward of fate between the divine and the human, some ultimate irrationality in the nature of things as they are.* There is, however, no continuity in Revelation taken as a whole; evi-dence of abrupt changes within it abounds: *from inanimate to an-imate nature, and from the dualism of man to the dualism of the God-man.* Seeking – starting with ourselves – a binding element for "all things visible and invisible," we turn to faith as a constant view of the world through the prism of our relationship with God. According to More, *religion is not an inference from what is outwardly observed or from the mechanism of reason, but a projection into the void, so to speak, of his own feeling of personal freedom, re-sponsibility, and purpose.* Of course, there are people, masses of people – no, not mentally sluggish, often conscientious and well-educated – who cannot think of any binding element of all things, who do not make any projections and generally move as if free from the dilemma of living in the world and simultaneous desire for "something more." *They appear never to have felt the stinging discontent of impermanence. I say to myself that the equanim-*

110 Ibid., p. 8.

ity of such men must be owing to some deficiency of that which distinguishes man as man (...) but these men, I insist, are not sceptics. The sceptic is one whose faculties are alert, and who is therefore bound to feel the force of the dilemma confronting him. In the age of humanitarianism, the position of the sceptic undoubtedly changes with the widespread conversion of imaginations, with the advent of the hegemony of economic ideals. Instead of the various forms of faith, the skeptic finds a shapeless indifference. The reason for "our present inclination" towards rejecting traditional religion is by no means an *increase of knowledge. It springs from an enfeebling of the emotions and a paralysis of what may be called the spiritual imagination. We have been made callous by the business of the world and have been habituated to the use of machinery,* thanks to which our earthly life has become, above all... absorbing. What remains is to ask a simple question, are *the troubles of our present civilization (...) not due to just this: the loss of hope* (for a happy, successful life in the faith) *and with that loss a sort of craven timidity before the high spiritual adventure that we call religion;* for – as More instructs us – *faith is the great adventure.*[111]

Faith as a great adventure – that's it! This adventure, however, means undertaking a course that has been abandoned; not inventing new lands for oneself or the sake of invention, but instead sailing towards goals long ago marked on the map of humanity. In the Christian version, it means *imitatio Christi,* and in general – undertaking for oneself, in one's own measure, the Creator's work. *These things I have spoken unto you, that in me ye might have peace. In the world ye shall have tribulation: but be of good cheer; I have overcome the world* (John 16:33). To overcome the world – that is: to overcome the formlessness of matter; to harness what of itself tends only towards nothingness, to the achievement of spiritual goals, to forging forms of civilization; a civilization oriented "upwards," suitable for the human soul – mine and yours. Our duty is – no more and no less – *to take our part in the cosmic conflict of forces into which we have been called, for which perhaps we were created.*

111 Id., *The Sceptical Approach...*, pp. 153-54, 166, 178–79, 189, 193.

Like cowardly recruits we have deserted our place in the ranks.[112] Let us then return to the ship of Christianity repentant before it is too late!

We can close our deliberations surrounding Paul Elmer More's theology with this dramatic appeal. It is evident that he was striving to revive a myth (according to his understanding of the notion of "myth"), which he claimed was as powerful – in his original intention – for us as it was for people who lived centuries ago. Christ does not age, but – people must be reminded of Christ. It seems that the great humanist saw himself in the role of a *logios, signifying one who is skilled to trace the operations of the logos, to distinguish its genuine expression in literature from shams, to know the truth, and so to dwell in the calm yet active leisure (scholê) of contemplation. The scholar, the* logios, *in that noble sense of the word, is he who by study and reflection has recovered the birthright of humanity and holds it in fee for the generations to come.*[113] Unfortunately, this sublime vocation, the legitimacy of which cannot be contested, was accompanied by a gloomy feeling of non-culpable failure. At least, this would appear to be the case from an incredibly moving statement at the end of *Pages from an Oxford Diary*. More writes: *my work, costly enough to myself, is about done, and will soon be forgotten. Occasionally a cloud darkens my reflections, when I think of vast ambitions that have shrivelled to insignificance in the performance. But I take comfort in remembering that, if I have not moved the world, I have moved myself (…) at times I am troubled by a longing, purer than ambition, for the gift of persuasion, for "that warning voice," clear and loud enough to rouse the world from its heavy slumber. If I could once before I leave speak out what I have known and felt of the sacred truth in such a manner that others should know and feel! But my voice is dull and confused; and it is hardly a cause for weeping not to be numbered among the prophets.*[114]

---

112 Id., *Pages from an Oxford...*, chapter XXV (no page numbers present).
113 Id., *Christ the Word...*, p. 301.
114 Id., *Pages from an Oxford...*, chapter XXXIII (no page numbers present). The phrase "that warning voice" likely comes from John Milton.

HUMANISM AS REALISM

It is hard not to think about this sad – and, in a sense, prophetic – confession as we sit today, almost a hundred years later, over the burned-out fire of the Humanist Movement. Why did they fail? What can we do? Here we have attempted to view the great work of More and Babbitt in the ancient mirror of theology, the same mirror that tells us that the reality surrounding us is not so much the rational product of an "enlightened" mind but the result of modern faith in humanity. After this exercise, we are surely aware of the relationship between the humanist response to modernity and the old religious approach to the ultimate questions. At the beginning of the first essay, we quoted Babbitt saying that the humanist is not concerned with defining God. Now we see that he needs this kind of definition after all; that it *must* be a definition that meets the requirements of nature and is, in that sense, *real*. The "equivalents" of genuine faith turn out to be impermanent, while living wisdom, born of a well-tended soul and reaching the level of Revelation, is of the utmost importance. In sum, for the humanist, humanity is worth as much as the lives of those who look lovingly at saints and philosophers while keeping their own feet firmly planted on the ground.

God is not dead. At most, He is saddened by our retreat. "Let him be an empty dream, or a shadow, or just a name" – reminisced about either way, whether reviled or longed for – He accompanies human experience, both in the times of masters of theology and in those of champions of obtuseness. May this experience draw as close to Him as possible! We cannot say what the future will bring. We know that we live for a short time only (how far we are from bodily immortality!), and as far as we think for ourselves, we *should* be able to face this world…somewhat effectively. As far as thinking is concerned, until our minds have been taken from us, only we decide where our mind reaches and for what purpose. Let us give More the floor one last time: *the man who is frightened by the impenetrable wall of mystery that everywhere surrounds us, had better cease to think at all.*[115] Amen!

115 Id., *Christ of the New...*, p. 18.

SELECTED LITERATURE

Babbitt I., *Democracy and Leadership*, Indianapolis 1979.

—, *Literature and the American College: Essays in Defense of the Humanities*, Boston–New York 1908.

—, *On Being Creative and Other Essays*, New York 1968.

—, *Representative Writings*, ed. G. A. Panichas, Lincoln – London 1981.

—, *Rousseau and Romanticism*, Boston–New York 1919.

—, *Spanish Character and Other Essays*, eds. F. Manchester, F. Giese, W. F. Giese, Boston–New York 1940.

—, *The Masters of Modern French Criticism*, Boston–New York 1912.

—, *The New Laokoon: An Essay on the Confusion of the Arts*, Boston–New York 1910.

Dakin A. H., *A Paul Elmer More Miscellany*, Portland, Maine 1950.

—, *Paul Elmer More*, Princeton, New Jersey 1960.

Eliot T. S., *Selected Essays*, London 1999.

Foerster N., *The American State University: Its Relation to Democracy*, Chapel Hill 1937.

Humanism and America: Essays on the Outlook of Modern Civilization, ed. N. Foerster, New York 1930.

Hulme T. E., *Speculations: Essays on Humanism and the Philosophy of Art*, ed. H. Read, London–New York 1936.

More P. E., *Christ the Word*, Princeton 1927.

—, *Hellenistic Philosophies*, Princeton–London 1923.

—, *On Being Human (New Shelburne Essays III)*, Princeton–London 1936.

—, *Pages from an Oxford Diary*, Princeton–London 1937.

HUMANISM AS REALISM

—, *Platonism*, Princeton–London 1917.

—, *Shelburne Essays First Series*, New York–London 1904.

—, *Shelburne Essays Second Series*, New York–London 1907.

—, *Shelburne Essays Third Series*, New York–London 1907.

—, *Shelburne Essays Fourth Series*, New York–London 1907.

—, *Shelburne Essays Fifth Series*, New York–London 1908.

—, *Shelburne Essays Sixth Series: Studies of Religious Dualism*, New York–London 1909.

—, *Shelburne Essays Seventh Series*, Boston–New York 1910.

—, *Shelburne Essays Eighth Series: The Drift of Romanticism*, New York–Boston 1913.

—, *Shelburne Essays Ninth Series: Aristocracy and Justice*, Boston–New York 1915.

—, *Shelburne Essays Tenth Series: With the Wits*, Boston–New York 1919.

—, *Shelburne Essays Eleventh Series: A New England Group and Others*, Boston–New York 1921.

—, *The Catholic Faith*, Princeton 1931.

—, *The Christ of the New Testament*, Princeton 1924.

—, *The Demon of The Absolute* (*New Shelburne Essays I*), Princeton 1928.

—, *The Religion of Plato*, Princeton–London 1921.

—, *The Sceptical Approach to Religion* (*New Shelburne Essays II*), Princeton 1934.

More P. E., C. M. Harris, *The Jessica Letters, An Editor's Romance*, New York–London 1904.*The Critique of Humanism: A Symposium*, ed. C. H. Grattan, New York 1930.

The Essential Paul Elmer More: A Selection of His Writings, ed. B. C. Lambert, New Rochelle, New York 1972.

INDEX

The index includes all persons mentioned in the main text and the book's footnotes. The pages where the name appears in the footnotes are in italics. References to Irving Babbitt and Paul Elmer More, to whose thoughts the book as a whole is devoted, are omitted from the index.

Alexander the Great 139
Alighieri Dante 28, 111
Arendt Hannah 129
Aristotle 15–17, 31, 51, 80, 116, 139, 154, 162, 245, 251, 255–56, 263, 275, 296–98, 306
Armada Paweł *220*
Arnold Matthew 15
Ashoka 139
Augustine of Hippo 20, 218–19, 252–55, 273, 275, 285, 288
Averroes 291
Bacon Francis 37–40, 48, 50–51, 138, 148, 151, 196, 205

Baum Maurice 263
Bellow Saul *114*
Berger Peter L. 224
Bergson Henri 59, 65
Bernard of Clairvaux 199
Bloom Allan *21*
Bonaparte Napoleon 118, 140, 146
Bossuet Jacques-Bénigne 20
Botev Hristo 58
Brague Rémi 229–*30*
Brennan Stephen C. XII

Buddha see: Gautama Siddhartha
Burke Edmund 129, 134–36, 157

Caligula 132
Che Guevara Ernesto 239
Churchill Winston 197
Cicero 16–17
Cohen Hermann 60
Combe William *181*
Comte August 32
Confucius 16, 235
Chernyshevsky Nikolay 192

Dakin Arthur Hazard XII, *5*, *131*, *141*, *174*, *184*, *209*, *257*, *264*, *303*, *305*, *307*
Darwin Charles 53–54, 111
Davies Robert M. XII
Descartes René 53, 78
Dewey John 111
Diderot Denis 255
Dilthey Wilhelm 65
Disraeli Benjamin 189, 197
Dostoevsky Fyodor 191–93
Duggan Francis X. XII

Einstein Albert 123

Eliot Thomas Stearns 24–26, 28, 61, 257, 268–69, 272
Elyot Thomas 17
Emerson Ralph Waldo 15

Fitzpatrick Sheila *113*
Foerster Norman *4*, *17*, 25–*26*, 28–*29*, 34, 46, 48, 61, 63, 92
Fra Angelico see: John of Fiesole
Francis of Assisi 91
Freud Zygmunt 40, 111
Fukuyama Francis 117, 124–*25*

Gandhi Mohandas Karamchand (Mahatma) 222
Gautama Siddhartha 28, 243–45, 247–48, 251, 254, 256
Gladstone William 32
Goethe Johann Wolfgang *279*
Górnicki Łukasz 17
Grattan C. Hartley 141–*42*

Harnack Adolf von 305
Hegel Georg Wilhelm Friedrich 111, 117–18, 121, 123–24, 157
Herder Johann Gottfried 32
Herford Charles Harold 32
Hitler Adolf 113, 182
Hobbes Thomas 139
Hoeveler J. David, Jr. XII, *130*
Hohenzollern William II 190
Homer 28
Hulme Thomas 59–69, 71, 77, 81, 196
Husserl Edmund 61

John Chrysostom 272, 298
John of Fiesole 63
Jesus Christ 89–90, 96, 211, 227, 246, 260, 262, 267, 271, 303, 305, 311
Johnson Paul 7

Kadłubek Wincenty 17
Kant Immanuel 7–8, 86, 157
Kirk Russell XII, 129
Kłodkowski Piotr *230*
Kochanowski Jan 17
Kojève Alexandre 117–19, 121
Kołakowski Leszek *7*, *41*, *286*, *295*
Kymlicka Will 116

Lenin Vladimir 132, 146, 150, 182, 222
Lilla Mark *7*, *220*
Lim Kim Hui *101*
Lippmann Walter 22, 103, 105, 138
Löwith Karl 8
Luther Martin 88

Machiavelli Niccolo` 104–06, 139, 153–54, 300
Manchester Frederick XII
Marx Karl 111, 121, 123, 176, 180, 182
Milton John *312*
More Louis Trenchard 124, *126*
Muhammad 228, 262
Munson Gorham B. *79*
Murphy Paul V. *105*

Nash George H. *129*
Nevin Thomas R. XII
Newman John Henry 57
Nietzsche Friedrich 8, 57, 65, 70–71, 122–23, 141, 179, 200
Norwid Cyprian Kamil 110
Nozick Robert 115

Pascal Blaise 69, 240
Paul of Tarsus 267
Plato 27, 72, 86, 116, 154–55, 157–58, 162–63, 208, 244, 261, 264, 267, 271–74, 278, 280–81, 284, 288, 292, 296, 298, 304

Index

Plotinus 293, 297
Pol Pot 146
Polybius 272
Poole Ernest 197–98
Popper Karl 157

Rawls John 115
Robespierre Maximilien 132
Rolle Richard 300
Rosen Stanley *118*, 210
Rousseau Jean-Jacques 32, 37–40,
 49, 57, 135, 137–39, 144–49,
 151, 154–55, 170, 175, 190, 196,
 206, 240
Russell Bertrand 61
Sainte-Beuve Charles-Augustin
 15

Savonarola Girolamo 300
Schmitt Carl *286*
Shafer Robert XII
Shakespeare William 160
Shepard Odell XII
Smith Adam 180
Socrates 4, 30, 148, 155, 158, 209,
 211, 244, 266, 280, 298
Sophocles 235
Spencer Herbert 54

Spengler Oswald 20
Stalin Joseph 7, 108, 112, 182
Strauss Leo 8, *79*, *104*, *106*, 109,
 119, 121, 129, 225
Streep Meryl 110, 126
Suchodolski Bogdan XII–XIII
Suslov Mikhail 114
St. Augustine see: Augustine of
 Hippo
St. Francis see: Francis of Assisi
St. Paul see: Paul of Tarsus
Świercz Piotr *78*

Tacitus 272
Tanner Stephen L. XII
Tesla Nikola 44–46, 49, 194
Thomas Aquinas 300
Tolstoy Leo 141

Valadier Paul *220*
Varro Marcus Terentius 218–19
Vlad the Impaler 132
Voegelin Eric 129

Wilson Woodrow 150, 183–84

Yarbrough Stephen R. XII